T0316349

IN SEARCH OF AN EAST ASIAN DEVELOPMENT MODEL

IN SEARCH OF AN EAST ASIAN DEVELOPMENT MODEL

Edited by

Peter L. Berger
AND
Hsin-Huang Michael Hsiao

Routledge
Taylor & Francis Group

LONDON AND NEW YORK

First published 1988 by Transaction Books

Published 2019 by Routledge
2 Park Square, Milton Park, Abingdon, Oxon OX14 4RN
52 Vanderbilt Avenue, New York, NY 10017

Routledge is an imprint of the Taylor & Francis Group, an informa business

Library of Congress Catalog Number: 87-19061

Library of Congress Cataloging-in-Publication Data

In search of an East Asian development model.

Papers originally presented at a conference sponsored by the Carnegie
Council on Ethics and International Affairs held in New York in June 1987.
Includes index.
1. East Asia—Economic policy—Congresses. 2. East Asia—Social life
and customs—Congresses. I. Berger, Peter L. II. Hsiao, H. H. Michael.
III. Carnegie Council on Ethics & International Affairs.
HC460.5.I5 1987   338.95   87-19061
ISBN 0-88738-149-9
ISBN 0-88738-686-5 (pbk.)

ISBN 13: 978-0-88738-686-2 (pbk)

Contents

Introduction   vii
About the Contributors   ix

Part I: Overview

 1. An East Asian Development Model?   3
    Peter L. Berger

 2. An East Asian Development Model: Empirical Explorations   12
    Hsin-Huang Michael Hsiao

Part II: Theoretical and Empirical Problems

 3. The New Asian Capitalism: An Economic Portrait   27
    Gustav Papanek

 4. The New Asian Capitalism: A Political Portrait   81
    Lucian W. Pye

 5. The Role of the Entrepreneur in the New Asian Capitalism   99
    S.G. Redding

Part III: Cultural and Social Features

 6. The Role of Christianity   115
    Jan Swyngedouw

 7. The Applicability of Asian Family Values to Other
    Sociocultural Settings   134
    Siu-lun Wong

Part IV: Individual Societies

 8. The Distinctive Features of Japanese Development:
    Basic Cultural Patterns and Politico-Economic Processes   155
    Iwao Munakata

 9. The Distinctive Features of Taiwan's Development   179
    Rong-I Wu

10. The Distinctive Features of South Korea's Development   197
    Kyong-Dong Kim

11. The Distinctive Features of Two City-States' Development:
Hong Kong and Singapore   220
    Pang Eng Fong

Index   239

Introduction

The papers collected in this volume were presented at a conference sponsored by the Carnegie Council on Ethics and International Affairs (formerly the Council on Religion and International Affairs). The conference, "In Search of an East Asian Development Model," was held at the Carnegie Council's headquarters in New York in June 1985. The idea for the conference and this book was that of Professor Peter Berger of Boston University and Professor Hsin-Huang Michael Hsiao of the Institute of Ethnology, Academia Sinica, Taipei, the co-directors of the conference. The purpose was to discover if there is any such thing as an East Asian development model. Was it rooted in common cultural characteristics which arose only in Asia and therefore had no relevance elsewhere, or did the cultural and social characteristics thus revealed have transcendent features, applicable at all times and in all places? Was the recognition of general Asian economic success a post facto situation, an attempt at later rationalizations to fit a logic and inevitability into a process that essentially lurched along without any particular direction?

Other related questions arise in these chapters. There is discussion of whether the Asian export-oriented economies were a product of a particular set of historical circumstances not likely to be repeated. Questions of values and philosophy are also discussed, as is the entrepreneurial element—an idea apparently at odds with Confucianism. This is a far-ranging discussion which sheds light in unexpected ways on the many facets of the very different countries who are the raw material for this fascinating search.

I would like to thank the Asia and the World Institute of the Republic of China on Taiwan for their intellectual and financial support of this conference. Specifically, I wish to express my heartfelt gratitude to Dr. Hon Li-wu, the distinguished chairman of this important research organization, and to Dr. Phillip Chen, president of the institute.

Robert J. Myers
President,
Carnegie Council on Ethics and
International Affairs

About the Contributors

Peter L. Berger is distinguished university professor of religion and sociology and director of the Institute for the Study of Economic Culture at Boston University. He is the author of many books and articles, including *The Capitalist Revolution, The Social Construction of Reality* (with Thomas Luckmann), *The Heretical Imperative*, and *Pyramids of Sacrifice: Political Ethics and Social Change*. From 1981 to 1983 he served as U.S. representative to the United Nations Working Group on the Right to Development.

Pang Eng Fong is associate professor at the School of Management of the National University of Singapore. During 1987-88 he will be visiting professor at the University of Michigan. He has held a number of posts at the National University of Singapore, including that of director of the University's Economic Research Center. He has also served as consultant to a number of international organizations. Among his publications are *Trade, Employment and Industrialisation in Singapore* (with Linda Lim), *Education, Manpower and Development in Singapore*, and articles in many international journals.

Hsin-Huang Michael Hsiao is research fellow, Institute of Ethnology, Academia Sinica, and professor of sociology, National Taiwan University. He was a Fulbright fellow at Boston University and Harvard University and visiting professor of sociology at Duke University. His publications include *Governmental Agricultural Strategies in Taiwan and South Korea* and *The Development of Agricultural Policies in Post-War Taiwan*.

Kyong-Dong Kim, professor of sociology at Seoul National University, received his Ph.D. from Cornell University. He has taught at North Carolina State University, was director of the Institute of Social Sciences of Seoul National University, and fellow of the Woodrow Wilson International Center for Scholars. Professor Kim has published over a dozen books and more than a hundred articles in both Korean and English. His most recent English-language publication is *Rethinking Development: Theories and Experiences*.

Iwao Munakata is professor of sociology in the Graduate Department of Social Science and Humanity at Sophia University. Dr. Munakata's research focuses on the sociology of religion and modernization. His published articles and papers include "Symbolic Structure of the Traditional Folk Religion in Japan" (Institute of International Relations, Sophia University); "Dualistic Model in the Cultural Approach to International Peace," *Peace Research in Japan*; and "Ambivalent Effects of Modernization on Traditional Folk Religion," *Japanese Journal of Religious Studies*.

Gustav Papanek is professor of economics and director of the Center for Asian Development Studies at Boston University. He served previously as the director of the Harvard Advisory Group to the Planning Commission and Ministry of Finance, Government of Indonesia, and as an agricultural economist with the U.S. Department of Agriculture. His recent books include *Development Strategy, Growth, Equity and the Political Process in Southern Asia, The Indonesian Economy* (editor), and *Decision Making for Economic Development* (co-author).

Lucian W. Pye is Ford Professor of Political Science and senior staff member of the Center for International Studies at the Massachusetts Institute of Technology. He is a member of the Council on Foreign Relations, a trustee of the Asia Foundation, and vice-chairman of the National Committee on U.S.-China Relations. Dr. Pye has conducted extensive field research in South Asia and Southeast Asia. His recent books include *Asian Power and Politics: Cultural Dimensions of Authority* (1985); *China: An Introduction* (3rd edition, 1983); *Chinese Commercial Negotiating Style* (1982); and *The Dynamics of Chinese Politics* (1981).

Gordon Redding is head of the Department of Management Studies at the University of Hong Kong, where he has worked since 1973. After a career in business, he received a doctorate in the field of organization. His principal research interests are in comparative management, and he has carried out extensive fieldwork throughout East and Southeast Asia. He also holds a visiting professorship at the Euro-Asia Centre, INSEAD.

Jan Swyngedouw is professor of religious studies (sociology of Japanese religion) and research fellow at the Institute for Religion and Culture at Nanzan University in Nagoya, Japan, and editor of the *Japanese Journal of Religious Studies*. Dr. Swyngedouw holds visiting professorships at Tokyo University, Tsukuba University, and Aichi University, among others, and has published several books and over 100 articles on Japanese culture and religion.

Siu-lun Wong is director of the Social Sciences Research Centre and senior lecturer in the Department of Sociology at the University of Hong Kong. He recently spent a year at Harvard as a Harvard-Yenching visiting scholar. His publications include *Sociology and Socialism in Contemporary China* and *Small-Scale Industry in a Laissez-Faire Economy*. His book *Shangai Industrialists in Hong Kong* is forthcoming.

Rong-I Wu is professor of economics, National Chung Hsing University, Taipei, where he previously served as chairman of the Department of Economics and director of the Institute of Economics. Rong-I Wu is a consultant to several government agencies and a part-time senior research fellow at the Taiwan Institute of Economic Research. He has published some 50 books and papers, including *The Strategy of Economic Development: A Case Study of Taiwan; The Impact of U.S. Investment on the Taiwan Economy*; and *Economic Infrastructure in Taiwan, ROC*.

PART I
OVERVIEW

1

An East Asian Development Model?

Peter L. Berger

For a long time now the focus of my work has been on the problems of modernization and development. An art collector will naturally be drawn to Florence, a mountain climber to the Himalayas. In very much the same way a social scientist interested in modernization will have his attention fixed on East Asia, to the point where he may reasonably conclude that this is the most interesting region in the world today. Needless to say, this in no way negates the other reasons for which one may be interested in this region—because of its importance in political and strategic terms, the splendors of its great civilization, its natural beauty or its sheer human vitality. I, for one, appreciate all of these, and I have also had a strong interest in the religious and philosophical traditions of Asia. But I can claim no particular competence in these areas. Allow me, then, to address an issue on which I can claim a measure of competence, namely, the question of whether Eastern Asia in general and Taiwan in particular can serve as a model relevant to other parts of the world, and, more particularly, whether there are cultural factors relevant to this issue.

The social sciences, for better or for worse, are a product of the West. They originated and developed during a period when the West was predominant throughout most of the world. Not surprisingly, when social scientists sought to explain the complex phenomenon we know as modernity—an aggregate of technological, economic, sociopolitical, and cultural processes—they looked on the societies of Europe and North America as marking the boundaries of the phenomenon. Later, after World War II, when the dissolution of the European empires led to the rapid development of new nations in what we now call the Third World, it also seemed natural to social scientists to look at this development through Western eyes; that is, they looked on it as a planetary expansion of the Western case, which remained the paradigmatic case for an understanding of modernity. We should not blame them too much for that (I'm thinking here of the growth of modernization theories in the 1950s and early 1960s); nor is it fair, in most instances, to accuse them of ethnocentrism. After all, modernity was a creation of the West, and it did expand from its Western base to other parts of the world. My point is, quite simply, that this Western-centered perspective is no longer adequate.

An analogy from the natural sciences may be useful here. A chemist trying to understand a particular chemical reaction will always carry out some sort of control experiment. The social scientist, of course, cannot carry on experiments of his own, but sometimes history provides him with the same experimental logic. Thus, anyone seeking to grasp modernity today may conjure up the image of a gigantic laboratory in which three test tubes are bubbling away, each containing a similar reaction ("modernization"), but with significantly different elements in each. There continues to be the case of advanced industrial capitalism in the West. There is also now the case of advanced industrial socialism, in the Soviet Union and in its European allies. The comparison between these two cases is very important, but it will not concern us here. But there is yet another case, that of advanced industrial capitalism in East Asia. It is my contention that this case is absolutely crucial for an understanding of modernity; it is, if you will, an essential "control experiment." In this logic, it is not just a question of understanding East Asia, but rather a question of understanding what happens elsewhere (including the West) in light of this Asian experience.

The countries I have in mind here are, of course, the successful capitalist ones in the region: Japan, the so-called Four Little Dragons—South Korea, Taiwan, Hong Kong and Singapore—and, increasingly, at least some of the countries of ASEAN besides Singapore. Their economic successes have powerfully impressed themselves on the consciousness of people everywhere (not always pleasurably i.e., the American automobile and steel industries). The same economic successes have induced both social scientists and politicians in other parts of the world to speak of an "East Asian development model." I recently met with a group of Senegalese intellectuals to discuss problems of African development; when they heard that I had just returned from East Asia, that was all they wanted to talk about. A few months ago I spent some time in Jamaica and, not really to my surprise, a question that kept coming up was what would have to happen to make Jamaica "another Taiwan" (incidentally, this thinking is very much present in the Caribbean Basin Initiative). I will return, briefly, to these practical implications at the end of my remarks here. But now let me return to the central theoretical issue.

It is my contention that these countries are sufficiently distinct, as compared with the West, that one is entitled to speak of them as a "second case" of capitalist modernity. I cannot substantiate this view in detail here, but let me list some of the distinctive features. There are, of course, salient economic features: high growth rates, sustained over many years; the remarkable fact that in some of these countries (Taiwan is probably the most important one) high growth has been associated, at least for a while, with diminishing income inequality[1]; an astounding improvement in the material standards of living of virtually the entire population; a highly active government role in shaping the development process (while East Asia certainly has capitalism, with the possible exception of Hong Kong, it certainly does not have laissez-faire capitalism); an underdeveloped welfare state (even in Japan); low tax rates and high savings rates (two probably interconnected facts); and an economy geared to exports.

Yet it is obvious, even to the most "hard-nosed" economists, that these economic features do not exist in a vacuum. Rather, they are linked to distinctive social and cultural features. Some of these include: a very strong, achievement-oriented work ethic; a highly developed sense of collective solidarity, both within the family and in artificial groupings beyond the family; the enormous prestige of education, with the concomitant motivation to provide the best education for one's children; and severe (some would say, brutally severe) meritocratic norms and institutions, which, while egalitarian in design, serve to select out elites when they are at an early age. Now, no one is likely to question that these social and cultural features are also, somehow, part of the "East Asian model" (economists, somewhat awkwardly, often refer to these features, often in a footnote, under the vague category of "human capital"). The question is to what extent the economic and the sociocultural features are causally linked. I think it is fair to say that at this point we don't know the answer to this, and that it would be very important indeed to get closer to an answer.

Let me return to the image of laboratory control experiment. Various historians and social scientists have assumed that the rise of individualism has been part and parcel of the "modernity reaction" (to stay with the language of the chemical laboratory). This is not an arbitrary or foolish assumption, as long as one limits one's attention to the Western case. The roots of Western individualism probably go back to very early, formative periods of Western civilization. It can be plausibly argued that this Western individualism provided a fertile soil for the birth of a number of important elements of modernity such as, for an important example, the birth of the capitalist entrepreneur. Conversely, as modernity came into being, it dissolved older, more collectively oriented communities and institutions, throwing the individual much more on himself, and thus fostering both the values and the social-psychological reality of individualism. A good deal of classical sociological thought was concerned with this shift, as in Ferdinand Toennies's notion of the change from *Gemeinschaft* to *Gesellschaft*, and Emile Durkheim's of the change from mechanical to organic solidarity. In other words, the development of modernity in the West suggests a reciprocal relationship with individualism: Western civilization generated a distinctive individualism that was very congenial to modernity; in turn, the process of modernization greatly accentuated this individualism, and, one may add, successfully exported individualism to other parts of the world. Not surprisingly, various theorists of modernization (for instance, Talcott Parsons) assumed that individualism (or, as he called it, "ego-orientation") is inevitably and intrinsically linked to modernity.

The East Asian experience, at the very least, makes this assumption less self-evident. To be sure, there has been successful exportation of Western-style individualism in this region as well (often to the chagrin of tradition-minded Asians). However, it can be plausibly argued that East Asia, even in its most modernized sectors, continues to adhere to values of collective solidarity and discipline that strike the Western observer as very different indeed from his accustomed values and patterns of conduct. The recent discussion about Japanese styles of business and industrial management has brought this feature into sharp relief. Could it be that East Asia has successfully generated a non-individualistic version of capitalist modernity? If so, the linkage between modernity, capitalism, and individualism has not been inevitable or intrinsic; rather, it would have to be reinterpreted as the outcome of contingent historical circumstances. If one reached such a conclusion, this would be much more than a reinterpretation of the past. Much more important, it would suggest the possibility of changes in this linkage in the future (changes that one might either welcome or deplore, depending on how committed one is to the values of Western individualism). Within the broad comparative logic that I have alluded to, one would then conclude that the specific aggregate of economic and sociocultural features that we know as industrial capitalism in the West could be disaggregated, perhaps reassembled in different ways (again, for better or for worse). I don't think that the evidence allows us to reach such a conclusion just yet. Thus the evidence of the inroads of individualism among young people in the East Asian societies is, as far as I'm familiar with it, uneven and inconclusive. But the very fact that the East Asian experience raises this question indicates its great importance as a vast "control experiment" that puts our assumptions about modernity to the test.

All of this reopens the questions, in an astonishingly fresh way, about the relation of modern capitalism and culture that preoccupied Max Weber in the early decades of this century. Weber's great work, *The Protestant Ethic and the Spirit of Capitalism*, continues to serve as a central point of reference for all who study this relation, even those who strongly disagree with Weber's thesis about the religious roots of capitalism and modernity in the West. Now, as is well known, Weber (also, one may say, in the mode of a vast, imaginary laboratory) wrote extensively on Asia, notably China and India, concluding that Asian cultures and religious traditions were deeply uncongenial to modernization. I think one may say today, quite simply, that Weber was wrong. I have imagined a number of times that the good German professor would come back to life today, say on top of a high-rise office building in downtown Taipei, that he would take one look out the window and say, "Well, I was wrong!" But to state that Weber was wrong—or, to put it more scientifically, that his theories about Asian culture have been empirically falsified—is not terribly interesting, except perhaps to disappointed Weber devotees. The much more interesting question is why he was wrong: what did he overlook? More specifically, are there cultural roots, and especially religio-ethical roots, of modern Asian capitalism? If so, what are they? Weber's questions were eminently important, even if some of his answers have to be discarded.

Again, let me say very frankly that I don't think we have, or can have, the answer to these questions at this time. An enormous amount of research and reflection will be required before we can come closer to some empirically supportable answers. But let me at least indicate some plausible areas of exploration.

For several years now the so-called post-Confucian hypothesis has enjoyed a certain vogue. It is essentially simple: both Japan and the newly industrialized countries of East Asia belong to the broad area of influence of Sinitic civilization, and there can be no doubt that Confucianism has been a very powerful force in all of them. The hypothesis is that a key variable in explaining the economic performance of these countries is Confucian ethics—or post-Confucian ethics, in the sense that the moral values in question are now relatively detached from the Confucian tradition proper and have become more widely diffused. Historical evidence on the spread of Confucian education and ideology is very relevant to this hypothesis, but equally important is empirical research into the sway of Confucian-derived values in the lives of ordinary people, many of whom have never read a Confucian classic and have had little education, Confucian or other. Robert Bellah has coined the happy phrase "bourgeois Confucianism" to distinguish this from the "high" Confucianism of the Mandarin elite of traditional China. The work currently being done by S.G. Redding and his associates at the University of Hong Kong on the norms of Chinese entrepreneurs is informed by precisely this point of view.

I'm strongly inclined to believe that, as evidence continues to come in, this hypothesis will be supported. It is inconceivable to me that at least some of the Confucian-derived values intended by the hypothesis—a positive attitude to the affairs of this world, a sustained lifestyle of discipline and self-cultivation, respect for authority, frugality, an overriding concern for stable family life—should not be relevant to the work ethic and the overall social attitudes of the region. At the same time, I strongly suspect that Confucianism is by no means the only cultural and religious factor in play. Other factors will have to be explored.

A very important area of exploration, I believe, is that of East Asian Buddhism. It is possible to make the argument that, as Buddhism crossed the Tibetan plateau and the great Himalayan passes, it underwent a profound transformation, changing from what was perhaps the most world-denying religion in human history to an emphatically world-affirming one. If so, this transformation was certainly the work of the Chinese mind, which, in its fundamental stance in the face of reality, is somewhere around the antipodes of the mind of India. To be sure, some of these world-affirming themes can already be found in Mahayana Buddhism in India, but it was in China and the other Mahayana countries of East Asia that salvation was located consistently in this world, culminating perhaps in the frequently reiterated proposition that *nirvana* and *samsara* are one and the same (or that the true body of the Buddha, the *dharmakaya*, is this world as we know it empirically). There are other East Asian traditions that must be explored to determine their effects, intended or unintended, on man's attitudes to the world of nature, to work in the world, and to the proper goals of life. I'm thinking here particularly of Taoism and Shinto.

Yet another important area of investigation, in the quest for a "spirit" of Asian modernity, would be folk religion. Allow me to tell a little story in this connection. When I was last in Taiwan, in 1982, I discussed the "post-Confucian hypothesis" with Professor Yih-yuan Li of the Academia Sinica. He was skeptical about the hypothesis and expressed the opinion that Chinese folk religion would be at least as important as Confucianism for the matter at hand. I was a little puzzled (partly, no doubt, because of my near-total ignorance in this area). A few weeks later, in what my old teacher Alfred Schutz used to call an "aha experience," I understood what Professor Li meant. I was in Singapore, on a tour of a part of the city in the company of a Singaporean anthropologist, when we came upon a spirit temple. We went in and talked to the medium, a young man who, as I recall, was an electrician by occupation. He conducted seances in the living room of his home and he gladly explained things to us. The center of the room was occupied by a bookshelf with several shelves, on which were arranged plaster-of-paris statuettes of different divinities and supernatural beings. On the top shelf, in the middle, was a statuette of Kuan Yiu, the Chinese Goddess of Mercy. All the other figures were placed hierarchically in relation to her. What impressed me was the manner in which the medium spoke about them. He would say something like this: "This fellow over here has been very bad. He is not good for anything and we have just demoted him, putting him down from the third to the fourth shelf. If he doesn't improve his performance, he will be thrown out completely. But this one has been very helpful to the community, so we have placed him very close to the Goddess.'' And so on. What struck me was that this man was speaking about supernatural beings in very much the same way, and indeed in the same tone of voice, that a corporation executive might speak about his staff. The little pantheon in the living room, then, could be seen as a sort of metaphysical table of organization.

All this, of course, suggests a very different hypothesis (I don't want to preempt what Professor Li has to say on the subject, but in my own mind I call it the "Li hypothesis"): the "great traditions," including Confucianism and Mahayana Buddhism, after all exist on a substratum of unsophisticated, deeply rooted attitudes to the world (cognitive as well as emotional). Could it be that, in the case of Sinitic civilization, it is in this substratum, rather than in the "great traditions," that we must seek the roots of this-worldliness, activism, pragmatism, and the like?[2]

Can other countries, be it in the Third World or in the West, learn from the East Asian experience? I suppose that nobody would deny that something can be learned from the experience of societies different from one's own, but the question rather intends the notion that East Asia might provide a "model" for others in the sense of a coherent and distinctive strategy of societal development. The answer to the question will hinge to a considerable degree on the role one will eventually ascribe to cultural factors in the economic performance of the region. Broadly speaking, two hypotheses are possible here, one "culturalist," the other "institutionalist." The first hypothesis would be to the effect that the economic success of Taiwan, for example, has been crucially determined by the fact that Taiwan is populated by Chinese people, whose attitudes to the world have been shaped by Chinese culture and Chinese social institutions. Having postulated this hypothesis, one may then explore which Chinese cultural patterns and themes have been important in shaping the "spirit" of modern Chinese capitalism. Alternatively, the second hypothesis would postulate that the economic success of Taiwan is only marginally due to such cultural factors, but is rather to be explained in terms of specific economic policies and practices that have nothing to do with the fact that the people executing them are Chinese. It goes without saying that each hypothesis will have very different implications for the possible "exportability"— that is, the "model" character—of the Taiwan experience. If the "institutionalists" are right, there is indeed a model to be exported; if the "culturalists" are right, one must be skeptical of such exportability. It makes sense to suggest to, say, Arabs or Latin Americans that they should adopt the fiscal or the trade policies of Taiwan; it makes no sense to suggest that they should adopt Confucian ethics.

Let me confess here that I'm not only uncertain as to which hypothesis to put my chips on, but while my intuitions as a social scientist (and especially as a sociologist formed very largely by a Weberian approach) are to the "culturalist" side, my moral and political prejudices draw me to the "institutionalist" hypothesis. It is, after all, the much more optimistic one. After pondering these questions for some years, my hunch, for whatever it is worth, is that the correct answer lies somewhere in the middle, between the two hypotheses starkly formulated. I will come back to this point.

Let me point out that the question of the relation between economic performance and cultural traditions is not only relevant to those who might want to learn from the East Asian experience—people like development planners who want to turn Jamaica into "another Taiwan," or American managers who believe that the Japanese hold the secrets of sustained productivity. The question is equally important to East Asia itself, especially as thoughtful people in the region think about the future. No one can dispute the economic (and, for that matter, the social) achievements of these societies. But will these achievements endure in future years?

Obviously this will hinge on a variety of political and economic developments that have nothing to do with the aforementioned two hypotheses: Will the region remain free of war? What will be the actions of the People's Republic of China and the Soviet Union with respect to the region? Will the international economic system continue to be favorable to the kind of development strategy adopted by these countries? What will be the trade policies of Western governments? And so on. But there is also this: if cultural factors are indeed important, as postulated by the "culturalist" hypothesis, then these countries have to be very much concerned with sustaining the cultural traditions at issue. I take it that this is a matter that greatly troubles Singapore's Prime Minister, Lee Kuan Yew, and the recent efforts to introduce a curriculum of Confucian ethics into the schools of Singapore reflects this concern. In this connection too there are important research agendas, for example on the adequacy of the various educational systems in the region and on the way in which attitudes change during the lifetime of individuals. At this time there is much debate in Japan over the educational system: Are its meritocratic norms too harsh? Do these testing mechanisms really select out the kind of elite that Japan may need in the future—innovative and independent-minded—or do they reproduce one generation after another of authority-bound, hard-working conformists? There is some evidence to the effect that young people in some of these countries (especially Japan) are more individualistic and less "collectivity-oriented" than their elders. But is this a sea change in attitudes, or is it simply a passing phenomenon of youth (before an individual settles down to "serious" life)? I don't think that we know at this point; it would obviously be very interesting to know.

Let me come back to my hunch in this matter, namely, that the answer probably lies in the middle between the two hypotheses. Economists use the term "comparative advantage": in international trade, when a country can produce a product relatively more cheaply than other products, it is said to have a comparative advantage in that product. Two countries with a comparative advantage in two different products can trade the products to their mutual benefit. Perhaps cultural factors operate in the same manner. And the distinctive cultural patterns of Sinitic civilization may be highly functional in the post–World War II period, producing the East Asian "economic miracle." There is no guarantee that this comparative advantage will continue in the future. On the other hand, cultural traits also change (although some anthropologists don't like to think so); they usually change spontaneously in response to new circumstances, but they occasionally change as a result of deliberate interventions by government (especially, of course, in educational policies). Therefore, I'm very much persuaded that it is an error to think of culture as a static, invariant reality.

I must come to an end, if not to a conclusion. I am aware that I have raised many more questions than I have answered. This, I am afraid, is of the nature of the beast we call social science. Contrary to what many people think, science can never give us certainty, only probabilities. But I hope that I have said enough to justify my initial proposition that East Asia is one of the most interesting areas in the world today. An economic and social experiment of enormous significance is being conducted in this region. What happens in these countries is of very great significance not only here but everywhere.

Notes

1. Economists speak here of an "anti-Kuznets effect," referring to Simon Kuznets's thesis, substantiated in most places, that high growth is associated with increasing inequality until a leveling process begins at a later stage.
2. This approach may apply to other civilizations as well. Anthropologists especially will be sympathetic to the idea that "high culture" is finally a manifestation on a different plane of underlying patterns and themes shared by everyone in a particular society.

2

An East Asian Development Model: Empirical Explorations[1]

Hsin-Huang Michael Hsiao

Since the 1970s, the development experiences of East Asia have increasingly become a focus of attention of those in social science circles, particularly those interested in development studies. Tremendous concentration was given to the delineation of the success story of the Asian newly industrialized countries (NICs), including Hong Kong, Korea, Singapore, and Taiwan. It goes without saying that the economic dynamism of Japan has gained fame among development and modernization experts since the 1960s. Moreover, practitioners and policymakers in the developed and developing world alike are even more anxious to find out what ingredients constitute the dynamism behind the success stories of East Asia, for counteractions or emulation. Much work has been devoted to describing the success in the aforementioned countries primarily in terms of economic performances.

More recent studies on the impressive economic records of the Asian NICs can be found in various economic journals and in different international and regional conferences. There seems to be little dispute over the economic performances of the Asian NICs regardless of the indicators used for evaluation or for comparison.[2] Many attempts have been made to explain how these countries in fact achieved their successes and, to a lesser extent, why.[3] One very interesting observation on all of this is that scholars and practitioners alike are anxious to transfer the experiences of the East Asian NICs in some way to other parts of the developing world. Two recent gatherings illustrate this: the first was the conference on "The Asian Development Model and the Caribbean Basin Initiative" held in Washington, D.C., by the Carnegie Council on Ethics and International Affairs of New York, on September 25–29, 1984; and the second was a workshop on "The Political Economy of Development in Latin America and East Asia," sponsored by the Center for

U.S.–Mexican Studies of the University of California at San Diego, held in La Jolla December 13–15, 1984.

There has been an unspoken intention—evident in both the meetings mentioned above—to determine the possibility of adapting certain traits, if not the whole package, from the East Asian development model to the Caribbean or Latin America, where development has been in trouble and is in great need of assistance. The various policy issues and institutional factors that have received the greatest attention are implicitly considered as critical variables in making the East Asian development model successful, though this does not eliminate social and cultural factors. Looking at the titles of papers presented at both meetings, one gets the impression that the role of the state has been most widely cited as the key agent in leading development in East Asia, followed by specific governmental policies to encourage economic growth in those countries, including land reform, agricultural policy, industrial strategy, export-led manufacturing policy, or labor policy. Many good delineations have been presented to sort out the successful policy factors that may be applied by Latin American or Caribbean policymakers.

Such policy discussions have been on an empirical level and have been factual in nature. The problems of cause and effect have also been clearly cautioned in discussions of the effects of specific state policies on various economic sectors. On balance, the discussion of the macro political-economic process has so far centered on concrete state actions and the general performance of the state. It is commonly maintained that the states in East Asia can by no means be depicted as ''soft'' in the sense of Gunnar Myrdal's reference to South Asia in the 1960s.[4] The effectiveness of the states' direct or indirect interference in the economic and market spheres in East Asia has been gradually evident among development experts. A new term can then be applied to the Asian NICs: ''developmental state.'' They can be anything but ''soft,'' ''passive,'' or ''minimalist.''[5]

This is particularly true as to the state's relative dominance in the agricultural sector in both Taiwan and South Korea.[6] Singapore is in no way a passive state, and even Hong Kong, under British colonial rule, cannot be termed a soft bureaucracy. The most impressive achievements have been manifested in these states' labor-intensive export-oriented policies, which have been deemed to be the prime movers of the rapid industrialization that indeed revolutionized the lives of more than 60 million people in a decade or two, including the poorest among them.[7] The view held by I.M.D. Little that the economic dynamism of the East Asian NICs ''can be attributed to good policies and the people'' is by and large shared by serious observers and scholars in world development studies.[8] But as illustrated above, the ''good policies'' are limited to domestic policies, and the ''people factor'' is only mentioned in terms of ''human resources.'' The wider, global political-economic context in which East Asian states are forced to operate in the postwar era is more or less viewed as a given and is not seriously analyzed. This leaves an analytical vacuum between the world-system dynamics and the domestic policymaking process. Consideration of the human factor as mainly a matter of static human endowments is, again, an oversimplification. It provides little insight to the question of how and why East Asian people could indeed have been mobilized to comply with various development policies. The cultural-psychological forces behind the East Asian development dynamism have so far not been dealt with thoroughly, although a great deal of reference has been made to them as a sort of unexplained residual factor. Even those serious culturalists who intend to explain the success story from a sociocultural perspective have not been very convincing, either due to their overly theoretical observations which are not sustained by empirical assessment, or to their narrow scope which takes only the community or village rather than the nation-state as the analytical unit. Peter Berger advocates an economic-cultural viewpoint that has merit in attempting to bring the various cultural forces that have driven people in East Asia to act as they have into the analysis of the region's macroeconomic dynamism since the 1960s.[9] However, much more solid empirical validation is greatly needed.

In this Chapter, I will attempt to bridge the gap between global economic dynamics and domestic policymaking and between culturally bound social-behavior patterns and economic dynamism at the national level by raising a series of empirical questions that can hopefully set the tone for the significant task of searching for an East Asian development model. I have no intention of drawing any empirical conclusions; rather I will only try to sort out what is known and what is yet to be learned in order to make the search for an East Asia development model not only possible but also fruitful.

The Global Political-Economic Context

There is genuine consensus that the economic growth and dynamism of the East Asian NICs has been the result of export-oriented industrialization, particularly the rapid booming of manufactures exports. Impressive performances in trade and export by the East Asian NICs have demonstrated the fact that they have successfully overcome the constraints of their limited natural resources by figuring out the most feasible development strategies, which involved using the world market as the preferred outlet for increased output. The importance of this strategy has been widely recognized. The markets in the industrially advanced countries, having experienced high growth, were readily accessible to manufactures exports from the developing countries. The mechanisms by which the East Asian NICs have harnessed the available world market for their export-led industrialization have also been well documented. The sequence of import-substitution industrialization (ISI) followed by export-substitution industrialization (EOI) are particularly noteworthy.[10] The East Asian NICs undertook the critical transition in industrialization strategies in the middle to late 1960s, when the world economy was extremely conducive to trade and exports. In a sense, the East Asian NICs are indeed blessed by favorable timing, and they have taken full advantage of such timing for their rapid industrialization take-off.

Japan was the first "late comer" in Asia to become a partner in the industrialized world, initially specializing in labor-intensive manufactures exports. Hong Kong then followed in Japan's footsteps. When Japan began in the mid-1960s to give up labor-intensive exports due to the constraints of labor costs, Korea, Taiwan, and Singapore started their export expansion, again largely depending on labor-intensive manufactures. The "Four Little Dragons" or "Gang of Four" have been fortunate enough to profit from the shift of comparative advantage in the international division of labor as historically assigned by the timing of the world economy, and, as "late-late comers," they indeed "hit the market" at the right time by filling the slot left by the "late comer" Japan.

The above analysis certainly provides useful insights into how Asian NICs became NICs, but two important empirical questions remain to be tackled. The first question concerns the timing of the world economy, and how this timing favored development of the East Asian NICs. The second question concerns why it was in East Asia that industrialization succeeded. So far these two issues have not been widely addressed, and only scattered discussions are available.

Almost all observers accept that from the 1960s onward the world economy had its own dynamics, or timing. But, the question of the timing of the East Asian NICs' entry into the world market and indeed their ability to "benefit" from incorporation should be taken as a crucial one, particularly in an empirical sense. Here it may be useful to look into the internal logic and dynamics (in Wallerstein's term, the "cyclic rhythm") of the postwar world capitalist system. The Asian NICs entered the world market at a time when the world system had been expanding and the capitalist countries (particularly the U.S.) enjoyed a great degree of overall economic growth. That the U.S. emerged as a unicentric core of the capitalist system after the war could be considered the most unique feature of the postwar system the East Asian NICs entered. Only the dominance of a hegemonic core state and the absence of major rivalry among core powers differentiated East Asia's situation of "dependence" from that of Latin America. The economic necessity of the American market for NICs' manufactured goods and the political imperatives of the U.S. cold war ideology vis-à-vis Soviet and Chinese communism in the region have established an "outer limit" for the activities of the East Asian allies of the

U.S., e.g., Japan, Taiwan, South Korea, and to a lesser extent, even Hong Kong and Singapore. As long as the outer limit—that is, to be capitalistic and anti-communist—is not breached the allies are free to pursue what could be considered by East Asian nationalists as "national interests" and "autonomy," even though these activities may prove devastating to domestic American industrial or labor interests in the future.

Therefore the timing of the East Asian incorporation into the U.S.–dominated world economy was indeed unique. One hypothesis advanced here is that the nature of the American hegemony, as it emerged from a trial-and-error process in the postwar era, could be much more open for the peripheral nations to escape from classic dependence than that which the dependency theorists observed in Latin America. One then has to look empirically into the very character of the role of the U.S. in East Asia.

One other related empirical question is why East Asia could be given such latitude in pursuing their interests received as such by U.S. foreign policymakers. Here geopolitical considerations come to the fore. The fact that East Asia was viewed as a bulwark against Soviet communism in the U.S. containment strategy formulated right after World War II helps one understand the multifaceted support which the capitalist-inclined states in this region received from the U.S., economically and militarily. As mentioned earlier, the outer limit for East Asian countries is to be anti-communist in national ideology and capitalist in development. Once the external linkages were established, a kind of exchange process was then underway. The East Asian countries seemed to take such external linkages as opportunities and "benevolence," and not as an inescapable death trap, despite the fact that they remained dependent on the U.S.

As Thomas Gold puts it, the ruling elites in East Asia have viewed the global economy as a challenge, as they realized that they were resource-poor, overpopulated, in vulnerable security situations, and unable to be self-reliant.[11] They also realized that they could take advantage of postwar political realities by granting political support to the emerging American power in the region. It would be inconceivable to ignore altogether the calculative capability of the East Asian states and their elites, given the limited choices available to them in the first place.

Once again, a serious empirical study into the ways in which the East Asian ruling elites calculated their own situations in postwar global political-economic contexts is needed. The compromises they have made in dealing with American foreign policymakers have to be documented. The potential conflicts that would result from such compromises within the states' machinery and local dominant elites and the solutions they have finally come up with in resolving conflicts are also of great interest. In other words, I do not suggest a "tyranny of the whole" approach, as Tony Smith did in his criticism of world-system theory.[12] Rather, the situation of the East Asian NICs should be examined from a broader historical, political, and economic framework by which the evolution of the states and their relations with external linkages can be better appreciated. Such recognition that external-internal linkages are to be seriously dealt with has gradually gained attention among scholars of the East Asian NICs.[13] The uniqueness of the world-economy timing in the postwar era, the new emergence of the dominant U.S. role in the region, and the geopolitical considerations of East Asia together constitute quite a different historical context from that of the rest of the developing countries.

To point out the importance of such a broader global political-economic perspective does not translate into providing answers to the questions posed earlier. Further empirical studies following this approach should be encouraged. Nevertheless, the unique world-system timing does constitute a historical ingredient of an East Asian development model.

State Structure and State-Society Relationships

As I briefly discussed at the beginning of this chapter, the role of the state in the process of East Asian development has been well noticed. Regardless of what terms are used to describe the states of East Asia, all scholars claim that the character of the state has played an active and leading role in development in each country. East Asian governments are relatively "autonomous" and "strong" vis-à-vis both external linkages with the U.S. and internal relations with local elites. The foregoing discussion provided some insight into why East Asian states have enjoyed a certain degree of relative autonomy in facing U.S. hegemony. The outer limit was cautiously and skillfully respected by the East Asian states, and, in turn, with external capital and even military support from the U.S., the states have gained an even better maneuvering position and more power in promoting certain economic sectors or favoring certain classes or social constituencies. In a sense the external dependence has not undercut state autonomy. On the contrary, it in fact enhanced state autonomy vis-à-vis the domestic classes and elites.

In this connection, one also has to look into the nature of the state in East Asia in the postwar era. It should be noted that the four states all shared a common colonial history before the war, which had a profound influence on the state structure after independence. The "overdeveloped" state bureaucracy that was inherited from the ex-colonial powers (Japan and Britain) and was created to control the indigenous population might be a legacy that led to compliance of the populace with state dominance.

Moreover, the traditional Oriental (Chinese, to be more specific) conception of the state as being more than a political control force also penetrated people's moral attitudes in East Asia; that conception even lasted until recent years. The Confucianist moral definition of the state has emphasized the aspect of the benevolent conduct of a leader or the state authority. East Asian tradition has long socialized people to respect "authority," which in modern times is represented by state bureaucracy. With such a political culture, East Asian states are certainly able to mobilize resources more autonomously, without being confronted with too much opposition from various sectors of the society.

Of course, one should not be naïve and assert that the political culture is the only factor that makes East Asian states strong and active. Without favorable world economic conditions and U.S. support, East Asian states probably could not have enjoyed such autonomy and strength in state-society relationships. Besides, without the successful implementation of land reform, which greatly weakened the potential opposition of the landed classes to industrialization in the cases of Taiwan and South Korea, and without the already favorable attitudes among local entrepreneurs to capitalist development in the two city-states, the East Asian NICs probably could not have mobilized resources in such a well-organized manner for capitalist industrial development.

In the above analysis I have tried hard to avoid the danger of reductionism. The East Asian NICs have indeed provided a very special historical case in that the state structure and state-society relationships can not be explained solely by either world-system reductionism or dominant-class reductionism. Complex external and internal forces have historically interacted with each other, and such interactions have resulted in the unique character of the relative autonomy of the East Asian NICs in the past several decades.

Equally important is to call for a comparative study of the dialectic relations between the state and class structures. In the East Asian NICs new classes were created by the state to pursue capitalist industrialization in the 1960s and onward. It has been observed that since the mid-1970s, the newly emergent working class and urban middle class have put increased pressures on the states in the East Asian NICs. The changing state-society relationships and coalitions might be another fruitful area for empirical research in the future. The character and evolution of such state-society dialectics will, to a large extent, shape the ways in which the East Asian NICs will adjust their management of capitalist development in the future.

Admittedly, much has been written about how East Asian states have successfully managed the external and internal constraints and assets to ensure their "national survival" over the past four decades. However, there is much more empirical investigation yet to be done.

The Cultural Factors

One of the most exciting but least studied areas of the East Asian success story has to do with the proper identification of the cultural factors in the process of capitalist development, which was in some ways alien to traditional Asia. So far there have been some interesting and illuminating discussions on the subject, though all have been in rather general and theoretical terms. Though a sizable part of the literature focuses on Japanese corporate culture and its impact on business/organizational management and behavior, very few studies really relate the cultural issue to macro regional economic dynamism at the empirical level.

It would be inconceivable to reject altogether the macroeconomic dynamism achieved by the collective efforts of the people in the region as having nothing to do with the cultural factors held in common. Cultural elements such as work ethics, thrift, diligence, respect for educational achievement, avoidance of overt conflict in social relations, loyalty to hierarchy and authority, stress on order and harmony, to name just a few, should have significant bearing on the dynamic economic activities practiced by workers, farmers, entrepreneurs, public servants, and even policymakers.

It would be equally unwise to maintain that cultural factors are the only causes of the region's success. In other words, neither a hard-nosed "policy thesis," which argues that the East Asian success was solely due to the "right" policies, nor a wholehearted "culture thesis," which only looks at the quality of culture for the ingredients of the big success, can realistically provide the whole picture.

Even with this conception in mind, and presuming it to be a plausible one, one is still confronted with several empirical problems. First, simply to say that culture in a very broad sense should have something to do with economic development is not terribly meaningful. But to delineate specific East Asian cultural traits or elements that could provide a "comparative advantage" in macroeconomic development processes is immensely important. Taking culture as a comparative advantage, as proposed by Peter Berger, is useful here.[14] In other words, the specific cultural roots of modern Asian capitalism are yet to be uncovered. In recent years, a very popular phrase is "post-Confucianism," later called "vulgar Confucianism" by Berger, which implies that Confucianist ethics practiced by ordinary people in their everyday lives could be an important variable in explaining the economic dynamism of East Asia. The Confucian-derived ethics and values toward work, family, and organizational authority are most relevant. A group of scholars is being assembled at Princeton University by Gilbert Rozman to study the impact of traditional sociocultural behavior in modern East Asia, and they are focusing exactly on the above social elements that are derived from "vulgar Confucianism."

Two ways of observing how these Confucianist ethics and values have been manifested in postwar East Asian society are to focus on two important realms: family and work organization. Other important cultural features include Buddhism, folk religion, and Christianity. It is good to note that the chapters in this book address each of the major East Asian cultural traditions and their respective roles in the development process. Similarly, several concrete traits derived from these cultural traditions are expected to be carefully delineated in these pages as well.

The second empirical problem is that in seeking to understand and appreciate the guarded "cultural thesis" as part of the complex interrelationship of culture and economics, cultural factors should not be interpreted as individual social behavior per se in the everyday life of the people. Rather they should be viewed as a set of orderly, institutionalized cultural arrangements at the societal level. Only at that level can one relate cultural behavior to macroeconomic activities. Again, one is not anxious to find in these cultural areas the "causes" of economic development; one can, however, expect to look for the "trigger" of development in East Asia. That is to say, the cultural factors could not act alone without other supporting political and economic conditions. It can also be added that the question is not to identify the cultural traits per se but to identify the political and economic environment in which these cultural factors are able to make economic activity dynamic and lively.

Michio Morishima's work on the role of Japanese Confucianist ethics in Japanese capitalism is relevant here.[15] He points out that the manner in which ideology has been utilized during the course of a country's history and that the content of that ideology (Confucianism) have played a crucial role in helping direct the possibilities of day to day economic activities. Roy Hofheinz and Kent Calder, on the other hand, seem to underestimate the "trigger" function of seemingly constant East Asian cultural factors in allowing the region's explosive economic growth in the past few decades. They merely note that "culture provides a background of values reinforcing respect for authority, promoting education and rewarding diligence."[16] It is a background indeed, and a necessary one, for culture is not a static medium but a genuine, dynamic trigger. Undoubtedly, more reflections are necessary to make such a view more plausible and empirically sound.

A third empirical problem concerns the linkage between the micro (cultural behavior) and the macro (national policymaking), and is equally important. The question of "right policy" is again relevant. During the past few decades, state policies for economic growth in the East Asian NICs have been presented by the government as offering probable and reasonable "opportunity," and they have been accepted as such by the people, particularly the entrepreneurial class. Inspired by the state strategies, the entrepreneurial class then was inclined to work to make them succeed. The state policymakers might have calculated that they did not have many options given the external and internal structures, and they had to take the chance. On the other hand, without the collective compliance on the part of the people, it is possible that the policy would not have been "right." The fact that people would be willing to follow state policies might have been due to the cultural factors listed earlier. Taking chances may not be a good explanation for any social scientist. But can a social scientist be so sure that everything that happens has absolutely nothing at all to do with such an unexplained chance factor?

One last point to be mentioned is the common sentiment evinced by the people in East Asia toward the issue of "national survival" in modern times. East Asians usually take their nation's survival as a real problem facing their societies, particularly in face of the challenges presented by modern Western society. People in the West, particularly in modern times, generally have not experienced this kind of national sentiment, which in East Asia has been a mix of cultural superiority and political inferiority. These attitudes may also have some direct and indirect influences on pushing people to work harder under the national ideology toward the goals of national strength and wealth.

Conclusions

As I stated at the beginning of this essay, the most exciting area in the world today is East Asia, where impressive economic and social progress has been witnessed over the past few decades. It is not surprising that so much attention has been given to this phenomenon. The efforts of social scientists to understand the reasons why East Asia has succeeded so well is equally exciting.

I have attempted to provide a brief empirical overview of the major issues brought about by recent studies of East Asian development. Three main concerns have been addressed here: the wider political economic context in which East Asia has progressed in the postwar era; the world economic system and its structural change, particularly the timing of East Asia's incorporation into the postwar U.S.-dominated world system, which was indeed unique as were the ways in which the U.S. exerted its hegemony after the war; and the geopolitical considerations, which provided East Asian countries some room to maneuver within the context of dependence, and which shaped considerably the relationships between East Asia and the world political economy.

Under the constraints provided by the timing of the world economy and the unique nature of the U.S. role in the region, the state structure and state-society relationships have been quite different from those in other parts of the developing world. Therefore, the strategic shift of state policy on economic development from one phase to another has been rather smooth. In addition, capitalist development via industrialization was much more successful in the relatively autonomous and "hard" states in East Asia than in other developing countries, and development efforts have not been confronted by severe opposition by the local dominant class.

The most praised "right" policies were made possible by effective mobilization of local and foreign resources. The states in East Asia might also have been greatly blessed with certain cultural factors that served as a "comparative advantage," allowing the economy to take off at the right moment. The "trigger" function of the major cultural factors in the East Asian development process must be appreciated.

Human history is full of uncertainties. The search for explanations of past history is even more so. Like one old Chinese saying, any big historical event is always made possible by three conditions: heavenly timing, geographic advantages, and human harmony. The East Asian development model as popularly depicted may in fact consist of the same three, yet unique, ingredients: world system timing, geopolitical considerations, and cultural factors. While this may seem fatalistic, a realistic overview of East Asian development history might just press one to feel that way. As to the extent these three ingredients have been interrelated and what their order of importance is remains a serious task facing serious social scientists.

Notes

1. The author wishes to thank Professor Peter L. Berger and Chin-chuan Lee for useful comments on an earlier version of this chapter.
2. John Wong, "Export-Oriented Industrial Development in East Asia," in John Tessitore and Susan Woolfson, eds., *The Asian Development Model and the Caribbean Basin Initiative* (New York: Council on Religion and International Affairs, 1985), pp. 49–63.
3. Robert Wade and Gordon White, eds., *Developmental States in East Asia: Capitalist and Socialist*, special issue of *IDS Bulletin* 15:2, 1984; and Roy Hofheinz and Kent Calder, *The Eastasia Edge* (New York: Basic Books, 1982).
4. Gunnar Myrdal, *Asian Drama: An Inquiry into the Poverty of Nations* (New York: Pantheon, 1968).
5. Robert Wade and Gordon White, eds., *Developmental States in East Asia*, op. cit.; Mick Moore, "Agriculture in Taiwan and South Korea: The Minimalist State?" in Robert Wade and Gordon White, eds., *Developmental States in East Asia*, op. cit., pp. 57–64; and Robert Wade, "South Korea's Agricultural Development: The Myths of the Passive State," *Pacific Viewpoint*, May 1983, pp. 11–28.

6. H.H. Michael Hsiao, *Government Agricultural Strategies in Taiwan and South Korea: A Macro Sociological Assessment* (Taipei: Institute of Ethnology, Academia Sinica, 1980); and H.H. Michael Hsiao, "Land Reform in East Asia Revisited: An Ingredient of an East Asian Development Model," in John Tessitore and Susan Woolfson, eds., *In Search of an East Asian Development Model*, op. cit., pp. 149–59.
7. I.M.D. Little, "The Experience and Causes of Rapid Labor-Intensive Development in Korea, Taiwan, Hong Kong, and Singapore, and the Possibilities of Emulation," ILO Working Paper WP11-1, ARTEP (Bangkok: ILO, 1979).
8. I.M.D. Little, "The Experience and Causes of Rapid Labor-Intensive Development in Korea," op. cit.
9. Peter L. Berger, "An East Asian Development Model?" *The Economic News* (Taipei), September 17–23, 1984; and Peter L. Berger, "Can the Caribbean Learn from East Asia?" *Caribbean Review* 13:2, February 1984, pp. 6–9.
10. Roy Hofheinz and Kent Calder, *The Eastasia Edge*, op. cit.; and John Wong, "Export-Oriented Industrial Development in East Asia," op. cit.
11. Thomas Gold, "Preface," in H.H. Michael Hsiao, ed., *Development and Underdevelopment: A Reader in the Sociology of Development* (Taipei: Chin-Lin Books, 1985).
12. Tony Smith, "The Underdevelopment of Development Literature: The Case of Dependency Theory," *World Politics* 31, 1979, pp. 247–88.
13. See Bruce Cummings, "The Origins and Development of the Northeast Asian Political Economy: Industrial Sectors, Product Cycles, and Political Consequences," *International Organization* 38:1, 1984, pp. 1–40; and Hagen Koo, "The Political Economy of Development in South Korea and Taiwan: The Interplay of World System, Class and State," paper presented at the Annual Meeting of the Asian Studies Association, San Francisco, September 1982.
14. Peter L. Berger, "An East Asian Development Model?" op. cit.
15. Michio Morishima, *Why Has Japan Succeeded?* (Cambridge: Cambridge University Press, 1982).
16. Roy Hofheinz and Kent Calder, *The Eastasia Edge*, op. cit.

PART II
THEORETICAL AND EMPIRICAL PROBLEMS

3

The New Asian Capitalism: An Economic Portrait

Gustav Papanek

The relevance of the East Asian development experience to the less developed world depends crucially on whether there is an identifiable economic model which underlies and largely explains the undoubted economic success of the five countries under review—South Korea, Singapore, Taiwan, Hong Kong, and Japan—and whether that model is transferable. There are two schools of thought on this question: those who believe that the explanation of East Asian economic success lies largely in the cultural realm, that is, in values, institutional structures, and social relations, and those who maintain that economic success can largely be explained by the economic strategy adopted by these countries.

Do not think that the former group includes no economists. Indeed, my late colleague, Paul Rosenstein-Rodan, believed that economists all too frequently abdicated their responsibility to trace the causes of economic events: "When doctors don't know what caused an illness, they call it psychosomatic; when economists cannot explain a phenomenon they call it social or cultural." On the subject of East Asian success, however, the explanation which gives primacy to economic strategy is gaining currency. The East Asian strategy is frequently referred to as "the Korean model," because Japan is classified as developed, Singapore and Hong Kong are considered atypical, and Taiwan presents awkward political problems. Increasingly, the fashion among politicians and businessmen, as well as economists, in the less developed countries (LDCs) and in international agencies has been to identify this "Korean model" as worthy of emulation, just as some talked in the past of an Indian, Russian, or Chinese model. This paper is an attempt to identify the economic strategy, that is, the set of policies, which explains the success of these countries, to speculate on the extent to which economic variables provide an adequate explanation, and, therefore, the extent to which the model has relevance for other countries.

The Indices of Success: Growth and Equity

The most obvious characteristic the East Asian countries share, and at the same time the outstanding index of their economic success, is the high rate of economic growth they achieved once they adopted a growth-oriented strategy. East Asia is the only part of the world that consistently outperformed all comparable countries in this respect over two to three decades. Indeed their rate of growth was generally about double that of other low-income countries (see Table 3.1).

The disparity was, in a real sense, even greater. During the early growth phase the low-income countries averaged a rate of population growth of 2.5

TABLE 3.1
Economic Growth

Countries	GNP Per Capita 1950[a] (1964$)	AVERAGE ANNUAL		GROWTH RATE GDP (%)		GNP Per Capita 1983[e] (current $)
		1950s[b]	1960s[c]	1970s[c]	1980–83[d]	
Japan	251	6.4[1]	10.5	5.2	3.8	10,120
All Industrialized Countries	n.a.	4.2	5.1	3.2	1.1	11,060
Singapore	434	5.4	8.8	8.4	8.6	6,620
Hong Kong	222	9.2	10.0	9.4	7.0	6,000
Taiwan	95	8.1	9.3	10.4	6.0	2,753[2]
South Korea	78	5.1 (4.7)[4]	8.6 (10.1)[4]	9.3	4.7	2,010
All Middle-Income Countries	n.a.	4.8	6.1	5.5	0.8[3]	1,310
All Oil-Importing, Middle-Income Countries	n.a.	n.a.	5.9	5.5	1.6	1,530
All Low-Income Countries	n.a.	3.9	4.5	4.7	5.2	260

Notes:
[1] Annual growth rate between 1952–60
[2] Converted to U.S. dollars by using the exchange rate NT$/US$ = 39.93 which was obtained from The Asia Society, Corporate Briefing, "Taiwan: An Economic and Political Update," January 1986
[3] Weighted average of growth rate of middle-income oil importers and oil exporters
[4] The first figure is for Korea as a whole, the second is for South Korea.
Sources:
[a] World Bank, *World Tables,* 2d ed., Economic Data Sheet I.
[b] World Bank, *World Tables,* 3d ed., vol. I, Economic Data Sheet I.
[c] World Bank, *World Development Report,* 1981, Table 2.
[d] IMF, *International Financial Statistics,* Supplement Series, No. 8, 1984, and World Bank, *World Development Report,* 1984, text tables.
[e] World Bank, *World Development Report,* 1985, Table 1.
[f] Council for Economic Planning and Development, Republic of China on Taiwan, *Statistical Data Book,* 1985.

percent per year. If data for the People's Republic of China are excluded from the discussion (since so much of the data has recently been reviewed and the revisions are often not yet incorporated in various data sources) the low-income countries have achieved a growth rate over the past 30 years of about 4 percent. Subtracting population growth gives a per capita growth rate of about 1.5 percent per year, which is barely perceptible and which means it would take about 50 years to double per capita income. In contrast, the per capita growth rate of East Asia has been four times as great, with per capita income doubling in about 10 years. By the 1970s the rate of population growth in East Asia had declined much more than in the low-income countries, worsening the gap.

The comparison with other low-income countries, primarily those in South Asia, may not seem the most appropriate one, because four of the East Asian countries are now in the upper middle–income group and one (Japan) is considered industrialized. It is easy to forget that after the Second World War the per capita income of the indigenous population in most of East Asia was more comparable to that of South Asia—the region which remains the heart of the poverty problem—than to Latin America, West Asia, or some countries in Africa. One of the reasons for the reference to a Korean model rather than to an East Asian one is that Japan is widely assumed to have been an industrialized or developed country, whose postwar experience is no more relevant to the problems of the low-income countries than the experience of Western Europe. It is true that Japan had a better infrastructure and industrial base than most less developed countries at the end of the war, but in terms of per capita income and the need to absorb productively a large pool of unemployed and underemployed labor, it was an LDC. Japan's per capita income was of the order of $200, and there were several million workers underemployed in agriculture or other low productivity work, demobilized, repatriated from the occupied areas, or dismissed from destroyed and closed industries. Therefore even the Japanese experience is relevant to the key problems of development.

Not only was growth in these countries rapid in comparison to other LDCs, it was also remarkably consistent and, above all, quite equitable. Unlike growth in China or in many resource-rich countries—rapid during some periods and slow or negative in others—East Asian growth outpaced that of comparable countries in *all* five- to ten-year periods once they adopted a consistent development model. What is even more unusual is that these were and remain reasonably egalitarian societies compared to other mixed economies. Only in Korea in the 1970s has income distribution become less egalitarian. In 1980 all were more egalitarian than the comparable countries (except Singapore for which we have no data) (see Table 3.8). An indirect measure of welfare, which is greatly affected by income distribution, is life expectancy: where income is unequally distributed the poor die young, or rather, their children die frequently. In the 1960s life expectancy in East Asia, excluding Japan, was about 50 percent greater than in low-income and 25 percent greater than in middle-income countries (see Table 3.10). By the 1970s the gap had shrunk, but was still about one quarter to one third. In the 1970s the Physical Quality of Life Index (PQLI), a composite of several welfare indicators, in East Asia was about one third higher than in all middle-income countries and double that in low-income countries (see Table 3.11).

In short, the outstanding characteristics of the East Asian development model are rapid, steady, and equitable growth from a base of very low per capita incomes at the end of the war.

Popular Explanations: Resources and Capitalism

These characteristics, however, define success but do not explain it. One partial, inadequate, and popular explanation points to the fact that all East Asian countries are poor in natural resources. Whether the causal linkage is phrased in terms of Toynbee-esque challenge-response terms, or in some other terms, this group of explanations is based on the notion that these countries had to work hard, invest much, and be innovative and entrepreneurial if they wanted to develop. The problem with this explanation is that there are many countries poor in natural resources that have not developed rapidly, South Asia and the Sahel countries in Africa among them, as well as some resource-rich countries that have used their resources wisely to support quite rapid growth, including Malaysia, Thailand, the Ivory Coast, and Botswana.

One element of truth in this argument is that resource-rich countries experience roller-coaster development which is difficult to manage. When there is strong demand for the products of such countries, wealth flows in with relatively little effort. It is a rare and unusual society and government that does not then go on a buying spree and instead husbands a substantial fraction of the wealth against the inevitable decline in demand. No one knows when, indeed even if, that decline will come. It is not wise politics for a government to impose austerity at a time when it is unnecessary in order to husband resources for another time—when another government may well be in power. The inclination is to spend the windfall, and that makes for difficult adjustment problems when the windfall is no longer available. East Asian economies have also been subject to the vagaries of the world market, especially the two city-states (Hong Kong and Singapore) in whose economy exports played an unusually important role, but the fluctuations in external demand have had a less critical importance for them than for the resource-rich states.

Another partial explanation, which has gained increasing currency recently because it so neatly fits the ideological preconceptions of the dominant political tendency in the U.S., is that these are countries that followed a capitalist strategy. This explanation suffers the same flaw as the earlier explanation: there are many other countries, especially in Latin America, that can be characterized as well or better as private-enterprise systems but that have experienced slow growth and rising inequality. Moreover, while Hong Kong is probably the purest private-enterprise economy in the world, it is stretching the definition of capitalism quite a bit to argue that the other four have minimal government intervention. The popular reference to "Japan Inc.," more recently followed by similar appellations for Korea, is based on the notion that government and business are closely involved with each other.

Probably the best way to measure the importance of a government's role in an economy is by the share of public investment in total investment.[1] Hong Kong has consistently been a highly market-oriented economy, while Singapore has been toward the dirigiste end of the spectrum. Taiwan was market-oriented in 1960s and dirigiste in the 1970s. Korea is similar to middle-income countries, but more market-oriented than the low-income areas. By the yardstick of public investment there appear to be no clear-cut, significant differences between the countries of East Asia and other countries (see Table 3.3); they are more market-oriented than most LDCs but not strongly so. Another measure, the size of the public enterprise sector in the economy, does not clearly distinguish Korea, presumably capitalist, from India, presumably socialist.[2] It is universally accepted that the government plays a far larger role in Japan than in most of the other developed economies. Attributing the success of these countries to "the magic of the marketplace" is therefore clearly inadequate. But some attributes of a private-enterprise economy have been crucial in the achievement of all five countries, an issue which is discussed further below.

A Crucial Common Factor: The High Rate of Investment

During their periods of rapid growth all five East Asian countries had above-average rates of investment, and some had among the highest rates in the world. Except in the 1950s, Japan has consistently invested at a rate about 50 percent above that for other developed countries and 25 percent or more above that for middle-income countries. The other four countries have had an investment rate which has been 20 percent to 100 percent above that of comparable countries (see Table 3.2; note that the average for middle-income countries includes the four East Asian ones, so that the figure for all other middle-income countries is lower). The higher rate of investment by itself explains two to four percentage points of the higher growth rate of the East Asian countries (see Table 3.3 for the "ICOR," which relates investment and growth rates and enables one to derive this figure).

Underlying the higher investment rates are three variables whose contribu-

TABLE 3.2
Investment and Savings
(as % of GDP)

Countries	1950s[a]			1960s[a]			1970s[b]			1980–1983[c]		
	Inv.[1]	Dom. Sav.[2]	For. Infl.[3]	Inv.	Dom. Sav.	For. Infl.	Inv.	Dom. Sav.	For. Infl.	Inv.	Dom. Sav.	For. Infl.
Japan	28.9	29.5	-0.6	36.0	36.5	-0.5	33.6	34.3	-0.7	30.3	31.5	-1.2
All Industrialized Countries	21.6	n.a.	n.a.	22.4	24.2	-1.8	22.4	23.5	-1.1	21.3	20.8	0.5
Singapore	11.4	-0.8	12.2	23.4	14.9	8.5	40.3	28.6	11.7	44.0	36.5	7.5
Hong Kong	9.1	9.2	-0.1	20.6	20.6	0.0	26.1	29.2	-3.1	28.8	24.5	4.3
Taiwan	18.1	10.7	7.4	21.4	18.4	3.0	29.9	31.4	-1.5	28.6	31.9	-3.3
South Korea	11.4	3.2	8.2	23.2	13.7	9.5	29.6	22.6	7.0	27.5	23.8	3.7
All Middle-Income Countries	n.a.			19.7	18.2	1.5	24.9	20.0	4.9	24.5	22.3	2.2
All Low-Income Countries	n.a.			16.3	13.4	2.9	19.3	18.6	2.9	24.8	22.0	2.8

Notes:
[1] Gross domestic investment
[2] Gross national savings (excluding net amount transferred from abroad)
[3] Foreign Inflow = Gross domestic investment − Gross national savings

Sources:
[a] World Bank, *World Tables*, 3d. ed., vol. 1, Economic Data Sheet I and Tables 3 and 9.
[b] World Bank, *World Development Report*, 1981–1985, Table 5; and World Bank, *World Tables*, 3d. ed., Tables 3 and 9.
[c] World Bank, *World Development Report*, 1982–1985, Table 5; and World Bank, *World Tables*, 3d. ed., Tables 3 and 9.
[d] Council for Economic Planning and Development, Republic of China, *Taiwan Statistical Data Book*, 1985.

tion is not uniform for the five countries: the rate of domestic savings, foreign aid, and foreign private investment. Since the Second World War, Japan has had an unusually high rate of savings, adequate not only to finance its exceptionally high rate of investment, but also to generate a surplus of savings, which has been exported to finance investment elsewhere (most recently to finance the large U.S. deficit in both government and international accounts). What is often overlooked in recent paeans of praise for this achievement and in drawing lessons from the Japanese experience for other countries is that during its early development Japan also drew heavily on foreign resources. Many countries, including the U.S. and Japan, have drawn heavily on foreign capital to finance early development. This is understandable: when any country begins the process of modern growth it is poor, and it is difficult to induce a poor people to further reduce their current consumption to finance investment. In the Japanese case foreign borrowing occurred much earlier, and in the postwar period a remarkable rate of domestic savings has been achieved.

In the 1950s both Korea and Taiwan financed well over half their investment with foreign aid. Both were aid success stories: foreign aid financed their initial growth spurt when their economies were in a shambles from civil war or war. That aid-financed growth enabled them to "graduate," to be able to finance investment without aid subsequently. In Korea, foreign inflows reached a remarkable 72 percent of investment. Korea continued to rely heavily on foreign resources, but beginning in the 1960s these took the form of foreign private investment and foreign commercial borrowing. Taiwan became a major exporter of capital as savings reached world-record levels and exceeded domestic investment needs.

Throughout its recent history, Singapore has relied heavily on foreign capital, both in the form of investment and borrowing, as Korea has in the last twenty years. Hong Kong, like Japan, has financed its investment with its own savings.

While aid was initially important to Korea and Taiwan, more important and characteristic was that all five countries have been able to induce private savers to finance an above-average rate of investment since the mid-1960s, at least. To explain the East Asian development model one needs to explain, not just to describe, this phenomenon. It is all the more remarkable because all of these countries, at one time or another and some for their entire postwar history, were high-risk places for savings and investment. The political and economic future of Japan and Singapore was in doubt immediately after the war, and the futures of the other three have been in doubt for much of the last 40 years. Three factors probably explain their ability to finance a high rate of investment despite this risk and uncertainty.

First, they have profited from a beneficent cycle: high growth facilitates high savings and investment, and high investment, in turn, facilitates high

TABLE 3.3
Economic Efficiency and Strategy

Countries	1950s ICOR[1]	1950s Exp. Grw.[a2]	1950s Share of pub. inv. (%)[b]	1960s ICOR	1960s Exp. Grw.[c]	1960s Share of pub. inv. (%)	1970s ICOR	1970s Exp. Grw.[c]	1970s Share of pub. inv. (%)	1980s ICOR	1980s Exp. Grw.	1980s Share of pub. inv. (%)
Japan	4.5	16	35	3.4	17	27	6.5	9	28	7.9	8	30
All industrial countries	5.1	7	35	4.4	8	31	7.0	6	30	19.4	5[d]	n.a.
Singapore	2.1	10[3]	n.a.	2.7	4	43	4.8	11	44	5.1	11[c]	34
Hong Kong	2.3	3[3]	n.a.	2.1	13	25	2.8	8	21	3.8	11	28
Taiwan	2.2	25[c]	48	2.3	23[c]	31	2.9	31[c]	58	4.8	15[c]	44
South Korea	2.2	0[3]	33	2.7	34	26	3.2	26	25	5.8	13	n.a.
All middle-income countries	n.a.	n.a.	35	3.2	5	38	4.5	4	28	30.6	−3[d]	n.a.
All oil-importing, middle-income countries	n.a.	n.a.	n.a.	n.a.	6	n.a.	n.a.	4	n.a.	n.a.	3[d]	n.a.
All low-income countries	n.a.	4	52	3.6	5	50	4.1	−1	50	4.8	5[d]	n.a.

Notes:

[1]ICOR = ratio between rate of investment and growth of GDP; i.e.: the rate of growth of the rate of investment

[2]Growth of export quantity index

[3]Growth of export value index

[4]Growth of export quantity index between 1980 and 1982.

Sources:

[a]IMF, *International Financial Statistics*, Supplement Series, No. 4, 1982.

[b]Japan, 1955, 1965, 1975 and 1982 figures: United Nations, *Yearbook of National Accounts Statistics*, 1962, 1976, and 1982.

Taiwan, 1955, 1965, 1975, and 1984 figures: *Taiwan Statistical Data Book*, 1985.

Korea, 1956, 1965, 1975 figures: United Nations, *Yearbook of National Accounts Statistics*, 1962, 1976.

Hong Kong, Government capital expenditure as a percentage of total gross domestic investment: Census and Statistics Department, *Hong Kong Annual Digest of Statistics*, 1978, 1985.

Singapore, 1966, 1975: Gustav F. Papanek and Oldrich Kyn, "Flattening the Kuznets Curve: The Effects of Income Distribution of Development, The Rate of Growth and Economic Strategy; Statistical Appendix," *Discussion Paper* No. 76A, Department of Economics, Boston University, October 1981.

Singapore, 1983 figure: Ministry of Trade and Industry, Republic of Singapore, *Economic Survey of Singapore 1984*.

Figures for industrialized, middle-, and low-income countries were obtained by taking simple average of the ratio of public investment of the countries, each group classified by the World Bank (see Gustav F. Papanek and Oldrich Kyn, op. cit., and World Bank, *World Development Report*, 1985).

[c]World Bank, *World Development Report*, 1981, Table 8.

[d]United Nations, *International Trade Statistics Yearbooks*, 1983, and World Bank, *World Development Report*, 1981, and 1984, Table 8.

[e]Council for Economic Planning and Development, Republic of China, *Taiwan Statistical Data Book*, 1985.

growth. It is widely accepted in economic analysis, and it makes good common sense, that it is easier to save out of rising incomes than out of stagnant incomes. With unusually rapid growth, a very high proportion of the population experienced rapidly rising incomes and was more willing and able to save. Foreigners too were more willing to invest in a rapidly growing economy than in a stagnant one. For foreign investors, rapid growth meant greater opportunities for profitable investment, and for foreign lenders it meant a rising ability to pay back loans.

Second, all five countries accepted, even encouraged, a high rate of return for private investors. The economic policies adopted made it possible for investors to become wealthy rather quickly. Unlike in the countries of South Asia and in some countries of Southeast Asia and elsewhere, there was little risk of nationalization, short of a radical change in the system. The risk was equally low that other policy changes (short of nationalization) would suddenly and rather arbitrarily deprive investors of the profits on their investments. In other countries the rate of return was highly dependent on particularistic decisions by specific government officials, which could turn a high profit into a major loss overnight, such decisions include, for instance, the decision on who is to be granted a license for the import of crucial inputs, or a loan from a government bank, or a permit to export particular goods, or on the price at which goods could be sold. In the five countries such profit-or-loss decisions were not controlled by government (e.g., imports were not subject to licenses) or were made within relatively stable and universalistic rules (e.g., exporters received preference over others in access to subsidized loans from government credit institutions).

Third, all were, at least at one time, austere societies, where status accrued to businessmen for expanding their empires, not for conspicuous consumption. The very political instability they faced made them societies under siege, and policies discouraged luxury consumption and encouraged enterprises that created jobs and earned foreign exchange. Imported luxury goods were expensive in Korea, Japan, and Taiwan (Hong Kong and Singapore were exceptions), and the political leadership in four of the countries (not Hong Kong) set an example in terms of austere, rather than luxurious, living. In Hong Kong the elite, recently traumatized by the refugee experience, were also willing to invest at a high rate rather than using their resources for expenditures. In some other Asian countries the government kept the prices of luxury imports relatively low (for those who had access to them), subsidized housing construction, and itself engaged in conspicuous investment, especially the construction of elegant and expensive offices.

It is clear that the considerable risk and uncertainty that investors faced in all of the East Asian countries at one time, with respect to the future of the country as a whole, was overcome and outweighed by the high probability of relatively high rates of return on most investments and by the relatively risk-free environment facing the investor within the country. The high rate of growth and the limit on arbitrary and personalized decisions by powerful government leaders made for more favorable incentives for saving and investment than in other Asian countries, where the country's future was more secure but the individual investor's future was more uncertain.

While a high rate of investment offers a partial explanation of the high rate of growth, the rate of investment was itself achieved primarily by the high growth earlier and the expectation that it would continue. It therefore remains to explain why these countries achieved a higher rate of growth for each unit of investment than most others.

The Key: Effective Economic Management

Utilizing Abundant Labor

The essence of the successful East Asian development model has been a set of economic policies, that is an economic strategy, which made for an efficient use of the resources of these societies—in short, effective economic management. The characteristics of a less developed economy dictate the determinants of economic efficiency. The essence of underdevelopment is a shortage of physical capital and of human skills—training, education, and experience—in modern industry, while the resource that is in abundant supply is unskilled labor. An effective development strategy is one which economizes on the scarce resources, uses the abundant resource lavishly, and rapidly increases the supply of scarce resources.

Another characteristic of many, though by no means all, LDCs is that agriculture has an ample, and often excessive, labor supply. As some increase in capital—machinery—takes place and as modern technology is applied to some operations, agriculture typically sheds labor in these societies; it can not efficiently absorb more labor. Labor productivity in the agricultural sector of these labor-abundant countries is already low, so for this abundant resource to be used efficiently it must be absorbed in the industrial sector.

For labor to be used efficiently in industry, development needs to emphasize labor-intensive activities which require relatively little scarce capital, skills, or technology. But at the low per capita incomes typical of LDCs, the domestic market for the products of such industries is saturated early in the development process. Further growth then requires breaking into the world market with efficiently produced, labor-intensive manufactured goods. The alternative is to produce increasingly capital-intensive and skill-intensive goods for the domestic market, but at declining efficiency as the economy's scarce resources are stretched too thin.

Therefore, as a logical corollary of the characteristics of many LDCs, and of most Asian LDCs, an efficient development strategy involves policies that encourage the rapid growth of labor-intensive manufactured exports, at least as soon as the domestic market is saturated with these goods. This is the most likely outcome in any case, if resources are allocated by the market, with a minimum of government involvement. In labor-abundant, capital- and skill-scarce economies, the cost of unskilled labor will be low and that of capital and trained or skilled labor high. Business and industry, in pursuit of profits and growth, will use the cheap labor extensively and will husband the expensive factors. More important, in deciding on the industries in which to invest, entrepreneurs will emphasize those that are labor-intensive. This is precisely what happened in Hong Kong, and the result was rapid, labor-intensive growth.

The Hong Kong pattern of development was more successful than that of many other countries in Asia, where government intervention in the economy created distortions. In an attempt to raise the income of organized labor and to benefit politically powerful groups in business and industry, government in these other countries raised the wages of labor in modern industry and lowered the cost of capital to the same sector.[3] The result was inefficient, slow, capital-intensive growth.

Government Intervention to Correct Distortions

While more efficient than the counterproductive strategies of many countries, the Hong Kong pattern was not ideal. It suffered from many of the problems inherent in a private enterprise economy, including:

(1) the short time-horizon of private decision makers, especially in LDCs: The risks facing the individual are inherently greater than for a society. At a minimum individuals are mortal, but there are also serious political risks. As a result individuals are reluctant to make the long-term investments which are desirable.

(2) inherent economic distortions in the prices facing private decision makers: The most important of these is a market cost of labor which is above the true cost to society of additional employment.[4] As a result, in the absence of government intervention, too little labor will be employed for efficiency.

(3) the existence of externalities, that is costs and benefits which the private decision–making unit imposes on, or provides to, others: One important externality for LDCs is the cost of selling in the world market. When a country first breaks into the world market for nonstandardized goods—that is, most manufactured products and processed agricultural goods—every firm must contend with the suspicion that its goods will be low quality. A firm that indeed exports low-quality products may be able to do so because little else is

expected, but it thereby imposes a cost on all other exporters from that country as it confirms the original suspicion. Conversely a firm that exports quality goods is conferring a benefit on all current and future exporters by helping to establish the country's reputation for quality. The country as a whole then should be willing to bear the costs of establishing the reputation of the country, but in a pure private-enterprise system these costs are borne by the individual exporting firm. Another important externality is the cost of training, broadly defined, especially that which takes the form of learning by doing. The pioneer in any industry in a country usually incurs large costs in learning how to operate in that industry. Later entrants can appropriate some of that learning without paying for it by hiring away some of the experienced workers, technicians, and managers. Again, society should bear the cost of this training, but it is borne by the pioneers in a private-enterprise economy.

The governments in the four East Asian countries other than Hong Kong adopted policies to compensate for these weaknesses of the private-enterprise system. Like other governments in Asia they intervened in the economy, hence the appellation of "Japan Inc." or "Korea Inc." is quite justified, but unlike many governments they intervened to compensate for distortions, not to aggravate them.

Most LDC governments made foreign exchange cheap. The result was to encourage imports and discourage manufactured exports. They then discouraged imports by a complex system of tariffs, quantitative restrictions, or both. These controls created distortions, often granting the highest effective subsidies to the least efficient industries. At the same time they raised the costs of exporting industries. Exports of manufactured goods therefore faced three hurdles: the costs of breaking into the world market; a foreign-exchange rate that did not reward exporters; and inflated costs for many of the imports they used as inputs.

None of the five East Asian countries imposed the last two handicaps on their exporters, or if the costs of imported inputs were high, they paid compensating subsidies. Instead of handicapping exporters, most of the countries quite deliberately used the exchange rate and a system of (mostly hidden) subsidies to encourage exports and discourage imports. Korea, for instance, roughly doubled the average effective cost of foreign exchange for imports from the late 1950s to 1965 as a result of the economic reform of the early 1960s.[5] Credit policies provided an additional incentive to exporters. After the reform, banks charged 26–28 percent to finance imports but only 6.5 percent to finance exports,[6] an effective subsidy of 10 percent on a loan of six months. There were also drawback schemes which refunded tariffs paid on imports. The other countries similarly used various direct and indirect measures to make it profitable to export non-traditional and initially labor-intensive exports. These policies simultaneously compensated for several weaknesses or distortions inherent in a private-enterprise economy. The implicit subsidy for manufactured and other non-traditional exports compensated for the external cost of breaking into the world market, and by subsidizing labor-intensive goods it indirectly subsidized the unskilled labor going into it.

The four countries other than Hong Kong also invested heavily in education, training, and adaptive research to compensate for the externality facing pioneer investors in learning by doing. Finally all had a medium- and long-run strategy for industrial development, sometimes called—somewhat pejoratively perhaps—"targeting." Government decided what industrial investment was desirable in the next decade and then provided various "incentives," really implicit subsidies, to make it profitable for private firms to invest in these activities. They thus again compensated for the weaknesses of the private sector, including the shorter-than-desirable time-horizon.

Competitive Pressure and Efficiency

While the governments of the four countries differed from those in many LDCs in counteracting rather than reinforcing weaknesses and distortions, all five East Asian governments differed in the extent to which they exposed their firms to the pressure of competition. It has been typical for many LDCs to shield their publicly owned enterprises almost completely from competitive pressures. The large, privately owned firms may be almost as fully protected because of the employment they generate or because they are well connected in the political system or both. When there is no competitive pressure it takes a very unusual manager to resist the myriad pressures, not least from powerful politicians or civil servants, to employ unneeded friends and relatives, to offer wages above the market to important groups or individuals, to spend extensively on important people and, above all, to be relaxed about the myriad inefficiencies the uprooting of which would be strenuous, unpleasant, and risky. It would also take a saint to keep prices at world levels, and since saints are scarce in all societies, in the absence of competitive pressures, costs and prices are high, well above those of competing imports. One consequence of high prices is that the costs are raised for all industries that purchase the output of these non-competitive firms to use as inputs in their own production. Then the purchasing industries need to be protected or subsidized to survive. The net result can be an industrial structure with pervasive high costs which is unable to compete on the world market and which presents a serious drain on the economy, in turn keeping growth down.

In contrast, the pressure of competition was fully effective in Hong Kong and was far more effective in the other four countries than in most LDCs. Even publicly owned enterprises were exposed to the pressure of competition because they had to compete in the world market. True, the exchange rate was relatively favorable to exporters, and, in addition, there were a variety of open and hidden subsidies, but most of these were not particularistic, reserved to a few favored and well-connected enterprises, but were open to all exporters. With this generally favorable environment, firms in most fields competed on a relatively even footing. And once they turned to exports, they had to compete with foreign firms.

Except for the two city-states, the countries did protect their infant industries quite extensively. The belief that these countries were free traders, exposing their infant firms to the bracing climate of world competition to harden them is as much of a myth as the belief that they operated a private-enterprise economy. (That the two city-states came quite close to an open economy, I suspect, has at least as much to do with their lack of choice as with ideological commitment—when you have a small and inherently unbalanced economy, a more autarkic approach is not really feasible.) However, these countries successfully made the transition in most cases from protecting infant industries to becoming driving exporters. Infant-industry protection was used to achieve the aim it is designed in trade theory to achieve—to get firms through the costly stage of learning by doing. After that, these governments did not continue to raise the level of protection nor did they prevent newcomers from eroding the protected position of established firms in the home market, as so many other countries did. Rather they forced established firms to export in order to continue to receive the implicit subsidies offered. That meant the firms had to compete in terms of price and quality with the best the world had to offer.

The distinction between public and large, private firms in these countries was more limited than elsewhere[7]: both received protection in the initial stages, both were subsidized when they exported, but both were to become sufficiently efficient to be able to compete before too long. In Japan, and to a far smaller extent elsewhere, public firms, once well established, were sold off to the private sector. That had the advantage of giving them more flexibility and reducing any tendency for government to protect them longer than needed, but it was not crucial. The essential element was that the export orientation of government policies forced all major firms to pay attention to cost and quality. None had the luxury of major firms elsewhere which can often ignore both because they are effectively protected from foreign competition being the sole firm one or a few firms producing for a domestic market which excludes foreign competitors. In addition, in Japan even the domestic market can be competitive, despite the minor role of import competition, as several large Japanese firms are in a fight for market shares.

The Crucial Elements in Effective Management

In short, there were several crucial elements in the good economic management of the East Asian countries. To the extent that government intervened in these economies, as it did extensively in four of the countries, it was to correct weaknesses and distortions in the market. In addition, a large part of the economy was under competitive pressure to reduce costs and improve quality because policies provided strong incentives to compete in the world market.

It is difficult to demonstrate conclusively the efficiency of these economies. One superficial and inadequate measure is the growth they managed to extract from the investment they put in place, but the rate of growth by itself does not necessarily indicate anything about the efficiency of the process. For example, an inefficient economy can grow quite rapidly if a strong authoritarian government manages to extract enough resources from the population to attain a high rate of investment. But the rate of growth extracted per unit of investment does indicate efficiency. Table 3.3 shows the ratio between investment and growth, the ICOR. The ICOR has been generally lower for the East Asian countries than for other countries in comparable stages of development (the low-income countries in the 1950s and the middle-income ones thereafter). However, such comparisons have no validity if made for a single year as the vagaries of the weather, in economies where agriculture is important, or of the world market, where trade is important, can easily swamp the effect of efficiency in the short term. But over a decade such short-term fluctuations cancel each other, and an ICOR that is 10–30 percent lower (more favorable) is significant. One exception to the overall trend appears to be Korea in 1980–83, but ICORs for the 1980s, which are based on figures for four full years, at most, should largely be ignored since one year of setback can distort the results. The more significant exception is Singapore in the 1970s; but, the relatively higher ICOR reflects the deliberate policy, inefficient in the short term, of raising the cost of labor to force a restructuring of the economy. By that time Singapore was also moving into the middle-income group, with capital more abundant and labor more scarce, which inevitably raises the ICOR as more investment is required for each additional unit of output. (This can be seen in the consistently higher ICOR of the industrialized countries.)

The ICOR is only a crude index of efficiency, partly because it measures only the efficiency of investment, not of all factors of production, and partly because the data on which it is based are flawed. But the fact that it is rather consistently lower over long periods for all five East Asian countries than for comparable countries does indicate that the East Asian development strategy made for an efficient use of scarce factors. The greater efficiency of investment accounts for roughly two percentage points in the growth rate, as compared to similar countries. This is approximately the same contribution to growth as that made by the higher rate of investment. In other words, the four middle-income countries averaged a growth rate very roughly four percentage points higher than comparable countries. Of that, approximately half was due to higher rates of investment and half to the greater efficiency with which that investment was used. For Japan much more of the difference was due to differences in investment rates, with less than a third of the difference in growth rate explained by Japan's greater efficiency in using investment.

I have so far offered an outline of the characteristics of the strategy which resulted in greater efficiency, yet I have not identified or analyzed, with any precision, the specific elements which the East Asian countries shared. That I will do in the next section, with respect to the aspects of growth, and the following section will deal with equity.

The Consequences:
Rapid, Labor-Intensive Growth of Industry and Industrial Exports

Speed

The leading sector in all five countries in East Asia was the production of industrial, or manufactured exports (see Table 3.4). In the 1950s the industrial sector in East Asia was not significantly different in size, as a share of national income, from comparable countries. Indeed, in all five it was smaller, although in view of their present industrial prowess that may seem hard to believe. Over the next 30 years they achieved a growth rate in manufacturing that was two to three times that of other countries. For the two countries where agriculture really mattered, Korea and Taiwan, because it constituted the largest share of national income in the 1950s, that sector's growth rate over the 30-year period also somewhat exceeded the rate of growth in comparable countries, although the differences were not great. It was rapid industrial growth that distinguished all five. Indeed, over twenty years the growth rate in industry ranged from ten percent per year in Japan to sixteen percent in Korea. These data are for value added at constant prices, not value of output, so they already take account of the increase in inputs used and in prices. They mean that, on the average, industry doubled the net value of its output every five years or so, or more than tenfold in twenty years.

Not only did industrial growth dominate the national income, it also was crucial in providing the foreign exchange required for development, which was possible because a large proportion of industrial production was exported. As a result, the East Asian countries achieved a rate of export growth that was generally from two to nine or ten times that of the average of comparable countries (see Table 3.3). There were substantial fluctuations in export growth for some of the East Asian countries, depending on the vagaries of the world market for the particular goods that dominated a particular country's exports and on internal policies. But, over the 30-odd years for which we have data, the East Asian countries' performance with respect to exports has exceeded that of other countries by a greater margin than for other economic

TABLE 3.4
Sectoral Structure and Growth
(rounded)

Countries	Share of GDP in Early 1950s[a]		AVERAGE ANNUAL REAL GROWTH RATE (%)								Sectoral Share of GDP in 1983[d]	
			1960s[b]			1970s[b]			1980–1983[c]			
	Ag[1]	Mf[2]	Ag	Mf	Sv[3]	Ag	Mf	Sv	Ag	Mf	Ag	Mf
Japan	25[4]	25[4]	2.1	13.6	11.7	−0.2	6.6	4.9	−1.4[x]	8.3	4.0	30.0
All Industrialized Countries	6[7]	29[7]	1.4	5.9	4.8	1.8	2.4	3.4	4.8[x]	0.4[x]	3.0	24.0
Singapore	4[7]	12[7]	5.0	13.0	7.7	1.6	9.3	8.5	1.0	4.8	1.0	24.0
Hong Kong	3[4]	12[4]	−2.3	13.6	n.a.	−2.5	10.2	10.1	−4.1[y]	5.5[y]	1.0	22.0
Taiwan[e]	36[5]	11[5]	4.6	15.9	9.0	2.9	15.2	10.9	0.6	3.5	8.8	34.0
South Korea	45[6]	12[6]	4.4	17.6	8.9	2.9	14.5	8.8	3.4	5.2	14.0	22.0
All Middle-Income Countries	24[7]	19[7]	3.5	7.3	5.5	3.0	5.5	6.0	3.0[x]	1.8[x]	15.0	21.0
All Low-Income Countries	50[7]	15[7]	2.2	5.5	3.8	2.3	3.4	4.6	3.3[x]	2.4[x]	37.0	14.0

Notes:

[1]Agriculture
[2]Manufacturing
[3]Service
[4]1950 Figure
[5]1952 Figure
[6]1955 Figure
[7]1960 Figure
[8]Average Figure 1980–82
[9]Since the GDP for Hong Kong was expressed in current prices, the growth rate for current-price GDP was first calculated and then deflated by using the GDP deflator obtained from: IMF, *International Financial Statistics*, Supplement Series, No. 8, p. 77

Sources:

[a]World Bank, *World Tables*, 3d. ed., vol. I, Table 4, and 1st ed., 1971.
[b]World Bank, *World Development Report*, 1981, Table 2
[c]United Nations. *Statistical Yearbook for Asia and the Pacific*, 1983, and World Bank, *World Development Report*, 1981, and 1984, Table 2.
[d]World Bank, *World Development Report*, 1985, Table 3.

45

indicators. Of course the postwar period saw a remarkable expansion of world trade, but it should be emphasized that in the early 1950s the East Asian countries' exports were less than 4 percent of total world exports, while 30 years later they contributed 13.5 percent.

Even more remarkable is the performance with respect to exports of manufactured goods. East Asian raw-material exports grew slowly, if at all, and in some cases declined. It was manufactures that determined their export success. In the early 1950s only about two percent of world exports were manufactured goods from East Asia, in the 1980s it was a remarkable eleven percent (see Table 3.5). Hong Kong, South Korea, and Taiwan had become the key players in the world market for textiles and garments, and Japan was dominant in a number of commodities.

Composition

The composition of exports is another crucial point. When East Asian countries first began the process of rapid development, they expanded exports that took advantage of their abundant unskilled labor. The manufactured exports of all these countries, including Japan, during their initial development spurt were dominated by textiles, garments, wigs, plywood, simple electrical and electronic goods, toys, and a whole host of miscellaneous products. These goods shared one set of characteristics: their production required large numbers of unskilled workers, relatively little capital, and few highly skilled and professional workers. As surplus labor was absorbed and wages rose and as training programs, experience, and high savings rates increased the supply of capital and skilled personnel, the countries gradually shifted to more capital- and skill-intensive products: consumer electronics (radios, TV sets, fans); higher-fashion and higher-skill garments; simple, and then more complex machinery; bicycles, then motorcycles, and finally automobiles; simple and then increasingly complex metal products, such as ships; high-quality shoes; and so on. While textiles and garments remain important in the exports of all except Singapore and Japan, the composition of their exports has become increasingly differentiated, as they have specialized.

The nature of specialization depended in part on the accident of where an industry began and in part on differences in the economies: Japan and Korea were in the best position, by virtue of their larger internal markets, to develop the automobile industry; Hong Kong and Singapore took advantage of their location to develop service activities. But each country followed the same strategy—unlike many LDCs—of emphasizing those exports which they could produce competitively because it took account of its factor endowment. The countries sometimes made mistakes. Korea probably shifted too soon to capital- and energy-intensive industries in the 1970s, especially in hindsight as the energy crisis and world recession made it difficult to compete. At the same time, Singapore probably raised wages too rapidly and as a result shifted too quickly to capital-intensive industries. But all five, more than nearly all other countries, played to their strengths and worked with and reinforced market forces rather than trying to swim against them.

Confounding Export Pessimism

Their export-oriented strategies should be seen in the context of that fact that many analysts had grave doubts that it was a feasible strategy. The decision by other countries to emphasize import substitution was a conscious one; it was based on the widespread assumption that manufactured exports could be expanded only slowly. Other LDCs, it was believed, could not afford and would not be willing to buy manufactured goods in any large quantity. The contention was that they and the industrialized countries were prejudiced against newcomers in the world market and, far more important, were determined to protect their own industries against competition. Therefore an export-oriented strategy was seen as unrealistic. As soon as it began to succeed, the developed countries would abort further expansion of LDC exports by imposing tariffs and quotas. This export pessimism was widespread and was a major factor in shaping development strategy in the 1950s and 1960s.

The East Asian countries proved it wrong. Or, rather, they proved that despite undoubted obstacles, quite remarkable rates of export growth could be achieved in manufactured goods. The 1970s provided an important test of the strategy. Despite two oil shocks and a recession, world trade continued to grow rapidly and so did the manufactured exports of the East Asian economies. Taiwan registered a 35 percent per year rate of growth, South Korea over 40 percent. The second test came in the 1980s when world trade almost stagnated and the East Asian countries had become major exporters of such goods as textiles and garments and were therefore obvious targets for protectionism. Yet the five showed a growth rate of industrial exports of 12.5 to 20 percent per year.

In the mid-1980s export pessimism again flourishes. The argument is that there is a fundamental change in attitudes in the developed world, that protectionism is such a powerful force that an export-oriented strategy would be foolhardy now. Moreover, it is argued by the pessimists that the East Asian countries other than Japan are "small"; even rapid growth of their exports does not threaten developed countries in the way the same strategy followed by a large country would.

There is something to these arguments, but it is doubtful that they are decisive in deciding on the applicability of the East Asian model. Even if it becomes more difficult to export in the future than it was in the past, it seems

TABLE 3.5
Growth of Exports and Imports

	Early 1950s (mil $ US)	AVERAGE ANNUAL GROWTH RATE[a]				1983 (mil $ US)
		1950s (mil $ US)	1960s	1970s	1980–83	
World						
Exports	78,180[1]	6.8	9.2	20.6	2.5	1,808,900
Imports	82,070[1]	6.7	9.2	20.2	2.7	1,880,500
Industrial Countries						
Exports	50,980[1]	7.7	10.0	19.0		
Imports	54,700[1]	7.8	10.0	19.8		
Japan						
Exports	1,348[1]	12.5	16.5	20.5	9.3	146,676
Primary commodities and fuel[5]	163[1]	12.4	8.4	12.9	5.5	3,227
Manufactured goods	1,185[1]	12.5	17.5	21.4	12.5	143,449
Metal manufactures[c]	299[1]					116,767
Chemicals	37[1]					11,189
Textiles	623[1]					6,312
Imports	2,399[1]	8.4[2]	16.0	23.0	7.2	146,992
Food, beverage, and tobacco	590[1]	0.3[3]	16.3	70.9	3.5	14,846
Intermediate goods	1,708[1]	11.3[3]	15.6	23.6	8.0	94,222
Capital goods	67[1]	30.4[2]	16.9	17.3	8.5	8,820
Consumer durable goods	12[1]	20.5[2]	25.9	29.2	4.8	588
Singapore						
Exports	1,026[1]	0.3[4]	3.4	20.8	10.5	21,833
Primary commodities and fuel[b]	652[1]	1.4[4]	3.3	16.5	7.4	10,764
Manufactured goods	374[1]	−0.6[4]	6.8	29.5	13.6	11,069

Metal manufactures[c]	62[1]				4,206
Chemicals	21[1]				3,564
Textiles	40[1]				454
Imports	1,337[3]	0.1[4]	4.8	21.0	12.5	28,158
Food, beverage, and tobacco	255[3]	−1.3[3]	3.9	10.6	9.4	1,830
Intermediate goods	888[3]	0.4[4]	3.6	21.3	12.9	15,290
Capital goods	91[3]	2.2[4]	18.0	27.6	12.9	8,532
Consumer durable goods	63[3]	4.1[4]	10.0	18.3	16.4	1,858
Hong Kong						
Exports	507[5]	1.8[6]	15.0	19.5	20.0	21,951
Primary commodities and fuel[b]	162[5]	−3.0[6]	4.2	18.5	27.0	1,910
Manufactured goods	345[5]	4.2[6]	16.9	19.5	19.8	20,041
Textiles	96[5]					8,397
Metal manufactures[c]	25[5]					7,235
Chemicals	84[5]					641
Imports	663[5]	4.5[6]	11.8	20.8	20.0	24,009
Food, beverage, and tobacco	192[5]	3.8[6]	8.6	13.9	18.4	2,953
Intermediate goods	361[5]	5.0[6]	11.3	19.3	17.8	11,140
Capital goods	34[5]	13.5[6]	18.6	24.3	21.5	5,402
Consumer durable goods	47[5]	5.8[6]	17.2	22.8	26.8	4,346
Taiwan						
Exports	128[7]	4.4[8]	21.0	31.5	14.0[11]	30,456[12]
Agricultural products	28[7]	20.9[8]	16.4	23.6	−6.5[11]	548[12]
Processed agricultural products	89[7]	2.4[8]	10.6	18.1	11.6[11]	1,553[12]
Industrial products	10[7]	24.4[8]	35.9	35.6	14.8[11]	28,355[12]
Textiles[d]	2[7]					8,466[12]
Electrical products	0[7]					6,578[12]
Metal products[c]	1[7]					2,479[12]
Machinery	0[7]					1,144[12]

(Continued)

TABLE 3.5
(Continued)

	Early 1950s (mil $ US)	AVERAGE ANNUAL GROWTH RATE[a]				1983 (mil $ US)
		1950s (mil $ US)	1960s	1970s	1980–83	
Imports	192[7]	3.1[8]	18.2	28.5	8.7[11]	21,959[12]
Agricultural and industrial raw materials	127[7]	3.7[8]	17.1	32.0	9.3[11]	15,152[12]
Consumption goods	38[7]	–9.2[8]	13.9	37.1	11.7[11]	1,669[12]
Capital goods	27[7]	11.9[8]	24.3	26.8	8.4[11]	5,182[12]
South Korea						
Exports	24[9]	–1.0[10]	41.5	37.5	13.0	24,445
Primary commodities and fuel	21[9]	–1.2[10]	24.9	30.2	6.3	2,078
Manufactured goods	3[9]	2.3[10]	71.4	41.5	13.8	22,367
Metal manufactures[c]	e[9]					8,835
Textiles	e[9]					8,075
Chemical	1[9]					1,678
Imports	243[9]	9.0[10]	22.4	29.0	7.5	26,192
Food, beverage, and tobacco	42[9]	14.2[10]	36.7	10.4	72.3	1,729
Intermediate goods	153[9]	8.9[10]	17.2	31.9	8.1	15,715
Capital goods	33[9]	7.5[10]	43.1	28.2	6.9	7,543
Consumer durable goods	10[9]	19.5[10]	31.6	30.8	7.7	943

Notes:
[a] Per cent change of value
[b] Consists of food, beverage, and tobacco, raw material, and fuel
[c] Includes basic metal
[d] Textile, leather, wood, paper, and related products

[c]Less than $1 million (US)

[1]1951 figure

[2]growth rate between 1951–59

[3]1957 figure

[4]growth rate between 1957–59

[5]1952 figure

[6]growth rate between 1952–59

[7]1953 figure

[8]growth rate between 1953–59

[9]1954 figure

[10]growth rate between 1954–59

[11]growth rate between 1980–84

[12]1984 figure

Sources:

World and Industrial countries trade and their growth rate 1950s–70s were obtained from: IMF, *International Financial Statistics*, Supplement Series, No. 4, 1982.

Trade of individual country and growth 1950s–70s was obtained from: United Nations, *International Trade Statistical Yearbooks*, various issues.

All 1980s trade figures were obtained from: United Nations, *Statistical Yearbook for Asia and the Pacific*, 1983.

very unlikely that minor exporters of manufactured goods, such as the South Asian, African, and most Latin American countries have reached a ceiling on their exports, which remain a fraction of those from East Asian countries. Manufactured exports from Pakistan in 1982 were less than $3 billion, from Indonesia less than $1 billion, and even from India, they were only about $8 billion. This is in contrast to over $20 billion for Korea, nearly $30 billion for Taiwan, and over $140 billion from Japan. Thus even the most populous countries in South and Southeast Asia have a long way to go before they threaten industry in the developed world to the same extent as the East Asian countries do. Of course their exports would be additional in the first instance and therefore especially difficult to absorb, but if they become efficient export producers they would gradually replace the middle-income East Asian countries in such industries as textiles and garments, just as the four "little tigers"—Singapore, Hong Kong, Taiwan, and Korea—earlier replaced Japan.

Moreover, if major countries in Southern Asia or elsewhere export more then they will also import more, stimulating world trade, helping to finance their own exports, and enhancing their own bargaining position in trade negotiations. Maybe it will be difficult for newcomers' exports to grow at 20 to 40 percent per year, as the East Asian countries have done, but that does not mean it is not possible to expand exports at 8 to 10 percent per year, which would be better than double the rate which low- or middle-income countries other than those in East Asia have achieved. Whatever the future of the East Asian model, there is no doubt that the growth in manufactured exports which those countries have registered represents their single most important achievement and demonstrates that export pessimism was at least overstated and probably unjustified.

The Labor Intensity of Exports

That East Asian industry was producing primarily for export made it possible to emphasize the production of goods which took full advantage of the countries' relative factor endowments, that is the relative abundance of labor. As Table 3.6 shows, the countries with the greatest supply of unskilled labor relied most heavily on labor to produce their manufactured goods, that is they had the lowest value added per worker. Both Japan and Singapore are labor abundant compared to the U.S. and much of Western Europe but are somewhat better endowed with capital and skills than the rest of East Asia; both countries had a more labor-intensive industry than the industrialized countries, but less than the other three East Asian countries. As capital and skills

TABLE 3.6
Value Added at Constant Prices per Worker in Manufacturing
(thousand $ U.S.)

Country	1950s (1955)	1960s (1965)	1970s (1975)	1980s (1980–1984)
Hong Kong[1]	n.a.	1.7	2.5	4.0[7]
	(147)[6]	(408)	(679)	(907)
Japan[2]	n.a.	4.7	11.1	17.1[7]
	(7560)	(11570)	(13460)	(13670)
South Korea[3]	n.a.	1.1	2.4	3.7
	(n.a.)	(800)	(2205)	(2872)
Singapore[4]	n.a.	2.9	2.8	3.4[8]
	(n.a.)	(52)	(218)	(338)
Taiwan[5]	1.4	2.9	4.0	6.6[9]
	(411)	(612)	(1518)	(2494)

Notes:
[1] at constant 1973 price
[2] at constant 1975 price
[3] at constant 1975 price
[4] at constant 1968 price
[5] at constant 1981 price
[6] Figures in parentheses are number of workers in manufacturing.
[7] 1980 figure
[8] 1981 figure
[9] 1984 figure

Sources:
Value added in manufacturing for all countries, except Taiwan, was obtained from: World Bank, *World Tables*, 3d. ed., Economic Data Sheet.

Number of workers employed in manufacturing and its index for the earlier year were obtained from: International Labour Office, *Yearbook of Labour Statistics*, various issues.

Value added and workers employed in manufacturing for Taiwan were obtained from: Council for Economic Planning and Development, Republic of China, *Taiwan Statistical Data Book*, 1985.

Value added in current price was adjusted by GDP deflator obtained by dividing GDP at constant 1981 price by GDP of current price.

increased, and as wages rose (see Table 3.7), all five became less labor intensive, with Japan, quite naturally, far less labor intensive than the other four. If East Asian industry had produced primarily for domestic consumption, it would soon have run out of demand for labor-intensive goods and would have rapidly become more capital- and skill-intensive, but by producing for export, it could continue to specialize in the industries in which it was most competitive, that is those with greater labor intensity.

TABLE 3.7
Growth Rate of Real Wage Rate

Country	Nominal Wage Rate in early 1950s ($ US)	AVERAGE ANNUAL GROWTH RATE OF REAL WAGE RATE				Nominal Wage Rate in 1980s ($ US)
		1950s	1960s	1970s	1980–84	
Japan						
—Textiles (per month)	29.2[1]	4.1[2]	7.0	5.3	0.2	851.2
—Construction (per month)	40.6[1]	6.2[2]	6.5	5.2	1.4	1280.3
—Agriculture (per day)	0.8[1]	2.8[2]	8.6	4.4	0.2	24.6
Singapore						
—Textiles (per hour)	0.19[1]	5.7[2]	5.4[3]	7.3	6.4	1.34
—Construction (per hour)	0.25[1]	1.3[2]	1.2	4.4	9.1	1.54
Hong Kong						
—Manufacturing (per day)	0.64[1]	0.8[2]	10.3	7.7	5.6	11.5
—Textiles (per day)	n.a.	n.a.	n.a.	6.5[4]	7.2	11.9
—Construction (per day)	n.a.	n.a.	n.a.	9.6[4]	−2.1	18.9
Taiwan						
—Textiles (per month)	11.8[5]	−1.5[6]	4.0	9.5	6.3[7]	282.9[8]
South Korea						
—Textiles (per month)	32.2[9]	10.2[11]	7.3	10.4	2.3	242.6
—Construction (per day)	5.1[9]	1.4[12]	n.a.	13.0	−2.4	472.2
—Agriculture (per day)	1.8[10]	n.a.	8.2	10.7	0.1	11.3

Notes:
[1] 1955 Figure
[2] Growth rate between 1955–59
[3] Growth rate between 1965–69
[4] Growth rate between 1975–79
[5] 1956 Figure
[6] Growth rate between 1956–59
[7] Growth rate between 1980–82
[8] 1982 Figure
[9] 1957 Figure
[10] 1959 Figure
[11] Growth rate between 1957–59
[12] Growth rate between 1955–59

TABLE 3.7
(*Continued*)

Sources:

ILO, *Yearbook of Labour Statistics*, various issues.

Directorate-General of Budget, The Republic of China, *Statistical Yearbook of the Republic of China*, 1983.

Council for Economic Planning and Development, The Republic of China, *Taiwan Statistical Data Book*, 1985.

Steven Chow and Gustav Papanek, "Laissez-Faire, Growth and Equity—Hong Kong," *The Economic Journal*, June 1981.

The Consequences:
Equitable Income Distribution and Reduction
in Poverty

Rising Real Wages

One crucial consequence of the strategy pursued by the East Asian countries was that the poor also benefited from rapid growth and that there was, in general, no worsening of income inequalities. With growth built around labor-intensive manufactured exports, there was a rapid increase in the demand for unskilled labor, the activity from which the poor derived most of their income. For instance, in Hong Kong some 730,000 jobs were created in medium- and large-scale industry between 1957 and 1979, a massive number in a labor force of 1.5 million. At the same time some jobs were lost in the lower-income, small-scale manufacturing sector, but the net gain was still around a third of the labor force.[8] Over 80 percent of the workers in industry were unskilled in 1974, an increase from 71 percent in 1951, so almost all the new employment was for unskilled workers, mostly in the garment, plastics, and electronics industries. The additional income in industry meant the creation of secondary jobs in construction, trade, and service occupations, many for unskilled workers as well. If one secondary job was created for each one in manufacturing, then industry, essentially producing for export, generated one million jobs in twenty-odd years in a country with a labor force of about 1.5 million.

Similarly dramatic proportional gains occurred in manufacturing employment in the other East Asian countries. Table 3.6 gives total employment in manufacturing. Comparing the mid-1950s with the mid-1980s years later, roughly two million jobs were created in Taiwan and six million in Japan, while in Korea the increase was two million in less than twenty years.

With rapidly rising demand for unskilled labor, real wages also rose rapidly (see Table 3.7). In the early 1950s they were very low indeed. Even in Japan they ranged from less than U.S. $1.00 per day in agriculture to less than $1.50 per day in the textile industry. In Hong Kong and Taiwan, industrial wages were not much above $.50 per day. In South Korea and Singapore, wages were high in U.S. dollars relative to other East Asian countries, because of the overvaluation of the currency. This was one reason for slow growth in the economy and in manufactured exports during that period. With economic reform, wages in U.S. dollars declined as the currency was devalued, a centerpiece of the reform, and then both countries joined the other three in the ''East Asian model'' of rapid growth in income based on rapid growth of manufactured exports.

During the five countries' periods of rapid growth, wages tended to rise between five and ten percent per year in real terms, which is at least as fast as the rate of growth in per capita income. Since these are real wages in agriculture, textiles, and construction, they are in most cases compensation primarily for unskilled labor. Unskilled workers in turn are the great majority of the poor, persons who derive their income primarily from selling their labor, with little physical or human capital to increase that income.

The slowdown in growth that affected these countries in the 1980s, in large part because of changes in the world economy, is reflected in the slowdown, stagnation, or decline in real wages as well. Japan and Korea were the principal sufferers in both respects (compare Tables 3.1 and 3.7). As growth slowed, so did the demand for labor and therefore real wages. That correlation confirms the stake which the poor have in rapid growth, as long as that growth is sufficiently labor intensive to assure them a reasonable share of its benefits.

Income Distribution

That the income of the majority of the poor increased, in most cases as rapidly as for other groups of the population, can also be seen in the income distribution data (see Table 3.8). Indeed, for Japan and Taiwan the share of the poorest twenty percent increased sharply over the 20–25 years for which data exist and was far higher than in comparable countries. For Hong Kong there was little change. Both there and in Taiwan the share of the richest twenty percent declined sharply, and the middle income groups, including some who are very poor by developed-country standards, gained. It was only in Korea that there was a major decline in the share of the poorest twenty percent in the early 1970s. It is no accident that this deterioration occurred at this point; it was then that Korea changed its strategy, placing much greater emphasis on capital- and skill-intensive industries such as steel and chemicals. But even after that decline, the share of the poorest twenty percent was still higher than for the average of comparable countries.

The Absolute Income of the Poor and Welfare Indicators

With income distribution improving and with a high rate of growth in average income, the absolute income of the poor increased very rapidly in all five countries. In Hong Kong the income per household, adjusted for inflation, more than doubled for the poorest twenty percent, more than tripled for the next poorest, and increased 360 percent for the third-poorest twenty percent of households between 1957 and 1979 (see Table 3.9).[9] That is quite a remarkable improvement for all but the very poorest in less than twenty years.

Hong Kong data suggest that Table 3.8 almost certainly understates the improvement for the poor by focusing on the poorest (and richest) twenty percent. In the East Asian countries, which generally had few welfare measures, the working poor benefited more from growth than the very poorest groups. Households with wage earners benefited from rapidly rising real wages. But families at the bottom of the income pyramid, often headed by a part-time worker or a handicapped person, benefited much less from rising wages. Table 8 therefore understates the improvement in income of the twenty to forty percent of the population who are poor, but not among the poorest twenty percent. In countries other than Hong Kong the real income of the poor also increased rapidly.

If income distribution remains unchanged while per capita income grows at six to eight percent, then the income of the poor obviously increases at the same rate. That means income doubles roughly every ten years and quadruples every twenty. If income distribution improves at the same time, then the rise is even more rapid. As a result, the real income of the poorest twenty percent increased seventeen-fold in Taiwan over thirty years, six-fold in Japan over eighteen years, and by 35 percent in Korea even in the ten years during which income distribution deteriorated (see Table 3.9).

The consequences can be seen in some direct measures of welfare. Life expectancy is one of these. While life expectancy figures are an average for all members of the population and are not specifically a measure for lower-income groups, they are useful as a measure of the well-being of lower-income groups: the wealthy in all modern societies already live quite long since they have access to nutritious food and good medical services; it is the poor whose life is prolonged as nutrition improves and health (and education) services become more widely available. As Table 3.10 shows, while life expectancy in Japan was slightly lower than in other industrialized countries in the early 1950s it was slightly higher in the early 1980s. The life expectancy in the other four countries seems to have been slightly higher than in most middle-income countries even in 1960 and substantially higher than in the low-income ones, and these East Asian countries subsequently kept their lead.

TABLE 3.8
Income Distribution
(percentage share of household income)

Country	1955 Low 20%	1955 High 20%	1960 Low 20%	1960 High 20%	1965 Low 20%	1965 High 20%	1970 Low 20%	1970 High 20%	1975 Low 20%	1975 High 20%	1980 Low 20%	1980 High 20%
Japan	n.a.	n.a.	4.8[1]	46.1[1]	5.4	43.7	8.8[2]	37.6[2]	n.a.	n.a.	8.7	37.5
All industrialized countries	4.5	47.8	4.5	47.8	5.4	43.6	5.4	43.6	6.3	37.0	6.3	37.0
Hong Kong	5.7[3]	65.2[3]	n.a.	n.a.	5.3[4]	57.7[4]	5.3[5]	52.6[5]	5.1[6]	50.3[6]	5.4	47.0
Taiwan	2.9[7]	61.8[7]	5.6	50.9	7.7[8]	41.1[8]	8.4	38.7	8.8[9]	38.6[9]	8.8	36.8
South Korea	n.a.	n.a.	n.a.	n.a.	9.4[10]	35.8[10]	7.1	44.5	5.7[6]	45.3[6]	n.a.	n.a.
All middle-income countries*	4.9	54.2	4.9	54.2	4.7	53.0	4.7	53.0	5.2	48.6	5.2	48.6
All low-income countries*	6.0	46.4	6.0	46.4	5.8	49.5	5.8	49.5	5.2	52.2	5.2	52.2
India	7.9[11]	42.4[11]	4.1	51.7	6.7	48.9	n.a.	n.a.	7.0	49.4	n.a.	n.a.
Pakistan	n.a.	n.a.	n.a.	n.a.	6.7[12]	45.3[12]	8.4	41.5	n.a.	n.a.	n.a.	n.a.
Bangladesh	n.a.	n.a.	n.a.	n.a.	6.9[12]	44.5[12]	n.a.	n.a.	6.2[13]	46.9[13]	n.a.	n.a.

Notes:

*The figures are averages for 1955–64; 1965–74; 1975–83. It was necessary to amalgamate data because otherwise the sample of available information would be too small. Even the averages still suffer small and changing sample size. Changes over time may therefore not be too significant.

[1] 1962 figure
[2] 1971 figure
[3] 1957 figure
[4] 1966 figure
[5] 1971 figure
[6] 1976 figure
[7] 1953 figure
[8] 1964 figure
[9] 1974 figure
[10] 1966 figure
[11] 1953–57 figure
[12] 1963–64 figure
[13] 1976–77 figure

Sources:

Japan: 1962–71 figures from: Shail Jain, *Size Distribution of Income: A Compilation of Data*, a World Bank Publication, 1979. 1980 figures from: World Bank, *World Development Report*, 1985.

Hong Kong: 1957–76 from: Steven Chow and Gustav Papanek, "Laissez-Faire Growth and Equity—Hong Kong" *The Economic Journal*, June 1981. 1980 figures from: World Bank, *World Development Report*, 1985.

Taiwan: 1953 and 1960 from: Shail Jain, op. cit. 1964–83 from: Council for Economic Planning and Development, Republic of China, *Taiwan Statistical Data Book*, various issues.

Korea: 1966 and 1970 from: Shail Jain, op. cit. 1976 from: World Bank, *World Development Report*, 1985.

India: 1953–65 from: Shail Jain, op. cit. 1975 from: World Bank, *World Development Report*, 1985.

Pakistan: Shail Jain, op. cit.

Bangladesh: Shail Jain, op. cit.

TABLE 3.9
Changes in Absolute Income of the Poor

Real Income	JAPAN[1]		TAIWAN[2]		SOUTH KOREA[3]		TAIWAN[4]	
	1962	1980	1953	1983	1966	1976	1957	1976
Poorest twenty percent of population	22.9	140.6	524	8,927	13.3	17.9	1.47	3.23
Third-poorest twenty percent of population	n.a.	n.a.	n.a.	n.a.	n.a.	n.a.	2.16	9.94

Notes:
[1]Base year is 1975; currency is yen.
[2]Base year is 1981; currency is NT dollars.
[3]Base year is 1975; currency is won.
[4]Base year is 1966; currency is HK dollars.
Sources:
See Table 3.1 for sources for average income and Table 3.8 for share of income groups.

They reached or approached the life expectancy of developed countries by 1970, except for Korea which was about ten percent behind (the middle-income countries then were more than twenty percent behind and the low-income ones nearly thirty percent behind). This at a time when their per capita incomes were substantially less.

A more complex index of welfare, the Physical Quality of Life Index (PQLI) shows similar results (see Table 3.11). Japan was ahead of the rest of the industrial countries in 1970 and the other four were substantially (22–30 percent) ahead of the middle-income group. The good performance of East Asia is partly due to the homogeneity of the population and to widespread health and education services, but also to a relatively egalitarian income distribution.

A Comparison with Other Countries

For many of the measures of well-being for the poor, the performance of the East Asian countries can be contrasted with that of countries in more slowly developing South and Southeast Asia. Based on the earlier discussion of factors affecting changes in real wages and the evidence on real wage changes in East Asia, one would expect wages in very slowly growing countries to stagnate. That is indeed the case for the low-income countries of South Asia included in one study.[10] During periods of stagnation in the economy wages stagnated also (they also stagnated during periods of rapid growth if

TABLE 3.10
Life Expectancy at Birth (years)

Country	1950			1960			1970			1983		
	Total	Male	Female	Total	Male	Female	Total	Male	Female	Total	Male	Female
Japan	57.9	56.2	59.6	68.0	65.7	70.4	72.4	69.9	75.2	77	74	79
All industrialized countries	n.a.	n.a.	n.a.	69.7	66.9	72.6	71.6	68.4	74.8	76	72	79
Singapore	60.5	58.8	62.1	64.5	62.8	66.2	68.7	66.7	70.9	73	70	75
Hong Kong	61.0	57.2	64.9	66.7	63.2	70.5	71.9	67.2	74.7	76	74	78
Taiwan	60.4¹	58.3¹	62.4¹	64.5	61.8	67.1	68.7	66.1	71.2	73	70	75
South Korea	52.4²	51.1²	53.7²	54.4	52.4	56.5	65.3	57.4	63.3	67	64	71
All middle-income countries	n.a.	n.a.	n.a.	50.1	48.5	51.1	55.1	53.4	56.8	61	59	63
All low-income countries				41.4	42.6	42.0	52.1	46.8	46.6	59	58	60
India	41.2	41.9	40.5	43.2	43.9	42.5	48.1	48.6	47.6	55	56	54
Pakistan	39.1	39.3	38.9	43.3	44.3	42.3	46.2	47.2	45.2	50	51	49
Bangladesh	37.7	38.0	37.5	37.3	37.8	36.8	41.6	42.1	41.1	50	49	50

Notes:
¹1953 figure
²1955 figure

Sources:
Taiwan: Directorate-General of Budget, Accounting and Statistics, The Republic of China, *Statistical Yearbook of the Republic of China*, 1983.

Other 1950s figures were obtained from: United Nations, *Demographic Yearbook*, various issues.
1960–70 figures from: World Bank, *World Tables*, 3d ed., vol. II.
1983 figures from: World Bank, *World Development Report*, 1985.

TABLE 3.11
The Physical Quality of Life Index
(PQLI)*

Country	1950s		1960s		1970s	
	1950	**1955**	**1960**	**1965**	**1970[1]**	**1975**
Japan			89		96	
All industrialized countries					92[2]	
Singapore					83	
Hong Kong			76		86	
Taiwan	63	71	77	82	87	90
South Korea		58[3]		76[4]	82	
All middle-income countries					66.7[5]	
All low-income countries					40[6]	
India	14		30		40	
Pakistan			—35—		38	
Bangladesh					35	

Notes:
*It is the composite index of three social indicators namely infant mortality, life expectancy and basic literacy.
[1]Early 1970s figure
[2]Weighted average figure of 38 high-income countries (per capita GNP $2,000 and over).
[3]1957 figure
[4]1968 figure
[5]Weighted average figure of 70 middle-income countries (per capita GNP of $300–$1,999).
[6]Weighted average figure of 42 low-income countries (per capita GNP of $300).
[7]1960s figure
Source:
Morris David Morris, *Measuring the Condition of the World's Poor: Physical Quality of Life Index*, (Overseas Development Council), 1979.

that growth was highly capital intensive). As a result, income distribution changed relatively little during periods of slow growth. With slow growth in per capita income and unchanged income distribution, the absolute income of the poor naturally grew slowly.

Based on real-wage data, one can conclude that in three of the countries of southern Asia studied the absolute income of the poorer groups increased by less than one percent per year over a 25 year period—indeed, in two of these countries it hardly changed at all. In the other two the increase in absolute income was somewhat higher, in part because the per capita income grew above the average for low-income countries and the growth was labor intensive, in part because in one country there were significant policies to redistribute income. At best, even in these two countries real wages doubled over 25 years. Contrast doubling at best or stagnation at worst in southern Asia with quintupling or better over the same time period in East Asia and it becomes evident which strategy was more successful in raising the income of the poor.

A comparison of the income-distribution data in Table 3.8 tells a somewhat similar story. For all low-income countries income distribution was somewhat more equal in the 1950s than it was in East Asia, but over time it seems to have become less equal. As a result of improvement in most East Asian countries and deterioration in all low-income ones, that relationship was reversed by 1975, with East Asia slightly more equal. On top of that the average growth rate was, of course, higher in East Asia (see Table 3.1) so the absolute income of the poor improved much less in the typical low-income country than in East Asia.

The Effect of Initial Conditions on Income Distribution

It has been argued that the relatively egalitarian development in East Asia was due not to the whole strategy they pursued, but to the asset redistribution which took place shortly after the war and the subsequent emphasis on manufactured exports. There is some basis for this argument, but it probably does not capture the most important reason.

In three of the countries—Japan, Korea, and Taiwan—there was an effective land reform program, which produced a more egalitarian distribution of land. It helped to spread widely the benefits of agricultural development and therefore contributed to an egalitarian income distribution. In Korea and Taiwan there were also few major industrial conglomerates and therefore little concentration of wealth in the business sector.

But the contribution of initial factors can be exaggerated. The experience of other countries suggests that differentiation in income and wealth can come quite quickly, even with a distribution that is initially egalitarian. Korean industry is a prime example. It has become highly concentrated, in part as a result of government credit programs and other policies which benefited the large conglomerates.[11] Agricultural land in Southeast Asia and in other rice cultures like Bangladesh was rather equally distributed in the 1950s, but inequality in the rural areas tended to increase under the pressure of population as the proportion of landless and land-poor increased. Moreover, in East Asia agriculture was of declining significance in the economy, so even if land remained equally distributed that fact would explain a declining part of an egalitarian income distribution overall. Finally there was no asset redistribution in Hong Kong and Singapore, so the developments in these countries cannot be attributed to initial conditions.

The emphasis on manufactured exports in East Asia contributed to equality because they were labor intensive. In a cross section study of factors in income distribution, no correlation was found between the importance of manufactured exports and equality.[12] The most plausible explanation is that some countries that are major exporters of manufactures are exporting capital- and skill-intensive goods, probably by providing significant subsidies. Manufactured exports as such do not contribute to an efficient and equitable development. They can be produced inefficiently and then exported if they receive a large implicit subsidy (e.g., through cheap loans, which need not be repaid; via large losses, absorbed by government; by firms producing for export being allowed to sell in a highly protected domestic market; and so on). It is only if they are produced efficiently and are labor intensive in labor-abundant countries that they contribute to rapid growth and equity.

In sum, while an egalitarian initial asset distribution contributed to equitable growth and the promotion of manufactured exports proved a good tool to promote continued equity, the essence of equitable growth, as it was of rapid growth, was a labor-intensive pattern of development in these labor-abundant countries. There appears to be no question that the East Asian strategy benefited the poor enormously. It probably led to an improvement in income distribution, but it definitely resulted in a very large increase in the absolute income of the lowest income groups. The poor just above the bottom twenty percent seem to have benefited even more. Since the strategy led to a high rate of growth as well as improvement in the well-being of the poor, a crucial element in equity, it was without doubt highly successful. It remains to be examined how readily this strategy is transferable.

Underlying Factors: How Transferable Is the East Asian Model?

Three broad areas can be identified which can influence economic performance and which are more or less subject to conscious policy manipulation. The relative importance of these areas will largely determine the extent to which the successful East Asian model can be transferred: government economic policies, which are readily subject to change; elements of the economy and society which can be changed through government policy, but not in the short term, such as the spread of education and the participation of women in the labor force; and aspects of culture broadly defined, which are difficult or impossible to influence by deliberate government policy, at least in the medium term.

The Role of Economic Policies

That specific government policies had an important role in economic success in East Asia has been a theme throughout this essay. Most salient have been policies with respect to prices and distribution and the extent to which governments aggravated or counteracted some of the distortions and weaknesses of a market economy. For both efficiency and equity, it has been argued earlier, it is crucial that labor remain low in cost as long as it is abundant and that capital and skill be high in cost as long as they are scarce. Table 3.6 and especially Table 3.7 provide evidence that the East Asian countries had very low labor costs by international standards during their periods of labor-abundant, labor-intensive rapid growth. The higher labor costs of Korea before its economic reform is typical of the distorted labor costs for organized industry in some other Asian countries.

Table 3.12 provides some very crude and partial information on the cost of capital. The real interest rate, that is the rate after taking account of price changes, in East Asia during the periods of rapid growth and capital scarcity ranged from one percent in relatively capital-abundant Hong Kong to nine percent in capital-scarce Taiwan and Korea, with Japan and Singapore in between. In contrast, the real rate in Korea before economic reform was strongly negative and in South Asia it ranged from an average of one percent to minus one percent.

More important for efficient, labor-intensive growth than the interest rate was the foreign-exchange rate. The contrast has already been stressed between the undervalued currency in East Asia and the overvalued currency in most of southern Asia. An overvalued currency made it cheap to buy imported machinery and expensive to use domestic labor and encouraged inefficient, capital-intensive industries producing for the home market.

In short, there clearly were major differences in the economic policies pursued by the East Asian countries which substantially affected their success and which could easily be adopted by other countries. In a later section I will consider whether there were some fundamental, noneconomic reasons why these policies were adopted in East Asia and not by many other countries.

The Role of Education, Female Labor Force Participation, and Technology Absorption

The most notable differences in factors that respond to policies only over a longer term were in the areas of education and women's participation in the economy. Literacy and educational participation were significantly higher in East Asia than in much of South Asia, even in the 1950s (see Tables 3.13 and 3.14). In East Asia the lowest rates of literacy in the 1950s, in Singapore and Taiwan, were around 50 percent, while in South Asia they were only 20 percent. Participation rates in primary education were 60–100 percent at that time in East Asia (other than Japan, where it was 100 percent) and 30–40 percent in South Asia (see Table 3.14). Much of the difference was due to differences in enrollment rates for girls. In East Asia 55 to 63 percent of the

TABLE 3.12
Nominal Annual Real Interest Rates
(percent per annum)

Country	1953	1957	1962	1967	1972	1977	1980
Japan							
—Nominal interest rate[1]	12.7	11.0	8.2	7.4	7.2	7.8	8.3
—Real interest rate	5.2	8.0	1.2	3.5	2.6	−0.5	0.4
Singapore							
—Nominal interest rate[2]	n.a.	n.a.	n.a.	8.0	7.5	7.0	13.6
—Real interest rate	n.a.	n.a.	n.a.	4.3	4.9	4.8	5.2
Hong Kong							
—Nominal interest rate[3]	n.a.	n.a.	n.a.	6.0	7.5	7.0	5.1
—Real interest rate	n.a.	n.a.	n.a.	−0.3	1.0	1.7	−10.3
Taiwan							
—Nominal interest rate[4]	27.0	19.8	15.8	13.3	11.3	10.8	16.2
—Real interest rate	8.2	12.3	13.5	10.0	8.3	3.8	−2.8
Korea							
—Nominal interest rate[5]	18.3	18.3	16.2	26.0	16.7	16.0	22.8
—Real interest rate	−26.6	−6.1	9.5	15.4	5.1	5.8	−5.9
Pakistan							
—Nominal interest rate[6]	n.a.	n.a.	n.a.	7.8	8.5	10.7	11.5
—Real interest rate	n.a.	n.a.	n.a.	−1.0	3.8	1.5	1.2
India							
—Nominal interest rate[7]	4.5	5.3	7.0	9.7	10.5	16.0	15.0
—Real interest rate	1.4	−0.8	3.8	−3.3	−17.1	8.4	3.9
—Nominal interest rate[8]	9.8	11.3	12.0	15.0	15.0	21.0	n.a.
—Real interest rate	6.7	5.2	8.8	2.0	−12.6	13.4	n.a.

Notes:

[1]Average of agreed interest rates on loans of all banks, Mutual Loan and Savings Bank and Credit Association

[2]Minimun lending rate

[3]The Hong Kong and Shanghai Banking Corporation's quoted best-lending rate

[4]Secured time loans in Taiwan District

[5]Commercial bank loans up to 1 year

[6]Scheduled bank advance rate for machinery

[7]Hundi rate of State Bank of India

[8]Bazaar bill rate in Bombay

Sources:

Japan: Statistics Bureau, *Japan Statistical Yearbook* 1961, 1985

Singapore, 1960–62: Chief Statistician, Department of Statistics, *Yearbook of Singapore,* 1974; 1982, 1983–84: Ministry of Trade and Industry, *Economic Survey of Singapore,* 1984.

Taiwan: Council for Economic Planning and Development, The Republic of China, *Taiwan Statistical Data Book,* 1969, 1984.

Hong Kong: Census and Statistics Department, Hong Kong, *Hong Kong Annual Digest of Statistics,* 1969, 1978, 1983.

Korea: National Bureau of Statistics, Republic of Korea, *Korea Statistical Yearbook,* 1967, 1977, 1981.

Pakistan: Government of Pakistan, Finance Division, *Pakistan Economic Survey,* 1978/79, 1984/85.

India: Department of Statistics, Ministry of Planning, *Statistical Abstract of India.*

Change in consumer price indices were obtained from: World Bank, *World Tables,* 1976; ILO, *Yearbook of Labour Statistics,* various issues; and IMF, *International Financial Statistics,* various issues.

girls were in primary school in the 1950s, even outside Japan, while in India it was 14 percent and in Pakistan only 6 percent.

The East Asian countries invested massively in education from the 1950s on. By the 1970s all their children, including girls, were in primary school and a third or more in secondary school. The older generation, which had not been formally educated earlier, produced relatively high rates of illiteracy, especially for women, but by the 1980s even that was below 20 percent. Considerable progress was also registered in South Asia, but even in the 1970s only in India were more than 50 percent of girls in primary school, while in Bangladesh it was 34 percent and in Pakistan 22 percent. At the secondary level the gap was even larger.

Another major difference in the educational system cannot be as readily documented: the nature of the training provided. Colonial heritage and current political pressures in South Asia have resulted in an educational system which is in large part poorly adapted to the needs of a modern society. It primarily has trained clerks at the secondary level, and lawyers, administrators, and liberal arts graduates at the higher level, rather than technicians, engineers, businessmen, and agriculturists. In the first few decades after independence, at least, many of the best students prepared for government service. A large proportion of the products of the educational system, especially in India, could not find suitable employment and formed a disaffected elite that contributed to social and political tensions rather than to economic productivity.

Partly as a result of more effective market pressures, especially in some countries, and partly as a result of a more authoritarian approach to education in others, the system in East Asia was more appropriate to the needs of the economy as a whole. In Korea, for instance, admissions to higher education were adjusted by government fiat to produce the skills that were deemed to be needed; to the extent that it was possible to forecast needs, the system was designed to assure that there were neither surpluses nor shortages in any skill or profession.

The differences in attitude toward female education, not only in the society as a whole but also in government policy, resulted over time in great differences in women's participation in the economy and especially in the industrial labor force. This is an area where data are quite unreliable, because definitions of "employment" vary and because, in some societies at least, female employment is deliberately underreported. Indeed, statistics of women working in agriculture are sometimes obviously absurd, with reported participation in census or survey data a small fraction of that reported in careful micro studies. Data on employment in organized manufacturing are more reliable.

Apparently the proportion of women in the industrial labor force in East Asia, except Japan, did not differ all that much from the proportion in South Asia in 1950 (see Table 3.15). But by the 1980s, with much higher educa-

TABLE 3.13
Percentage of Illiteracy
(age level: 15 + years)

Country	1950s			1960s			1970s			1980s		
	Total	Male	Female	Total	Male	Female	Total	Male	Female	Total	Male	Female
Japan	n.a.	n.a.	n.a.	2.2[6]	1.0[6]	3.3[6]	n.a.	n.a.	n.a.	n.a.	n.a.	n.a.
Singapore	53.5[5]	35.3[1]	77.4[1]	50.2[7]	32.3[7]	70.8[7]	31.1[12]	17.0[12]	45.7[12]	8.2[17]	6.6[17]	11.3[17]
Hong Kong	n.a.	n.a.	n.a.	29.6[8]	8.2[8]	51.0[8]	25.5[13]	9.2[13]	41.6[13]	n.a.	n.a.	n.a.
Taiwan	49.9[2]	37.9[2]	62.3[2]	27.1[9]	16.7[9]	38.1[9]	20.6[14]	10.7[14]	31.9[14]	11.0[18]	5.1[18]	17.5[18]
South Korea	23.2[3]	12.6[3]	33.3[3]	29.4[6]	16.6[6]	41.8[6]	12.4[12]	5.6[12]	19.0[12]	n.a.	n.a.	n.a.
India	80.7[4]	70.6[4]	91.6[4]	76.3[10]	66.1[10]	87.2[10]	65.9[13]	52.3[13]	80.6[13]	63.8[19]	53.5[19]	75.1[19]
Pakistan	81.1[5]	74.7[5]	88.3[5]	81.2[11]	71.1[11]	92.6[11]	79.3[15]	70.4[15]	89.7[15]	73.8[20]	64.0[20]	84.8[20]
Bangladesh	n.a.	n.a.	n.a.	78.4[11]	66.6[11]	91.3[11]	74.2[16]	62.7[16]	86.8[16]	n.a.	n.a.	n.a.

Notes:
[1]Year of census 1947
[2]Year of census 1950 (Age level 6+)
[3]Year of census 1955
[4]Year of census 1951

[5]Year of census 1951 (All ages)
[6]Year of census 1960
[7]Year of census 1957
[8]Year of census 1960
[9]1960 figure (Age level 6+)
[10]Year of census 1961 (All ages)
[11]Year of census 1961
[12]Year of census 1970
[13]Year of census 1971
[14]1970 figure (Age level 9+)
[15]Year of census 1972
[16]Year of census 1974
[17]Year of census 1980
[18]1982 figure (Age level 9+)
[19]Year of census 1981 (All ages)
[20]Year of census 1981

Sources:
UNESCO, *Statistical Yearbook*, various issues; and Directorate-General of Budget, Accounting and Statistics, the Republic of China, *Statistical Yearbook*, 1983.

TABLE 3.14

Education

(enrollment of all ages as percentage of the school-age population)

COUNTRIES	1950s				1960s[4]				1970s[5]				1980s[6]			
	PRIMARY		SECONDARY		PRIMARY		SECONDARY		PRIMARY		SECONDARY		PRIMARY		SECONDARY	
	Total	Female	Total	Female	Total	Female	Total	Female	Total	Female	Total	Female	Total	Female	Total	Female
Japan	100[1]	97[1]	71[1]	64[1]	103	102	74	73	99	99	86	86	101	101	91	91
All industri-alized countries	n.a.	n.a.	n.a.	n.a.	114	112	64	52	109	109	81	71	102	103	89	86
Singapore	80[2]	55[2]	8[2]	5[2]	111	101	32	26	106	102	46	45	107	105	55	58
Hong Kong	61[3]	55[3]	32[3]	26[3]	87	79	20	18	117	115	36	31	109	107	62	65
Taiwan	79[1]	63[1]	11[1]	6[1]	67	47	37	n.a.	104	n.a.	47	n.a.	n.a.	n.a.	n.a.	n.a.
South Korea	83[1]	n.a.	16[1]	6[1]	94	98	27	14	103	103	42	32	119	108	80	74

All middle-income countries	n.a.	n.a.	n.a.	n.a.	75	67	14	11	84	78	25	21	100	95	39	38
India	28[1]	14[1]	4[1]	1[1]	61	40	20	10	73	56	26	15	72	57	30	20
Pakistan	37	6	14	3	30	13	11	3	40	22	13	5	57[7]	30[7]	15[7]	8[7]
Bangladesh	n.a.	n.a.	n.a.	n.a.	47	26	8	1	52	34	19	8	63	48	15	7

Total: total (male and female) enrollment of all ages as percentage of the population of the corresponding school age.

Female: enrollment of female (all ages) as percentage of the population of females of the corresponding school age.

Notes:

[1] 1950 Figure
[2] 1951 Figure
[3] 1955 Figure
[4] 1960 Figure
[5] 1970 Figure
[6] 1980 Figure
[7] 1979 Figure

Sources:

1950s: UNESCO, *Statistical Yearbook*, various issues.
1960s–80s: World Bank, *World Tables*, 3d ed., vol. II.

TABLE 3.15
Economically Active Female Ratio in Manufacturing[1]

Country	1950s		1960s		1970s		1980s
	1950	1955	1960	1965	1970	1975	1980–83
Japan	28.7	36.6	32.5	34.3	35.8	33.9	39.6[11]
Singapore	11.4[2]	18.4[5]	n.a.	n.a.	33.6	44.2[9]	43.4[11]
Hong Kong	n.a.	n.a.	n.a.	43.1[7]	41.7[8]	46.1[10]	48.5[11]
Taiwan	11.2[3]	11.7	11.6	11.8	29.4	40.8	44.4[12]
South Korea	n.a.	n.a.	26.5	30.2	35.9	39.2[9]	38.2[11]
India	11.9[4]		27.1[6]		12.8[8]		14.6[13]
Pakistan	8.0[4]		10.5[6]		n.a.		5.9[13]

Notes:
[1]Economically active females in manufacturing over economically active population in manufacturing.
[2]1947 figure
[3]1953 figure
[4]1951 figure
[5]1957 figure
[6]1961 figure
[7]1966 figure
[8]1971 figure
[9]1977 figure
[10]1976 figure
[11]1983 figure
[12]1982 figure
[13]1981 figure
Sources:
   ILO, *Yearbook of Labour Statistics*, various issues.
   Directorate-General of Budget, Accounting and Statistics, The Republic of China, *Statistical Yearbook of the Republic of China* 1983.

tional participation of girls, the development of industries that actually preferred women workers, and a more accepting social attitude, female participation in the industrial labor force in East Asia was roughly triple what it was in India and seven times what it was in Pakistan. That means the East Asian countries had a much larger labor force to draw on and one that, for a variety of reasons, was lower paid. Moreover, the society did not have to incur the cost of infrastructure as additional workers moved into the city to take industrial jobs: most of the women workers would already be resident there as a member of an urban family. For all these reasons, greater female participation gave both industry and government a cost advantage in East Asia. That advantage may increase, as there is a trend to employ more women in that region, while in the two South Asian countries no such trend emerges from the data.

   Finally, the East Asian countries took a number of concrete steps to obtain access to the technology and markets for the export industries they were developing. Singapore encouraged massive foreign private investment, while Korea and Japan relied more heavily on licensing agreements for their access to technology. Korea and Japan also developed institutions that did adaptive research initially and served as channels for foreign technology, and both fostered large trading houses that had the resources to develop a foreign marketing network. All five countries used foreign companies when needed to gain market access. This sometimes meant selling under the foreign firms' brand names until a knowledge of the foreign markets was acquired and a reputation was established; then East Asian firms would begin to export under their own names.

It is plausible that all these steps made a difference in their success as exporters of manufactured goods and more broadly in the development effort. A literate labor force can more readily absorb and use new agricultural technology, for instance, than one that is almost wholly illiterate. Greater participation of women in the labor force adds to productivity in government, banking, professions, trade, and services generally, not just in industry. But explanations of East Asian success which stress the investment in education probably overstate its importance as a causal factor. For instance, the South Asian countries, most notably India, were not seriously handicapped by inadequate investment in education. The educational system may have in relative terms neglected technical and engineering training, but there were a reported 30,000 unemployed engineers in India at one time. Given the size and growth rate of the industrial sector, even the existing educational system produced a sufficient number of trained people to staff it and still leave a surplus. Similarly, the proportion of persons in secondary school in South Asia was low compared to East Asia, but the absolute numbers were so large and the needs of a slowly growing economy so limited that there is no evidence that this imposed any special constraints on economic growth. This point is strengthened by a comparison with Latin America, where a number of countries had rates of literacy and educational participation in the 1950s quite comparable to those in East Asia, but did not achieve high growth rates. In parts of Africa, and some countries elsewhere, inadequate and inappropriate education may have put a serious constraint on growth, but it was not a major factor in other countries.

Inadequate participation of women in the organized labor force similarly had only limited effects on growth. The countries of South Asia suffered from disguised unemployment, as did some countries in Southeast Asia. Wages were quite low, even for men. Adding women to the organized industrial labor force in larger numbers would have made a marginal difference to costs for the manufacturing sector, but it was not a significant factor. Moreover, women worked hard in agriculture, especially in processing and animal husbandry, and in a variety of activities in the informal sector that were poorly paid or produced irregular income, so they contributed to the economy, even if their contribution to modern industry was more limited than in East Asia. Their low participation rates in the modern urban sector was more significant because of the additional costs for infrastructure it imposed. In addition, in both East Asia and in parts of South Asia their limited role in professional and managerial positions was a handicap. But it does not help explain the higher growth rates of East Asia, since in these occupations the role of women in East Asia was even more limited than in some countries in South Asia.

Therefore, both education and women's employment do not seem to have played a major role in higher growth in East Asia in the 1950s and 1960s. Yet, they may have been more important in the 1970s. By then the four East Asian countries, other than Japan, were beginning to move to more skill-intensive industries which required a stronger education base. The reservoir of underemployed was nearing exhaustion, so participation of women in the industrial labor force was more crucial for continued growth (Japan had reached the same point earlier, but so had the developed countries with which it is compared).

Throughout the period since the 1950s, limited educational opportunities and limited opportunities for women to obtain regular, reasonably well-paid industrial employment was of greater significance for equity than for growth. It is the lower-income groups who are disproportionately excluded when educational facilities are inadequate, and it is they who most need the additional income women can bring in. Cross-section studies confirm that the spread of education is favorable for an egalitarian income distribution.[13] The rapid extension of primary education to the entire population and of secondary education to a substantial proportion of the population and the growth in employment opportunities for women therefore was a significant factor in the continued egalitarian income distribution in East Asia.

To sum up, until recently neither education nor women's participation in the labor force were major factors in explaining the higher growth rate in East Asia than in South or Southeast Asia. The greater ability of East Asia to adopt and adapt modern technology also was more important recently than in the first twenty years of development. The early industries in all countries tend to have simple technologies readily obtainable with their machinery. Even Pakistan, with practically no indigenous industrial tradition and negligible foreign investment, found it quite feasible to set up a textile industry *de novo*, which later competed effectively in the world market. The suppliers of machinery provided initial access to the technology involved, essentially on a turn-key basis. It is when India tried to develop a competitive automobile industry that problems of access to the latest technology arose.

The Role of Culture

It is even more difficult, especially for an economist, to analyze the importance to East Asian success of the culture of the region. Elements in the region's culture that have been emphasized as important to development, at least with respect to some of the countries, include discipline, respect for authority and for education, thrift, this-worldliness, cultural homogeneity, and the fluidity of class structures. As with many such ex-post explanations, at least some of these characteristics could be interpreted as being unfavorable as well as favorable to rapid growth. Several might be seen as undesirable for innovation, for entrepreneurship. The education which was respected tended to be scholarly and not practical, and so on. On an *a priori* basis only some of these characteristics would seem clearly favorable to rapid growth, and it requires someone familiar with the cultures of the five countries, their similarities as well as their differences, to carry this analysis further.

The comparative perspective can be helpful in providing some indication of the importance of cultural factors. First, in the postwar period, Korea initially followed a more dirigiste and inward-looking strategy. During that period its growth rate was less than five percent. After economic reform, implying a fundamental change in strategy, the growth rate more than doubled to ten percent. Presumably the cultural environment, broadly defined, did not change with economic strategy. The five-percentage-point increase may thus be a very crude measure of the contribution the change in strategy made to the growth rate. It is very crude indeed because other factors did not remain unchanged. In the earlier period, for instance, Korea was recovering from the ravages of the war, which usually contributes to a very high growth rate, and was receiving massive inflows of foreign aid, which has the same effect. On the other hand, in the later period it may have benefited more from U.S. expenditures in connection with the Vietnam War. Other factors may have changed as well. But the correlation between changed strategy and most economic indicators, including growth, is so close and clear, that it provides powerful evidence that changes in policies have been at least as important as cultural factors in explaining high growth.

One can make similar but less clear-cut comparisons for Singapore and for the Nationalist government in China. Singapore followed a more mixed strategy in the 1950s and had slow growth. The Nationalists' economic policies on the mainland were a disaster, while different policies in Taiwan resulted in one of the outstanding economic success stories of the last 30 years. But these comparisons are much less clear-cut than for Korea, because other factors more clearly changed as well. Both Singapore and Mainland China passed through political and physical turmoil, far worse in the case of the latter, that might itself explain the more modest growth rate. Therefore one can not make too much of these examples.

Another comparison is possible with the one country in South and Southeast Asia that is as resource poor as the East Asian countries and that adopted a similar market-oriented strategy in the 1960s: Pakistan's growth rate during that decade was not quite seven percent. The difference from East Asian growth rates of nine to ten percent in the same decade can be attributed to cultural factors, to differences in external circumstances (e.g., the effects of the Vietnam War), or to the fact that Pakistan did not adopt a market-oriented strategy, based on manufactured exports, to the same extent.

Among economic indicators several differences stand out. Pakistan's rate of investment was lower—below twenty percent rather than 21–36 percent— and it did not provide the same strong incentives to export, in the form of a favorable effective foreign-exchange rate, as those which rapidly pushed up East Asian exports. Pakistan's savings rates were somewhat lower, which can either be attributed to differences in the attitude towards thrift or to less effective economic incentives (see the lower interest rate in Table 3.12 for instance).

There is no satisfactory way for clearly distinguishing the effect on the growth rate of cultural as against economic-policy variables. But it does seem significant that East Asia, that is the countries with a Chinese-based culture, and only those countries, achieved a consistently higher growth rate than any other region and without the benefits, and costs, of profitable raw-material exports. It seems reasonable that some part of the explanation lies in the noneconomic realm, but there are three arguments for the proposition that these noneconomic factors explain only a small part of the success. First, one can provide a good, coherent economic rationale for the East Asian countries' success. Second, the success in three cases occurred only after these countries changed economic strategy. Culture was invariant, economic policies changed, and, almost simultaneously, economic performance changed. Third, other countries with quite different cultures also were successful in achieving growth and equity when they followed a similar strategy.

Political Factors and Economic Strategy

There remains a fundamental question: Why did these countries adopt a successful economic strategy and why did so many other countries fail to do so? While some element in their culture could provide an explanation, the reason could equally lie in their political situation and perhaps in historical accident.

All five East Asian countries were guided by elites that were, in a sense, under siege. Japan had lost a war and like the other major loser, Germany, had the incentive of trying to recoup its position. The elites of the other four also felt that they had to deliver if they were to survive. South Korea was in competition with the North, Taiwan with the Mainland; Hong Kong was populated by refugees, with a colonial government whose legitimacy was always in question, while Singapore was a Chinese island in a Malay sea. These are circumstances which might well induce a leadership to limit diversion of resources to its private benefit, and instead to use resources to benefit the majority of the population.

One other element is worth mentioning: economic success tends to set up a beneficent cycle which can reinforce the adoption of policies that further strengthen that success. When economic policies produce benefits for a large proportion of the population they strengthen the political position of those who advocated them in the government and those who decided on their adoption. That makes it easier for them to advocate and adopt further steps that improve the functioning of the economy. The demonstration effect of Japan's success exerted a powerful influence on the region, encouraging other governments to try the Japanese model in the first instance. Foreign aid donors, especially the U.S., also strongly encouraged that experiment. Early and quick success with that model—the Korean economy turned around in a relatively short period of time—then made it easier to pursue the same strategy more widely and consistently.

In short, there are no clear conclusions on the extent to which culture was a determining factor in the economic success of the East Asian countries. It may well be that the same economic strategy in other countries would not yield the same outstanding results in terms of both growth and equity. But there are good reasons to believe that it would be almost equally successful.

Summing Up: The Lessons of East Asia

The lessons of the East Asian experience are therefore quite optimistic. There are three major elements affecting economic performance that may not be reproduced elsewhere: societies and elites under pressure to perform; a relatively egalitarian distribution of wealth, including land, as a result of historical circumstances; and a set of cultural attributes, some of which were favorable for economic performance. But the principal element in economic success was the strategy adopted, which should be readily reproducible elsewhere.

The central elements of that strategy were: (1) a set of prices and other incentives which made it profitable to invest in activities which heavily used abundant unskilled labor and conserved scarce capital and skilled labor; (2) extensive government intervention in the economy in four of the countries, which compensated for weaknesses and distortions that exist in market economies, including measures to further encourage labor-intensive activities and to meet the costs of breaking into the world market; (3) wide scope for competitive pressures, primarily by providing strong incentives for industry to compete in the world market. This fostered efficiency and was a factor in promoting labor-intensive activities since, in labor-abundant countries, these were the most competitive; (4) high returns to investors and an environment in which arbitrary, personalistic decisions were limited. This provided incentives for both domestic and foreign investors to save and invest sufficiently to overcome their hesitation due to uncertainty about these countries' future.

As a result of the strategy there was extremely rapid and consistent growth of labor-intensive manufactured exports. Together with its indirect effects, the rapid expansion of industry resulted in the highest growth rate of national income over two to three decades achieved in any region in the world.

Since growth was labor intensive, it meant rapidly escalating demand for unskilled workers. This in turn raised their wages and meant that the poor, who derive income primarily from selling their unskilled labor, benefited from growth more or less proportionately. The strategy therefore led to a rapid decline in poverty. That these countries had a relatively egalitarian distribution of wealth in the 1950s helped in spreading widely the benefits of growth, as did the rapid expansion of education and of women's participation in the labor force. But the fundamental reason for growth being both rapid and egalitarian was the labor-intensive nature of the strategy.

The success of the strategy was not due, in any fundamental sense, to the commitment to private enterprise or to its export orientation, as sometimes averred. Four of the countries were far from traditional private-enterprise economies. Governments intervened heavily in economic decisions. It is true that even without government intervention, a pure market economy in a labor-abundant society will result in a labor-intensive pattern of investment and, especially if the economy is small, in substantial exports, since the domestic market can absorb only a limited amount of labor-intensive goods and cannot efficiently produce capital- and skill-intensive ones. The market will also assure a degree of efficiency as a result of competitive pressures. But a market economy also has some problems and failures, including the possibility that it will price labor at a higher level than desirable for efficiency and that externalities in exporting will discourage exports. Government intervention can meet both problems, and that is what four of the governments did to a varying extent. These governments used the market to accomplish national objectives efficiently. They complemented the market by intervening in areas where it functioned less well.

Exports similarly were means to the end of efficiency. Indeed the three countries that were not city-states and therefore had a sizable domestic market often developed industry first behind protective barriers to serve the domestic market and then moved to exports once the infant-industry stage had been left behind. Exports at that stage were helpful in achieving two of the central elements of the strategy: labor intensity and competitive pressures for efficiency.

It is not clear that other countries adopting a similar strategy will achieve the same growth rates, or the same degree of equity, because many of their circumstances will differ. They could be more or less successful, depending on such factors as the impact of their human and natural resource endowment, their location, historical accidents with respect to such matters as the nature of the goods they are producing, and their culture, broadly defined. Whether they can and will adopt the East Asian model also depends on their political system and the costs and benefits that the model will allocate to particular groups. But it seems clear that the essence of the model is eminently transferable and will yield the same success with respect to growth and equity.

The East Asian countries did not adopt the model in a pure form. Their governments introduced some distortions in the economy which resulted in a loss of efficiency and equity, because growth and overall equity are not the only goals which a government pursues. Any government which can ignore other objectives, usually political in the broadest sense of that term, could well achieve even better results than the East Asian pioneers.

Notes

1. See Gustav Papanek and Oldrich Kyn, "The Effect on Income Distribution of Development, the Growth Rate and Economic Strategy," *Journal of Development Economics* 21, 1986.
2. Leroy P. Jones and Gustav Papanek, "The Efficiency of Public Enterprise in Less Developed Countries," in G. Ram Reddy, ed., *Government and Public Enterprise* (London: Frank Cass, 1983).
3. For a discussion of the mechanism and its political rationale, see Gustav Papanek, "Capitalism and Income Distribution," in Peter Berger and Philip Marcus, eds., *The Calculus of Hope* (Lanham, MD: University Press of America, 1986); and Gustav Papanek, *Lectures on Development Strategy, Growth, Equity and the Political Process in Southern Asia* (Pakistan Institute of Development Economics, 1986).
4. See Gustav Papanek, "Capitalism and Income Distribution," op. cit.; and Michael Manove and Gustav Papanek, with Harendra K. Dey, "Tied Rents and Wage Determination in Labor Abundant Countries," unpublished working paper, 1986.
5. D.C. Cole and P. Lyman, *Korean Development* (Cambridge: Harvard University Press, 1971).
6. Ibid.
7. See Leroy P. Jones and Sakong Il, *Government, Business and Entrepreneurship in Economic Development: The Korean Case* (Cambridge: Harvard University Press, 1980) (Korean translation: Seoul: KDI Press, 1981).
8. Stephen Chow and Gustav Papanek, "Laissez-Faire Growth and Equity— Hong Kong," *Economic Journal*, June 1981.

9. See also Stephen Chow and Gustav Papanek, ibid.
10. Gustav Papanek, "Capitalism and Income Distribution," op. cit.
11. See Leroy P. Jones and Sakong Il, *Government, Business and Entrepreneurship in Economic Development*, op. cit.; and Suk-chae Lee, "Growth Strategy and Income Distribution: Analysis of the Korean Experience," unpublished Ph.D. dissertation, Boston University, 1982.
12. Gustav Papanek and Oldrich Kyn, "The Effect on Income Distribution of Development, the Growth Rate and Economic Strategy," op. cit.
13. Ibid.

4

The New Asian Capitalism:
A Political Portrait

Lucian W. Pye

Although it may be reasonable to classify the East Asian countries as a single category economically, with Japan setting a pattern which the others will be following, this is not so easily done with respect to their political systems. Political evolution in Japan, Korea, Taiwan, to say nothing of Hong Kong and Singapore, differs significantly, nor are there reasons to assume that the other East Asian countries will emulate Japan politically. Today, Japan is a well institutionalized democracy, while both South Korea and the Republic of China on Taiwan (ROC) are systems that are partially democratic and partially authoritarian. Singapore has a parliamentary government with regularized elections, but it is also a one-party system ruled by a strong-willed leader. Hong Kong remains a British colony destined to again become a part of China in 1997. The military looms large in South Korea and the ROC, for both are parts of divided nations which confront hostile Communist enemies. The political history of Korea, the former Hermit Kingdom and Japanese colony, bears little resemblance to the story of the Kuomintang's rise and fall in China and its subsequent problems of unifying Mainlanders and Taiwanese in a place that was expected to be only a temporary island retreat. While Singapore and Hong Kong share a history of being British colonies, the former was guided toward independence, while the latter has been denied such a prospect; hence their constitutional developments have been strikingly different.

There is also considerable variety in the ways in which these East Asian governments manage their respective economies. Certainly MITI's (Ministry of International Trade and Industry) style of influencing Japanese companies is different from the way the Seoul government directs the huge Korean industrial groups and the way the ROC Finance Ministry treats the smaller and more numerous Taiwanese enterprises. The Hong Kong colonial government makes only limited interventions into an essentially laissez-faire economy, while the Singaporean authorities keep track of and guide much of the commercial and industrial activities in their city-state.

In spite of these historical differences and the variations in their political economies, there are valid reasons for treating the East Asian political systems as a common category and for asking whether in their few common features they represent an appropriate model for other developing countries. Although it is necessary to keep in mind the differences among the five, it is equally important to note that their similarities leap out and demand attention when they are compared with the developing countries of Africa and Latin America.

Furthermore, it is known that most countries of Southeast Asia—particularly Malaysia, Thailand, Indonesia, and even the Philippines—are seeking to follow the East Asian model of export-led growth guided by firm governmental policies. The prime minister of Malaysia has spoken explicitly about "looking to the East," that is to Korea and Japan, for answers to his country's development policies. Even the People's Republic of China, in its current pragmatic phase, has implicitly acknowledged that it might have something to learn from its East Asian neighbors.

The political features that the East Asian systems have in common are, first, their shared Confucian cultural traditions, and second, their close involvement with the United States, both in terms of direct U.S. interventions—as during the occupation of Japan, the Korean War and Korea's subsequent recovery, and the years of substantial economic and military aid to Taiwan—and in terms of their continuing dependence upon access to the U.S. market. The combination of the historical Confucian tradition and the decision to become closely associated with the United States in a contemporary world situation in which the likely alternative was Communist rule has led to many common political and governmental practices among the East Asian states.

Indeed, the economic successes of the East Asian states have attracted so much attention that Westerners seem unaware that these same societies have developed some equally novel political forms. In economics, a veritable new industry has emerged around the production of studies and theories about management and economic strategies in Japan and the "four little dragons," the "gang of four," or the NICs. The names abound to hail the economic "miracles," but we do not yet have any widely accepted name for the distinctive type of political system that has emerged out of the uniting of Confucianism and advanced capitalism. Although Japan is seen universally as a democracy, albeit with only a "one-and-a-half party" system, Korea, Taiwan, and Singapore are defined as "quasi-authoritarian" or "semi-authoritarian," yet they bear little resemblance to Latin American authoritarian systems in that they stress equality over gross economic disparities.

The East Asian countries, Japan excepted, have authoritarian systems—but again, this is not quite true; they do not conform to the general model of authoritarian governments as they are known in the rest of the world. In East Asia power is monopolized by a relatively small elite, dissent is not easily tolerated, political controls tend to reinforce a dominant party or ruling group, and boundaries are set on press freedom—all of which add up to authoritarianism by any definition. Yet, there is another side to the East Asian governments. They tend to recognize merit, extol technocratic skills, encourage national development, and generally press for modernization and egalitarian economic development. Leaders cling to their rights of power, but they can be broadly supportive of all who contribute to national development, just as long as they are not also politically unruly and disruptive.

In short, the systems are paternalistic. They seek to nurture legitimate social and economic activities, and they are generally responsive to the dependency needs of populations that tend to look to authority for problem solving. They are also authoritarian in that they are hypersensitive to any threat to their power and status.

It is generally assumed that the East Asian NICs are following the economic model of Japan and developing a form of capitalism that is strongly supported by, and dependent upon, government. It has also been suggested by a few observers that the "four little dragons" will develop politically along the lines of Japan. For example, some people see the possibility of this happening in Taiwan, with the Kuomintang becoming the functional equivalent of Japan's Liberal Democratic Party (LDP), even to the point of having a variety of factions, and the *dang wai* performing the role of the opposition. In general, however, the East Asian model of paternalistic authoritarianism has been harsher with political opponents than has the Japanese. Indeed, it would be incorrect to call them "soft authoritarian" systems because they can be very stern and strict in administering punishment to those they feel to be inappropriately challenging them.

Before we analyze the evolution of these paternalistic authoritarian systems it may be helpful to summarize their common characteristics. We can do this by proposing the following model that consists of a dozen boldly stated propositions. Of course modifications would be needed to describe each of the separate countries because of their individual differences. In the main, however, the propositions seek to capture the essential features of the East Asian political systems at a level of generality useful for judging their appropriateness as models for other developing countries. The fact that it is possible to construct such a model seems to suggest that there is such a thing as a category of East Asian political systems. It goes without saying that the model is the least applicable to the British colony of Hong Kong.

The East Asian Political Model

1. In East Asian political cultures, authority is expected to combine, with grace and benevolence, both elitism and sympathy—that is, aloof dignity and nurturing concern. The cultures revere hierarchy, accepting gradations of rank and merit as natural, but they also expect rulers to be concerned about the livelihood of the masses.
2. It therefore follows that East Asian governments are the unquestioned dominant institutions in their societies, but in each country the government is expected to manifest paternalistic concern for all the people. All segments of the society are expected to yield to the government as the guiding force of the collectivity, but in return rulers should be supportive of everyone who displays proper awe.
3. The Confucian ideal of rule by an educated elite has given way to rule by technocrats who are assumed to be knowledgeable about, and sympathetic toward, the interests of all segments of society. They must also, however, be deferential to their political masters.
4. In practical economic terms, paternalistic government in East Asia means protecting domestic industries against foreign competition, championing exports in a vigorously nationalistic fashion, and supporting a spirit of national consensus that encourages cooperation among all elements of society—including, especially, labor and management—and prevents unseemly competition among business enterprises. In East Asia the state is not seen as being only in competition with other states, sovereignty versus sovereignty, but rather the state is both a guardian against foreign private actors and an active force in helping domestic enterprises to conquer foreign markets. The American idea that government should foster competition and oppose trusts seems absurd to East Asians. Instead, East Asian governments feel obligated to bring together the most powerful combinations of enterprises possible to accelerate economic growth and strengthen the nation against all other nations.
5. In return for nurturing a corporatist spirit throughout society, East Asian governments feel they should have the right to limit real dissent. Adversarial relationships are muted, and critics are taught the benefits of conformity. Paternalistic authority in East Asia legitimizes patronage, and hence government can support chosen private enterprises. Authority can play favorites, depending upon who is most responsive in honoring it. Blatant corruption is, however, no longer acceptable.
6. Political leadership involves setting national goals and priorities, mobilizing resources and public attention for collective tasks, and squashing debates that might dilute the national will. Government sees itself as the embodiment of the national destiny, and hence it has the obligation to tell everyone what needs to be done and censor divisive ideas and initiatives.
7. Except in Japan, leadership means rule by a dominant figure, an ultimate authority on all problems. Consequently the question of succession be-

comes a process dangerous to the stability of the entire system. The Achilles heel of all the NICs is precisely the question of what will come after the current strong man.

8. In East Asia the predictability necessary for economic prosperity lies less in a system of laws and more in the leadership's commitment to its professed policies and principles. The rule of law is secondary to the sincerity of officials and the steadfastness of individual leaders in carrying out their programs. The adversarial, indeed game-playing, spirit of Western legal practices is seen as whimsical when contrasted with the reassuring consistency in judgment of stolid officials with long terms of office.

9. Although traditional Confucian political authority was expected to be omnicompetent, modernization and the humiliating shock of defeat in war have made contemporary East Asian authority respectful of other forms of skill and merit. While ultimate political authority in East Asia still pretends to omnipotence, scope is given to lesser authorities—just so long as they keep their place and show proper deference. The heirs to Confucianism have thus avoided, as much as possible, unseemly clashes of authority in favor of established hierarchies of power.

10. In contrast to traditional Confucianism which despised the marketplace, political legitimacy in East Asia has become inordinately dependent upon continued national economic progress. The criterion of legitimacy, to a dangerous degree, has become success in advancing economic development. The more insecure the government, the greater the pressures on industry to expand. Any period of prolonged stagnation can cause a crisis of authority.

11. The paternalism of East Asian authority is complemented by a psychology of dependency among the people, which seems to make some apparently authoritarian practices acceptable—just so long as welfare is nurtured—but if authority should falter, explosive anger could result. What may seem to Westerners as unbecoming authoritarian practices are often accepted as appropriate by East Asians. But if the government fails to be nurturing and appears weak and unauthoritative, the people feel they have a right to be angry. Political authority in East Asia is expected to protect the cultural values of their societies, while encouraging the adoption of foreign technologies. Today, however, the values that need protecting have been diluted by acculturation, although some technologies are Asian innovations.

12. In East Asia, and especially in Korea and Taiwan, the military is recognized as a powerful institution, but there is profound ambivalence about what its future role should be because it is not clear whether armies are a drain or a support to the main task of national economic growth. The military establishments in Korea and Taiwan remain the ladder to political leadership, but direct military rule is no longer acceptable, and the demand for collective vigilance against a foreign military threat has become somewhat trivialized by repetition.

The Confucian Paradox

The model we have just outlined reflects in most aspects its Confucian roots. Yet there is an astonishing paradox: the East Asian countries that are now having such striking economic successes shared a Confucian heritage which was traditionally scornful of merchants and materialistic accomplishments. Conventional wisdom has long held that Confucianism was a drag on economic development. Yet, today we find that other countries in Asia with different cultural roots are finding it difficult to emulate the East Asian economic model, precisely because they lack those qualities inherent in that Confucian legacy. The paradox thus becomes a mystery which needs to be resolved before it can be decided whether there is such a thing as an East Asian model which can be relevant for other developing areas or whether these countries are *sui generis* precisely because of their Confucian roots.

As a start in untangling this puzzle, we need to take note of three critical features of the Confucian tradition which at one time impeded economic progress but which have endured and now seem to support the paternalistic authoritarianism that is compatible with East Asian capitalism.

First, there is the strong ethical-moral basis of government in the Confucian tradition that both sets limits on the pragmatic uses of power and requires that authority act with compassion for the people. It is this ethical-moral dimension of the Confucian sense of legitimacy that seems to make the East Asian governments feel that they not only have the right to intervene in people's lives but that they have a definite obligation to do so if it can help improve the people's condition. At one time such interventions tended to be detrimental to economic growth, but that is no longer the case now that government officials know more about how economies grow. In short, the Confucian tradition had to be coupled with advances in economics as an intellectual discipline in order to produce the economic miracles of East Asia. The new mandarins had to be schooled in the wisdom of Western economic theories and practices.

Second, and closely related, is an elitist view of the sociopolitical order which justifies the existence of hierarchy but which is ambivalent as to whether the criterion for status should be the manifestation of virtue or of merit, the goodness of a "virtuocracy," or the skills of a meritocracy. In traditional Confucianism stress was placed mainly on the virtues of the upright man who embodied leadership. In recent times the idea of rule by an educated elite has meant the legitimization of technocrats in government. Those who rule know best what is good for everyone because they are the best trained and have the appropriate skills. In this tradition the common man should defer to his intellectual betters.

The third quality is the Confucian stress on harmony, which in applied politics gets translated into a demand for consensus and conformity and, on the opposite side of the coin, a belief that individualism can only be a manifestation of selfishness and a vulgar craving to attract attention to the self. The value of harmony also means scorn for those who would disrupt the social order by dissent and by engaging in oppositional activities. Rulers are expected to preserve order, prevent social confusion, and thus keep in check any and all who are likely to disrupt the smooth flow of economic and social life. This valuing of harmony in Confucian political cultures places obstacles in the way of political critics, labor agitators, student rebels, and other challengers of the status quo.

Nationalism as the Basis of Modernization

In the East Asian systems of today, including the Japanese, these traditional Confucian qualities still exist. What is new is an expansion in perspective: the traditional Confucian group-oriented, rather than individual-oriented, outlook has been extended to go beyond family and clan to include the nation. The powerful sense of nationalism in all East Asian societies stems first from the traditional emphasis upon the collectivity which became the nation after the Western impact.

The first shock to the Confucian world was the arrival of a technologically more advanced West, with its stress upon the importance of the nation-state as the basic political unit. The Chinese, the Japanese, and in time the Koreans all responded in the same way: they sought to distinguish between their fundamental Confucian or traditional cultural values and what they denigrated as mere technology, a lesser aspect of culture. The Chinese, for example, advanced the dichotomy of *t'i-yung*, in which *t'i* stood for the essence, the highest value, which, of course, was their Confucian traditional culture, and *yung* which was only the practical, the utilitarian, and hence the technology of the "barbarian."[1] The strategy that followed from this distinction was that it would be all right to utilize Western technology to protect superior Chinese values, as though it would be possible to control social change so neatly. (The Chinese Communists are in a sense still trying to maintain such a distinction under their "open door" policy by saying they will keep out the "corrupt" features of bourgeois culture—"spiritual pollution"—while at the same time protecting basic Chinese values which now, ironically, stem largely from imported Marxist-Leninist socialism.)

In Japan there was a similar dichotomy which took the form of the slogan *wakon yosai*, "Japanese spirit, Western technology" and which, during the Meiji era, became the call for national mobilization. In Korea Confucianism reinforced a sense of nationalism, first, by giving the traditional aristocracy, or *yangban* class, a stronger sense of collective responsibility than it originally had, and second, by providing a basis for national pride during the period of Japanese colonial rule—for the Koreans could remind themselves that it was they who gave Confucianism to Japan and the Japanese could be seen as second-rate Confucianists as compared to their Korean teachers.

This early version of East Asian nationalism soon took the form of a "search for wealth and power."[2] In Japan the slogan was *fukoku kyohei*, "rich nation, strong army," in China it was *fu-min ch'iang-kuo*, "rich people, strong nation." Only in Japan, with its historical tradition of cultural borrowing, did this initial phase of nationalism result in effective modernization. In all the countries, however, the new formula of wealth and power served to shift the rationale of legitimacy away from the Confucian view of rule by moral example to a more utilitarian obligation of the state to encourage economic development. (Ironically, in South Korea the opposition politicians are challenging the thesis that legitimacy can be based on mere success in economic policies, and they are insisting that there should be a return to Confucian virtues; on the other hand the government insists that Confucianism calls for the discipline necessary for continued economic growth.[3])

Thus, in East Asia, long before the theories of economic development and nation-building became popular in the Third World, governments were concerning themselves with questions of how public policies might be able to further economic progress and state-building. In this sense, the East Asian countries had a substantial head start over the rest of the non-Western world in striving for economic growth. Elsewhere colonial administration concentrated more on law and order, constitutional development, and support for Western economic enterprises.

Paternalism Becomes Patronage

The initial efforts at economic development of this early phase of East Asian nationalism were not especially impressive, except in Japan. The traditional paternalistic version of authority provided no clear sense of how best to realize the new goals of wealth and power. It was Japanese paternalism which first hit upon the solution that was most consistent with Confucian virtues: the use of patronage. The story of how the Meiji government built up the private enterprises which became the *zaibatsu* has been told too many times to warrant recapitulating here.[4] For our analysis the only point that needs stressing is that the nurturing, supportive role of government in helping worthy but dependent private efforts was very much in line with Confucian ideals about how benevolent authority should be kind to those in need.

Hence it was not surprising that in all the Confucian countries that have sought capitalistic development, the response of government has eventually been one of providing patronage and guidance to those in the private sector found to be worthy.[5] While still on the mainland, the Kuomintang was somewhat ambivalent about building a version of bureaucratic capitalism which might enrich some friends of government or encourage independent entrepreneurs to prosper; but by the time the Nationalists moved to Taiwan, preference clearly was for the latter alternative.[6] (In Taiwan today, the state-run enterprises are generally less successful and lack potential buyers in the private sector.) In Korea, President Syngman Rhee's version of paternalistic-patronage focused mainly on agriculture and land reform, and it was President Park Chung Hee who caused the state to create the huge industrial groups that now are at the center of the nation's phenomenal growth.[7]

The Need for a Second Shock

Before bringing the historical account up to the present, we need to take note of the fact that the contemporary political and economic configurations of East Asia were critically shaped by a second major shock which shattered the traditional Confucian sense of cultural superiority and made genuine learning from the outside world possible. The first shock brought only the acknowledgment of Western technological superiority. In each case of successful development there had to be a second and far more profound shock—humiliating defeat in war.

For Japan it was the defeat in the Second World War and the American occupation that destroyed the warrior tradition and ended the earlier Confucian sense of cultural superiority. In seeking to regain self-esteem, the Japanese channeled their energies into economic development and the consolidation of a democratic polity—much as Germany did.[8] In Taiwan, the Kuomintang experienced profound humiliation in being beaten by what they considered to be only a peasant army. Consequently they had little resistance to reform and were more vigorous than before in paternalistically supporting capitalistic developments.[9] Korea was totally torn apart by war, and in rebuilding, government had to take the lead; it could not be complacent because of the continuing threat from the North.[10] (One of the most important questions that can be asked about the People's Republic is whether the shock of the Cultural Revolution has been the functional equivalent of the defeats experienced by other East Asian countries, and whether China is in a state of readiness for effective learning from abroad.)

The Nationalization of Risks

Many features of the paternalistic authoritarianism of East Asia are critical in explaining the nature of the capitalistic developments in those societies, but possibly the most important feature that emerged from the patronage process, especially after the second shock, has been the readiness of the government to assume much of the risks usually taken by the private entrepreneurs in other capitalistic systems. The spirit of paternalism, when fueled by anxieties about possible national failure, has made the East Asian governments ready to shelter businessmen from economic failures. In a sense, they have nationalized risks and made entrepreneurs into more dependent figures than is normal in a capitalist system.[11]

The relationship of government and business goes well beyond guidance and indicative planning to include protection against the risk of failure. In Korea and Taiwan the government has prodded industrialists to move into ever higher levels of technology while promising to protect the domestic market. Less often have been cases in which government has counseled against new departures and has not given initial protection to enterprises which are prepared to assume the risks themselves—as when MITI in Japan advised against the development of a domestic automobile industry. But as soon as government recognizes its mistake, the paternalistic spirit once again asserts itself and shelter and support are provided.[12]

Mercantilism Becomes Corporatism

The strong sense of group orientation basic to the Confucian tradition has reinforced East Asian nationalism and has produced a vivid awareness of the boundary lines between foreigners and compatriots. East Asian governments can thus operate with confidence that there is a national consensus that home markets should be shielded and competition abroad facilitated. Indeed, feelings of a deep divide between "us" and "foreigners" in the East Asian cultures have made mercantilism second nature.[13] Governments and citizens automatically agree that it is more honorable to sell abroad than to import. In these countries people do not have to be told to buy domestic products rather than imports.

The transition in East Asia with the development of industrial capitalism was not, as in the West, from mercantilism to free trade; instead, the paternalistic tradition has made the transition one toward a form of corporatism. The state, in its nurturance of industry, has concentrated on making enterprises internationally competitive.[14] This has meant that policies have been designed to insure harmonious industrial relations while keeping wages in check. In Korea, in particular, the government has been active in controlling wages so as to insure that exports remain competitive. The result is that labor's main opponent is often the government rather than the employers.[15]

Government's ideal, of course, is to create a bonding sense of family between labor, industry, and government. In return for pressures on labor to keep wage demands low, governments have insisted that employers should provide paternalistic security for labor; therefore, in the early stages of East

Asian industrial development companies rather than governments have had to bear the burden of welfare costs. In Korea and Taiwan, social security is still primarily the province of private companies, or even more often it is left to the families themselves. In Japan, however, the transition toward state-run welfare has begun, and given the paternalistic tradition, the cost of social services has mushroomed very rapidly.

This raises a fundamental question about the future of East Asian political paternalism: Will these governments in time feel obligated to protect their people's livelihood to the point of providing social services equal to, if not greater than, that provided by Western welfare states where the tradition of a more individualistic ethic provides some restraints? The ballooning of pensions and health-care costs in Japan probably indicate a similar trend in Korea and Taiwan as their governments become more affluent. If this comes about before there is an expansion of political pluralism, the state is likely to try even harder to achieve consensus because paternalistic authority in East Asia generally assumes that dependency should produce conformity in a properly socialized citizenry.

Strong Sovereignty, Weak Establishment

Paternalistic authority, especially in Korea and Taiwan, is lonely authority. The sense that the state should stand alone goes beyond just hostility toward political opposition and competition. Sovereignty should also be monolithic in the sense that the ultimate authority is expected to have competence in all areas. There are few limits to the acceptable scope of government.

Moreover, in the Confucian tradition authority was not easily divided; hence, centralized decision making was the norm. Just as the father was assumed to be omnipotent, so was the ruler, and all lesser authorities had to bow to the ultimate one. With modernization, this created serious problems because it has generally not been easy for authority to be allocated according to specialization. Responsibility still lies with the sovereign, and such power tends to be personalized; it is not treated as a function of specialized institutions or technical competence.

In Korea, decision making is concentrated in the Blue House; in Taiwan everyone looks to the President's Office. Nothing is final until these ultimate authorities pass on it. Concentrating authority in this way has also increased its vulnerability. Complaints have a single target. Even if the man at the top is spared, it is still the central government that will be held at fault. The system of patronage which creates power through the dispensing of favors also focuses criticism on government as the only competent authority.

In Korea, in particular, and to a lesser degree in Taiwan, the government is highly visible but is not surrounded by rings of supporting authority, and thus there is no establishment capable of reinforcing the social and political order. In a sense, the king must rule alone without the support of nobles with autonomous bases of power. In Korea, the government has created some extraordinary economic groups—true empires in international competition. Yet politically, they are minor factors, for everyone knows that their strength comes from the favors of government. Similarly, the country has a highly developed system of higher education, but the leading academics are not a voice of established authority: professors have influence only when they join government, but then they lose credibility with the public. The Korean press is rich but not powerful. In short, if government falters, there are no other institutions capable of performing as an establishment to hold together the social order until government can right itself. The exception, of course, in both countries is the army.

The situation in Taiwan is not as extreme. In addition to government there is the Kuomintang with its various factions, a large number of elected opposition politicians who have a vested interest in political evolution rather than chaos, and numerous business enterprises that are independent enough of governmental patronage to be able to act as autonomous interests. Yet, even so, government towers over all other institutions, and operates largely without the benefit of a supporting establishment. There is no group of leaders outside of the party or the government who could confidently advise the political authorities and quietly help shape policy.

Historically, the situation was different in Japan because Confucianism was modified by an elaborate system of centralized feudalism which implanted in the Japanese political culture a respect for specialization and a tolerance for divisions of authority according to technical competence that was unique in East Asia. Although government may now pose as the ultimate guiding force, in practice there is autonomy in vast areas of decision making, and thus governmental authority does not stand alone. Indeed, instead of the traditional Chinese Confucian ideal of an omnipotent authority and a sovereign authority which had the last say in all significant matters, the Japanese version of Confucianism allowed for deference to persons having various forms of skill and merit. In modern times this has meant that the different realms of specialization have not only deferred to each other's competencies, but they have actually respected the criteria of others in recruiting for their own. Thus the government places absolute faith in the relevance of academic merit in its search for competence, and in turn, business assumes that government's measurement of merit is a proper guide in hiring former government officials. Consequently, merit is diffused throughout the Japanese system and is not just concentrated in government. The Confucian idea of a hierarchy of merit persists, but there is an un-Confucian respect for a great variety of skills. At the same time the system is integrated by mutual respect for the different forms of merit.

Stability is Idealized but Succession is Uncertain

In all of the East Asian paternalistic systems of authority, the ideal of government has been stability based on the predictability of official behavior in all possible respects. Although the Confucian tradition favored rule by superior men, not by arbitrary laws, still the principle of government was that officials should avoid doing the unexpected or acting whimsically. The rule of predictability has, of course, been a major factor facilitating economic growth. Businessmen can feel that government will be consistent and its procedures will be orderly.

Historically, this was not characteristic of Chinese Confucian rule. In China, government, especially in modern times, was often highly erratic, and the ideal of rule by men and not by laws allowed for uncertainty and at times corruption. It was what we have called the ''second major shock'' that forced each of the East Asian systems to become more law-abiding and hence more predictable.

Yet, so far only Japan has been able to realize the ultimate test of stability, that of political succession through orderly procedures. In Korea, succession has been only by coup d'état; in Taiwan the only succession has been dynastic—the passing of power from father to son. Even in Japan competition over succession has been restricted to the informal play of factional politics in the LDP, and thus the process is not regulated by legally defined institutional procedures. Fortunately, in Japan the bureaucratic procedures of government are so institutionalized that succession at the prime minister's level usually does not signal dramatic policy changes.

In Singapore, anxiety over the eventual need to pass power on from the twenty-year stewardship of Prime Minister Lee Kuan Yew to a second generation of leadership has stimulated talk of the need to have a more stable system of government than is provided by parliamentary democracy. First Deputy Prime Minister Goh Chok Tong, a likely successor, has spoken out in favor of a one-party system with a few marginal ''peripheral parties'' to represent ''sectional interests.'' Prime Minister Lee's son, Lee Hsein Loong, another potential successor, has denounced the idea of ''protest voting'' against the ruling party and has called for ''national unity'' as the only hope for a stable political future.

Thus, in Korea, Taiwan, and Singapore the greatest uncertainty for the political system surrounds this question of succession. Since there has been no constitutional transferal of power in the three countries, people are not certain as to whether they should believe pledges of the respective incumbents that their successors will take office according to the appropriate existing laws. The more general expectation is that succession will produce some form of a political earthquake of uncertain intensity. This is the uncertainty which always prevails in authoritarian systems, especially when the supreme ruler seems to embody the destiny of the state.

Legitimacy Crises

This brings us to the troublesome fact that the failure of the East Asian countries to keep pace politically with their economic achievements has left all, except Japan, with some legitimacy problems. The root of the difficulties has been the need to find another basis for legitimacy to replace the traditional Confucian ideal of rule by morally superior men of proven mastery of the classics.

Ironically, Japan has been spared this crisis for two reasons. First, out of its defeat in war it had an American-drafted constitution imposed upon it, and, second, its ruling politicians have established solid relationships with the people in their respective constituencies. Although they have lost the legitimacy associated with their god-emperor, the Japanese have found an equally powerful source of justification for government's authority in the skills with which they have mastered a foreign-imposed system and made it indelibly their own.

The Kuomintang on Taiwan has had more difficulty with the concept of legitimacy, especially since it has had to cling to the myth of being the government of all of China when in fact it was a defeated remnant with an urgent obligation to justify its rule over an ethnically different majority—the Taiwanese. Historically, after the end of the monarchy in China, the Kuomintang took the lead in trying to devise a new and modern basis of legitimacy to replace the Confucian ideals of government by hierarchy and in support of a harmonious social order. Sun Yat-sen and Chiang Kai-shek hoped to find a new basis of legitimacy in the idea of a "national will." Out of a combination of the Three People's Principles, the Five Power Constitution, and a nationalistic, if not racial, appeal to all people of Chinese blood, the Kuomintang molded a new and more authoritative basis for government.

But the humiliation of military defeat turned those ideals into a memory of something that might have been. While not abandoning those ideas, the Kuomintang has had to search for something additional to justify continued rule. The initial answer was the pragmatic political pay-offs of economic success and of a rising standard of living. The achievements of Taiwan capitalism brought political stability and thus a degree of legitimacy. Economic growth also reduced tensions between the 2 million Mainlanders who arrived with

Chiang's defeated armies and the 16 million Taiwanese. The economic miracle thus became a political miracle as well because it was the Taiwanese who benefited most. They were the ones who gained from land reform and who became the new industrialists, while the Mainlanders were frozen with government salaries and the life of military officers. The entrepreneurs of Taiwan's industrial growth are predominantly Taiwanese, while the bureaucrats and the managers of the generally inefficient state enterprises are Mainlanders.

Indeed, the anomaly of Taiwan is that it has had an economically disadvantaged "outsider" "ethnic" minority as its ruling class and a "native" majority "ethnic" group that has prospered. The great accomplishment of Chiang Ching-kuo has been to bridge the gap between Mainlanders and Taiwanese and to recruit Taiwanese into both the Kuomintang and the government in proportion to their numbers in the population. The problem of finding jobs in industry for Mainlanders had been made more difficult because of the clannishness of the Taiwanese. The tide is clearly turning: about 75 percent of the Kuomintang are now Taiwanese, and in popular elections it is Taiwanese who are winning either as Kuomintang candidates or as *dangwai* people.

The expanding role of Taiwanese in government and politics has therefore reduced the legitimacy problem. Yet it will not go away entirely, first, because of uncertainty over what will happen at the time of succession after President Chiang Ching-kuo, and second, because there is the unfathomable question of Taiwan's ultimate destiny, especially with respect to relations with the regime in Beijing. Will there be reunification? If so, under what conditions? If not, will the two go their separate ways in peace or with abiding tensions? These questions for the future do, to some degree, cloud current perceptions of the government.

The legitimacy crisis in Korea can be more simply stated, but is possibly harder to predict. With every Korean transferal of power coming through coups, there are not only those who see the current regime as illegitimate, but even more widespread is the uncertainty over what will happen after the current term of office of President Chun Doo Hwan. Although he has promised to step down and permit elections in 1988, there remains considerable skepticism—especially since many Koreans cannot imagine him passing up the glory of presiding over the Seoul Olympic games.

Whereas in Taiwan there is, in addition to the army, a major civilian political party, the Kuomintang, in Korea the ruling generals have not as yet built a comparable political party. Therefore, the general expectation is that President Chun Doo Hwan's successor will come out of the ranks of the army, using the state bureaucracy and other arms of government to prevail over any civilian opposition. Hence, the frustrations of the opposition will continue, questions of legitimacy will remain unresolved, and political tranquility will depend largely upon the vast majority of the population feeling that they have an economic stake in the status quo.

The Concluding Paradox

This brings us to a final paradox in the relationship of East Asian capitalism to their respective political systems: Whereas historically Confucianism in the region reinforced state power in ways that inhibited economic development, today the rulers, who are the heirs of that tradition, would be politically vulnerable were it not for the legitimacy they gain from the economic successes of their peoples. Once Confucianist rulers looked with disdain upon the merchant class and exploited them as best they could, but now the East Asian rulers' prime concern is continued economic progress.

In Japan political development has gone beyond the point of being hypersensitive to economic performance. This is because successful Japanese politicians have concentrated their paternalistic style of authority on building enduring relationships with their electoral constituencies, working to make the patronage system bring benefits in return for votes. Beyond these practical needs, Japanese politicians can leave much of the managing of government to skilled, professional bureaucrats, who in their turn understand the need to be sympathetic to the interests of business. Business and labor are just as quick to appreciate the advantages of cooperating with government. In the melding of interests in such a modified corporatist system, it is no doubt true that some will benefit more than others, but the lines are so blurred that it is not at all obvious who the serious losers are at any given moment. Moreover, any effort to force into the open a clearer accounting of benefits could upset the entire system and damage everyone's interests.

Taiwan, as we have seen, may be moving toward a comparable Japanese model. With more elections and a greater need to bend to the demands of constituents, a system of patronage politics is evolving which is consistent with a paternalistic ideal of authority. A basic tension remains, however, because the Old Guard Kuomintang politicians, who do not have to face elections, continue to distrust both the popularly elected Taiwanese officials and the modern technocratically trained bureaucrats who they suspect will adhere more to rationality than to sanctified principles. As long as economic growth continues, and both the technocrats and the Taiwanese politicians attribute the miracle to the Three People's Principles, the Old Guard will cause little trouble. But should the economy sour, then the potential for mutual recrimination could seriously strain the political system.

In Korea, political stability is even more sensitive to economic progress. Traditional Korean respect for hierarchy and deference to authority operate to provide social tranquility as long as life is improving—and life has improved in Korea beyond the imaginations of most people of only a few years ago. Yet beneath the surface Koreans have a way of accumulating frustrations so that the potential for angry explosions is always present when things no longer go well. It is precisely their exaggerated expectations about what authority should be able to accomplish that makes Koreans initially so willing to defer to authority, but that also suddenly legitimizes their anger when they believe authority has let them down.

Indeed, it is this sense of dependency which makes the Confucian tradition of paternalistic authority so effective in working for the collective goal of national economic development. Yet, that same spirit of dependency can become an angry explosive force when authority has failed to provide the expected benefits. Thus, as long as economic progress continues, the East Asian political systems will operate well with their quasi-authoritarian institutions, but disappointment over the expected benefits from governments can produce explosive reactions against the failure of paternalistic authority. The ultimate safety valve for the East Asian system is the one fashioned by the Japanese politicians: mutual respect and binding ties between paternalistic leaders and dependent, but articulate, constituents.

Notes

1. Joseph R. Levenson, *Confucian China and Its Modern Fate*, 3 vols. (Berkeley: University of California Press, 1958, 1964, 1968), vol. 3.
2. Benjamin Schwartz, *In Search of Wealth and Power: Yen Fu and the West* (Cambridge: Harvard University Press, 1964), pp. 38–39.
3. See Sungjoo Han, *The Failure of Democracy in South Korea* (Berkeley: University of California Press, 1974).
4. See Johannes Hirschmeier, *The Origin of Entrepreneurship in Meiji Japan* (Cambridge: Harvard University Press, 1964); and Bryan K. Marshall, *Capitalism and Nationalism in Prewar Japan: The Ideology of the Business Elite, 1868–1941* (Stanford: Stanford University Press, 1967).
5. Chalmers Johnson, *MITI and the Japanese Miracle: The Growth of Industrial Policy, 1925–1975* (Stanford: Stanford University Press, 1982).
6. Shirley W.Y. Kuo, Gustav Ranis, and John C.H. Fei, *The Taiwan Success Story* (Boulder, CO: Westview Press, 1981).
7. See Edward S. Mason et al., *The Economic and Social Modernization of the Republic of Korea* (Cambridge: Cambridge University Press, 1980); and Leroy P. Jones and Sakong Il, *Government, Business, and Entrepreneurship in Economic Development* (Cambridge: Harvard University Press, 1980).
8. See Ellis S. Krauss, Thomas P. Rohlan, and Patricia G. Steinhoff, eds., *Conflict in Japan* (Honolulu: University of Hawaii Press, 1984).
9. See Ralph N. Clough, *Island China* (Cambridge: Harvard University Press, 1978), chap. 3; and Ch'en Ch'eng, *Land Reform in Taiwan* (Taipei: China Publishing Co., 1961).
10. Harold C. Hinton, *Korea under New Leadership* (New York: Praeger, 1983), p. 24.

11. Leroy P. Jones and Sakong Il, *Government, Business, and Entrepreneurship in Economic Development*, op. cit.
12. Chalmers Johnson, *MITI and the Japanese Miracle*, op. cit.
13. Rodney Clark, *The Japanese Company* (New Haven: Yale University Press, 1979).
14. William W. Lockwood, *The Economic Development of Japan: Growth and Structural Change, 1868–1938* (London: Oxford University Press, 1955).
15. See Vincent Brandt, *A Korean Village* (Cambridge: Harvard University Press, 1972), and Vincent Brandt, "Sociocultural Aspects of Political Participation in Rural Korea," *The Journal of Korean Studies*, 1979, pp. 205–44.

5

The Role of the Entrepreneur in the New Asian Capitalism

S.G. Redding

This chapter addresses the question of entrepreneurship in the context of the new capitalist systems of Asia, and is thus concerned primarily with assessing how much of the explanation for dramatic economic growth is attributable to certain key actors in the economic system. These key actors go under the general heading "entrepreneurs," a category which of course contains variety. It should however be clearly stated, at the outset, that a monocausal model is not implied. The determinants of economic growth are inevitably complex, multiple, and interconnected, and any explanation must take account of reciprocal effects and the dangers of historicism.[1]

It is, however, of some value to take one special aspect of the total model, and examine the way it takes its place in more complete attempts at explanation. By this means it may be possible to illuminate the larger debate between more universal models. In this context, there are two competing paradigms between which the question of entrepreneurialism is sandwiched. These are: the structuralist argument which uses institutions as prime determinants, and the cultural argument which uses individual values to explain especially efficient systems of cooperation. The entrepreneurial role may be seen as a link between these two, and we shall conclude that, untidy though it may be, both are needed for a proper understanding.

The chapter will proceed by considering the central question of entrepreneurial contribution via the following aspects:

1. The structural model.
2. The cultural model.
3. The nature of entrepreneurialism.
4. Varying patterns of entrepreneurial activity in Asia.
5. The place of the entrepreneurial factor in larger models of development.

The Structural Model

In a recent review of Japanese political economy, Chalmers Johnson outlined what he sees as three alternative paradigms used to explain Japanese postwar economic growth.[2] The titles assigned to them are the "Mac-Arthurian," the "Venetian," and the "Nihonjinron" (or cultural uniqueness theory). The MacArthurian view sees the country as being like a child protected, and to some degree spoiled, by a rich uncle, and so far still able to indulge in selfishness. Although no longer in vogue today in the West, Johnson notes significantly that this view "has many adherents among people who have lived the longest and most intimately with the Japanese, including many who have great respect for Japan's economic achievements."

As the Venetian view is of main concern in this section, we shall pass briefly to the Nihonjinron model before returning to the Venetian for more detailed examination. The Nihonjinron view explains Japanese success entirely in terms of cultural uniqueness, stressing such features as cooperativeness and identity with the work group, intergroup competition, sacrifice for common goals, etc. Johnson sees the weaknesses of this approach to be partly theoretical and partly practical. In terms of theory, culture does not stand close scrutiny as a main cause. As he observes: "Japan's culture was at least not an obstacle to development. But then neither was it an obstacle to militarism, elitism, emperor worship, colonialism, or many other things that the Japanese understandably prefer to forget." The practical weaknesses of this view are dangerous outcomes of ethnocentrism and need not concern us here.

It is Johnson's Venetian model which we might use to illuminate the structuralist approach. In using the Japanese case, and Johnson's explanation of it, as an example, we do so to illustrate how parallel descriptions could be, and have been, developed for other countries in the region.

The title Venetian is used to highlight the rationality of the "trading nation" as a distinct type of political economy and to stress how such an economy relies on certain institutional innovations. In the Japanese (and historically the Venetian) case these produced key wealth-creating features: flexible government-business relationships, tranquil labor relations, high savings, high levels of education, mechanisms for changing the industrial structure, and equitable distribution of wealth.

These patterns of societal behavior are seen to rest on four structural underpinnings which together characterize the "capitalist developmental state."[3] The key components are:

1. Stable rule by a political-bureaucratic elite immune to political pressures which would undermine economic growth or security.

2. Cooperation between public and private sectors under an overall plan for guidance.
3. Heavy and continuing investment in education for everyone, combined with policies to ensure equitable distribution of national income.
4. A government that understands the need to use and respect methods of intervention based on the price mechanism.

These structures within the body politic are replicated in Korea and Taiwan and could be argued to exist, in forms which still show the underlying aims but which are local interpretations of them, in Hong Kong and Singapore. The key point is that such a special combination of elements within the political economy of capitalism diverges from the Western equivalent, but achieves similarity across certain Asian countries, thus providing a strong argument for the structure itself determining the growth.

In the context of our theme, however, a possibly unconscious contradiction, and certainly a significant reminder to himself, appears in Johnson's main book on the capitalist developmental state, *MITI and the Japanese Miracle*. The title page is faced by a quotation from Peter Drucker:

> "It is only managers—not nature or laws of economics or governments—that make resources productive."[4]

There is no more appropriate theme for this chapter.

The Cultural Model

The most obvious vehicle for the cultural explanation, which stands as an alternative to the structural, is the post-Confucian hypothesis. Early attempts at formulating this abound,[5] but possibly the best known is that of H. Kahn, who argues that the key determinants of economic growth in East Asia are a set of cultural values.[6] He discusses them in terms of four components, as follows:

1. Family socialization sponsoring sobriety; education; skills acquisition; seriousness about tasks, job, family and obligations.
2. Tendency to help the group (whatever its basis).
3. Sense of hierarchy and the naturalness of it.
4. Sense of complementarity of relations (which together with point three provides a sense of fairness and equity in institutions).

A parallel finding using the same basic approach is visible in comparative management theory, and is exemplified in the work of Hofstede, Haire, Ghiselli, and Porter, England and Lee, and McClelland.[7] To be fair to the field of comparative management, however, it should be noted that its explanandum is not normally national economic growth, but usually organizational efficiency and managerial behavior.

The majority of writers who have addressed the question of economic growth in East Asia tend to have incorporated cultural effects without necessarily assigning them the central role.[8] There is however one major exception to this, which is the field of economics, and development economics particularly. Here is a field which has largely refused to assign any weight to the cultural factor, and which appears to have suffered in its capacity to predict, as a result.[9] Some bridge-building is, however, now taking place and there are signs of some willingness among economists to broaden the base of explanation.[10]

The Nature of Entrepreneurialism

We have suggested that the entrepreneurial role is a kind of fulcrum between two theories—the structural, based on institutions, and the cultural based on sociocultural values. In terms of the institutional aspect of the society, the entrepreneur creates and represents the basic institutional component. In terms of the values of people, he is responsible for acting as a catalyst to release the energy they contain as potential. It is my contention that these two models are not mutually exclusive but in fact are complementary to each other. To examine this further, some consideration must now be given to the nature of the entrepreneurial role.

A convenient and important distinction is that between entrepreneur and manager. This is normally dealt with by saying that an entrepreneur *initiates* new economic activity, and a manager keeps ongoing activities running. Schumpeter's work is seminal in this field and contains a point which is commonly overlooked. This is that the central component is the formation of "new combinations of means of production," and this comprises much more than starting a business.[11] Behavior of an entrepreneur, to meet Schumpeter's definition, includes:

1. *The introduction of a new good*, that is, one with which consumers are not yet familiar, or of a new quality of good.
2. *The introduction of a new method of production*, that is, one not yet tested by experience in the branch of manufacture concerned, which need by no means be founded upon a scientifically new discovery, and can also exist in a new way of handling a commodity commercially.
3. *The opening of a new market*, that is, a market into which the particular branch of manufacture of the country in question has not previously entered, whether or not this market existed before.
4. *The conquest of a new source of supply* of raw materials or half-manufactured goods, again irrespective of whether this source already exists or whether it has first to be created.

5. *The carrying out of a new organization of any industry*, like the creation of a monopoly position . . . or the breaking up of a monopoly position.

The implications of this wide model of entrepreneurship were examined by Jones and Sakong in one of the key studies of entrepreneurship in East Asia, using Korea as a base.[12] I will return to this important study in the next section, but a pause is justified here to take on board what appears to be a crucial idea for the understanding of how entrepreneurship works.

Jones and Sakong point out that most of the literature on the subject treats the entrepreneur as a sole agent who is either there to the benefit of the system or absent to the detriment of it. The hidden assumption is that he does it all himself. In fact, economic systems themselves contribute helpful mechanisms or circumstances, or alternatively hindrances, and the entrepreneur cannot be the sole agent for innovation except in the rarest of cases. Instead, an analysis of the bundle of activities which constitute entrepreneurship, yields the following:

1. Perception of a new economic activity, including:
   a. new products,
   b. new processes of production,
   c. new markets.
2. Evaluation of the profitability of a new opportunity.
3. Gaining command of financial resources.
4. Plant design, technology, and construction supervision.
5. Recruiting and training new personnel.
6. Dealing with government.
7. Dealing with suppliers and purchasers.

For the complete performance of this bundle of activities, the entrepreneur can either do them himself or hire people. In essence, his role is to ensure that they are all done, regardless of which (if any) he does himself. Jones and Sakong, in contrasting this view with that prevailing in the literature, use the following analogy for the entrepreneur:

> He is like a lens that focuses the energies of others, and we therefore term this pure and unavoidable task the 'lenticular' function.

It is now possible to speculate about variations in the nature of the entrepreneurial function in different economies and, in particular, to note some possible grounds for contrast within East Asia.

In a developed economy, it is possible to hire people to carry out each of the seven functions above and for their training to be such that they will carry them out efficiently. In an economy where such skills are generally sparse, leaving the entire burden to the individual entrepreneur may be expecting too much. In an economy where the problems inherent in carrying out the seven functions are simplified, such as by light government control, easy financing, etc., it could be argued that a single entrepreneur might take on the whole seven. In a culture where trust is low between people not of the same kin, it may prove difficult for the entrepreneur to share such functions, or delegate them to professional outsiders. (Such speculations will be recalled in a later section of this chapter which attempts generalizations.)

Varying Patterns within the Region

The region will be divided for analysis into four categories, namely, Japan, Korea, the Overseas Chinese, and indigenous, non-Singaporean ASEAN. It is perhaps appropriate to begin a review of entrepreneurship in the region with the detailed study of Korea by Jones and Sakong,[13] as it appears to have examined the topic more deeply than any other study and to have reached some conclusions of general significance.

Examining the growth of manufacturing companies from 1962 to 1974, they reach the important conclusion that "the traditional entrepreneurial act— foundation of a new firm by a new entrepreneur—is of minor consequence in Korea." They propose that the sources of real growth in value added are as follows:

Growth in average size (old firms at new size) 72%
Growth in number of firms (new firms at old size) 3%
Gross product (new firms at incremental size) 25%
                                                                          100%

The question, as they see it, is posed as follows:

> What has to be explained is not how new entrepreneurs were found, but how old firms grew, and why new firms were so much larger than the old. The critical question is not net *entry*, but *expansion*. The problem is less entrepreneurial *quantity*, than *quality*.

The quality referred to takes us back to the lenticular quality of ensuring that the seven entrepreneurial functions are carried out. The key is not so much inventiveness and being risk-prone, but what one might term organizing ability. Many firms fail initially, roughly a quarter have failed after four years, and morbidity runs at 10 to 15 percent after six years. The survivors tend to have expanded rapidly, and it is on their shoulders that the economy rests. It does not rest on the large number of newcomers churning around at the bottom.

The capacity for growth of organizations is attributed in the Korean case to two main forces which operated from the 1960s onwards. First, there was the opportunity to learn by doing, fostered partly by government dedication to economic growth. Second, there was a differentiation of the entrepreneurial task into parts which were increasingly handled by employees, the market, government, and professional specialists. The increase in the quality of entrepreneurship is thus systemic, and the entrepreneur himself falls into place as a partial contributor to the total. The key skill appears to lie in the managerial process of coordination, and a universal component comes to the surface,[14] in line with Drucker's reminder.

Turning now to the case of Japan, there is prima facie evidence that the position is similar to that of Korea, although an exact parallel study to that of Jones and Sakong is not available. The nearest would appear to be that of Okochi and Yasuoka,[15] but it deals with an earlier period. Industry studies are extensive and detailed, but the precise workings of the entrepreneurial process, except for a proliferation of hagiographies, is not described.[16] As Johnson has noted (citing Roberts), Japan's miraculous emergence has been described exhaustively "yet very little of the literature provides credible explanations of how it was done, or by whom."[17]

A description of the postwar economic growth by Imai does, however, suggest parallels with what is known from the Korean study. He describes the workings of Japan's dual economy in the following terms:

> In the process of the postwar economic growth, large oligopolistic firms grew up through introducing innovations of large-scale technology which enabled them to enjoy advantages of mass production and mass marketing. They gave the driving force of rapid growth, thereby expanding industrial fields subject to large-scale production. On the other hand, however, the process of rapid growth, accompanied by changes in the industrial structure, diversified consumer demands and helped to create a great many opportunities for different kinds of goods to be produced in small lots by small firms, thereby giving rise to the new types of distribution and services. Such opportunities created favourable conditions for the growth and development of firms of various sizes, including small firms.[18]

Movements of firms were traced and showed substantial upward shifts in size among small- and medium-size firms, as well as mortality rates that were very similar to those reported for Korea. If the context of entrepreneurialism, and the apparent results, are similar in Korea and Japan, then perhaps similar conclusions may be allowed about the crucial nature of managerial coordinative skills and the importance of environmental contributions to the entrepreneurial process.

The Overseas Chinese form a highly significant economic group when seen together and may be analyzed as one category in light of their highly consistent business behavior across the region. They are taken here to comprise the

Chinese of Hong Kong, Singapore, and Taiwan. It is also valid to include the minority groups in the Philippines, Indonesia, Malaysia, and Thailand, because these groups have significant economic power in these countries.

Of considerable interest in the context of entrepreneurialism is the difference in the Overseas Chinese behavior pattern to that found in Korea and Japan. The standard form of organization is the Chinese family business, and even large companies retain this fundamental characteristic. There is thus an inevitable built-in barrier to growth and, in consequence, size remains restricted. There is evidence to suggest that in Hong Kong firms are becoming smaller and the average size (by employees) in the manufacturing sector has shown the following trend:[19]

1954	44.6
1964	40.0
1970	27.8
1974	19.1
1984	18.4

Redding and Hicks have argued that this indicates a different pattern of development from that elsewhere and that it has led to a special adaptation influenced by both structural and cultural features.[20] Speculations about the workings of this system, based on the idea of molecular organizations and the role of organizational networks, are now the focuses of new research in Hong Kong.[21] Indications of internal structural differences between Chinese and Japanese organizations are also now clear.[22]

Regrettably for the Overseas Chinese, there is no study to indicate the pattern of entry and exit of companies to and from the economy or to show the patterns of growth. It is, however, possible to speculate that the preponderance of small firms leaves the economy more reliant on entrepreneurial initiation of companies than on the managerial coordinative skills which foster new combinations. It would appear that the combinations favored by the Overseas Chinese are networks of companies making up an organizational set. This is the functional equivalent of a large company elsewhere but is differently structured. It may be depicted as shown in Figure 4.1.

If this pattern is normal, and the literature on Overseas Chinese management suggests that it is,[23] then questions arise as to why the Chinese form of economic organization rests on the family business unit and why larger-scale entities are relatively rare. In the context of the entrepreneurial process, why is there more reliance on the initiation stage, and less on the coordinative stage? Alternatively, is the molecular form of networked "organization" the Chinese answer to coordination? Rather than answer these questions here, I will carry them forward as inputs to the final section of the chapter which attempts some model building.

The ASEAN countries have been examined by a number of scholars, gener-

FIGURE 5.1
Organizational Set for Export Operation in Hong Kong
(An Ideal Typical Construction)

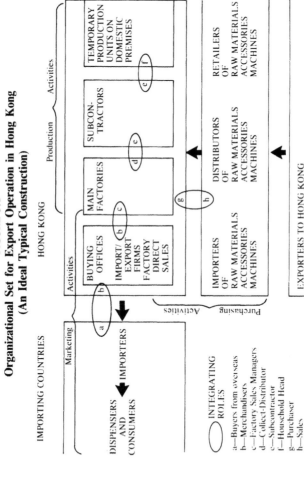

Source: S.G. Redding and S. Tam, "Networks and Molecular Organizations: An Exploratory View of Chinese Firms in Hong Kong." Academy of International Business, Hong Kong Conference, 1985.

ally attempting to address the question of why entrepreneurship is absent among the indigenous population. Charlesworth's work in Malaysia was set against his statement that:

> The fundamental thesis of this report is that Bumiputras in the business world experience considerable role conflict between social and economic roles and that this conflict impedes development of their entrepreneurial potential.[24]

Similarly, Lasserre examined the Indonesian position and drew up advice on the basis of a similar assumption, and Ayal's study comparing values in Thailand and Japan also reached the same position in concluding that certain societal values acted as barriers to economic development in hindering the innovative and risk-prone phases of entrepreneurial behavior, thus preventing the initiation of the organizing process which later could respond to managerial skill.[25] It is not surprising then that a recent review of indigenous entrepreneurs in the ASEAN countries by Yoshihara should acknowledge the dominance of foreign companies in most modern economic sectors and "the commanding position the Chinese occupy in the economy."[26] In accord with such findings, it is proposed that ASEAN indigenous entrepreneurship be considered as problematic, rather than as a source of study in itself, and that the problems implied for consideration be carried forward theoretically.

The Entrepreneurial Factor in Larger Models

It may be useful to divide the entrepreneurial function into two main parts, following Jones and Sakong's interpretation of Schumpeter, and to see it as:

1. Initiating/inventing/creating a company.
2. Lenticular activities of coordination which foster growth of the organization.

I would propose that causation flows one way from a set of societal values into the process of initiating (although some reverse effects from the display of success may influence values in the long term). Similarly, certain values influence the coordination process. The set of structural features are seen as being reciprocally connected with the entrepreneurial process, as they contain it and have much influence in shaping it. The use of the model lies in bringing out the different distribution of both values and structural components in different countries and in suggesting their dampening or enhancing effects.

The list of values which contribute to the enhancement of entrepreneurship derives from the work of Ayal, Lasserre, Charlesworth, and Ryan,[27] but details of the functioning of these connections will not be examined here. The

FIGURE 5.2

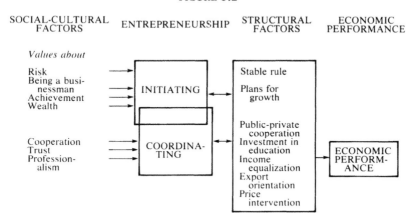

The list of values which contribute to the enhancement of entrepreneurship derives from the work of Ayal, Lasserre, Charlesworth, and Ryan,[27] but details of the functioning of these connections will not be examined here. The list of structural factors is influenced by Johnson, but also by the work of other writers on East Asian countries outside Japan, in particular Chen and Little.[28]

list of structural factors is influenced by Johnson, but also by the work of other writers on East Asian countries outside Japan, in particular Chen and Little.[28]

The propositions which the model might illuminate (and which must necessarily be the subjects of more specifically focused research) are the following:

1. Japan and Korea have both values and structural factors which facilitate and enhance entrepreneurship in both its main features, *initiating* and *coordinating*.

2. The Overseas Chinese have values which facilitate the *initiating* phase of entrepreneurship but which place barriers to the higher levels of *coordination* necessary for growth of the individual firm to a large scale. Some compensation is achieved with a hybrid form of coordination which allows firm size to remain small but achieves large task units of a molecular kind, made up of small firms.

3. Structural factors, in the Overseas Chinese case, are difficult to generalize about because of the variety of environments, but may be taken to be conducive to both initiation and coordination in Taiwan, Hong Kong, and Singapore (given the limits to coordination already noted in point two).

4. For ASEAN indigenous groups, sociocultural values act as barriers to the crucial first stage of *initiating*, and structural factors are not so directly conducive to entrepreneurial *initiation* or *coordination*, as they are in the strong cases of Japan and Korea.

These propositions are hypothetical, and it will be necessary for more empirical evidence to be gathered before a better understanding of the phenomena is achieved. In essence, what is suggested is a more discriminating use of the idea of entrepreneurship. It clearly has a central place in any model of economic development, but it is not a simple act. Being intertwined with the structural component of an economy and owing its existence to the sociocultural features of a society, it provides a useful unifying concept between disciplines which often seem to prefer mutual exclusivity to cooperation, and which regularly try to claim a monopoly of explanatory power.

Notes

1. S.G. Redding, "Causation and Research Models in Comparative Management for Asia," conference proceedings of the Academy of International Business, Hawaii, 1980.
2. Chalmers Johnson, "The Role of Japan in the Pacific-Asian Region and Japanese Relations with the U.S., PRC, and USSR," Conference on the Pacific-Asian Region, Shanghai Institute for International Studies and Institute of East Asian Studies, University of California, Berkeley, May 1985.
3. Chalmers Johnson, *MITI and the Japanese Miracle* (Stanford: Stanford University Press, 1982).
4. Ibid.
5. See, for example, R. McFarquar, "The Post-Confucian Challenge," *The Economist*, February 9, 1980, pp. 67–72; and E.B. Ayal, "Value Systems and Economic Development in Japan and Thailand," in R.O. Tilman, ed., *Man, State and Society in Contemporary Southeast Asia* (New York: Praeger, 1969).
6. H. Kah, *World Economic Development: 1979 and Beyond* (London: Croom Helm, 1979).
7. G. Hofstede, *Culture's Consequences* (London: Sage Publications, 1980); M. Haire, E.E. Ghiselli, and L.W. Porter, *Managerial Thinking: An International Study* (New York: John Wiley, 1966); G.W. England and R. Lee, "The Relationship between Managerial Values and Managerial Success in the United States, Japan, India and Australia," *Journal of Applied Psychology* 10, pp. 161–68; and D. McClelland, *The Achieving Society* (New York: Irvington Publishers, 1976).
8. Typical here is R. Hofheinz, Jr. and E. Kent Calder, *The Eastasia Edge* (New York: Basic Books, 1982).
9. See G.L. Hicks and S.G. Redding, "The Story of the East Asian Economic Miracle," *Euro-Asia Business Review*, 1983, part 1, vol. 2, no. 3; part 2, vol. 2, no. 4.
10. See, for example, Kwan-yiu Edward Chen, "The Newly Industrializing Countries in Asia: Growth Experience and Prospects," Working Paper No. 55 (Hong Kong: Economics Department, University of Hong Kong, 1985).
11. J.A. Schumpeter, *The Theory of Economic Development* (Cambridge: Harvard University Press, 1980).

12. L.P. Jones and I.L. Sakong, *Government, Business, and Entrepreneurship in Economic Development: The Korean Case* (Cambridge: Harvard University Press, 1980).
13. Ibid.
14. See C. Barnard, *The Functions of the Executive* (Cambridge: Harvard University Press, 1938); and H. Mintzberg, *The Structuring of Organizations* (Englewood Cliffs, NJ: Prentice-Hall, 1979).
15. Akio Okochi and Chigeaki Yasuoka, eds., *Family Business in the Era of Industrial Growth* (Tokyo: University of Tokyo Press, 1984).
16. For reviews see Toshimasa Tsuruta, "Industry Studies of Japan: A Survey," and Kazunori Echigo, "Japanese Studies of Industrial Organization," in Kazuo Sato, ed., *Industry and Business in Japan* (London: Croom Helm, 1980).
17. Chalmers Johnson, *MITI and the Japanese Miracle*, op. cit.
18. Kenichi Imai, "Japan's Industrial Organization," in Kazuo Sato, ed., *Industry and Business in Japan*, op. cit., p. 103.
19. Hong Kong Government Census and Statistics Department Annual Digest.
20. S.G. Redding and G.L. Hicks, "The Smaller the Better: The Declining Size of the Hong Kong Manufacturing Firm," Mong Kwok Ping Management Data Bank Working Paper (Hong Kong: University of Hong Kong, 1985).
21. S.G. Redding and S. Tam, "Networks and Molecular Organizations: An Exploratory View of Chinese Firms in Hong Kong," Academy of International Business, Hong Kong conference, 1985.
22. See S.G. Redding and D.S. Pugh, "The Formal and the Informal: Japanese and Chinese Organization Structures," in S.R. Clegg, D. Dunphy, and S.G. Redding, eds., *The Enterprise and Management in East Asia* (Hong Kong: Centre of Asian Studies, University of Hong Kong, forthcoming).
23. See L.Y.C. Lim and L.A.P. Gosling, eds., *The Chinese in Southeast Asia* (Singapore: Maruzen Asia, 1983); R. Silin, *Leadership and Values* (Cambridge: Harvard University Press, 1934); and S.G. Redding and G.Y.Y. Wong, "The Psychology of Chinese Organizational Behaviour," in M.H. Bond, ed., *The Psychology of Chinese People* (Hong Kong: Oxford University Press, 1986).
24. H.K. Charlesworth, "Increasing the Number of Bumiputra Entrepreneurs," working paper (MARA Institute of Technology, 1974), p. 5.
25. P. Lasserre, "A Contribution to the Study of Entrepreneurship Development in Indonesia," working paper (Euro-Asia Centre, Insead, April 1979); E.B. Ayal, "Value Systems and Economic Development in Japan and Thailand," op. cit.
26. K. Yoshihara, "Indigenous Entrepreneurs in the ASEAN Countries," *Singapore Economic Review* 29, October 1984.
27. E.B. Ayal, "Value Systems and Economic Development in Japan and Thailand," op. cit.; P. Lasserre, "A Contribution to the Study of Entrepreneurship Development in Indonesia," op. cit.; H.K. Charlesworth, "Increasing the Number of Bumiputra Entrepreneurs," op. cit.; and E.J. Ryan, "The Value System of a Chinese Community in Java," unpublished doctoral dissertation, Harvard University, 1961.
28. Chalmers Johnson, *MITI and the Japanese Miracle*, op. cit.; Kwan-yiu Edward Chen, *Hyper-Growth in Asian Economies: A Comparative Study of Hong Kong, Japan, Korea, Singapore and Taiwan* (London: Macmillan, 1979); and I.M.D. Little, "The Experience and Causes of Rapid Labour-Intensive Development in Korea, Taiwan Province, Hong Kong and Singapore, and the Possibilities of Emulation," in Eddie Lee, ed., *Export-Led Industrialization and Development* (Geneva: International Labor Office, 1981).

PART III
CULTURAL AND SOCIAL FEATURES

6

The Role of Christianity

Jan Swyngedouw

That sociologists and other students of East Asian societies, in trying to find an explanation for what is now increasingly called the "East Asian development model," look first of all for a functional analogue to the "Protestant ethic" within the Eastern ethico-religious traditions themselves comes as no surprise. Indeed, differences with what happened in the West are, at first sight, related to the peculiar social and cultural setting of East Asia. It is these differences that nowadays capture the attention and that ask for an interpretation. On the other hand, nobody would dare to deny that much of what is being accomplished in the East is also intrinsically linked to an impulse from the West. Therefore, if we take into account that modernization, Westernization, and Christianity are "so intimately intertwined that no one could take them apart,"[1] it rather strikes me that relatively few authors dealing with this subject explicitly refer to the role Christianity has played and might still play in the process.[2]

In dealing with this issue, we are beset with a host of problems. There is of course the first and basic question: To what extent are economic and sociocultural factors in fact linked together, with "culturalist" and "institutionalist" hypotheses opposed to each other and the "in-betweeners" trying to have the best of both worlds? The question becomes still more complicated if we focus on the ethico-religious factor in culture, which brings us at once to the issue of secularization and urges us, moreover, to make a distinction between the ethico-religious roots of culture and institutions on the one hand, and the (ongoing) role of this factor in present-day society on the other hand.[3]

Furthermore, are we indeed able to speak about an "East Asian development model" as one particular model distinct from an equally particular Western capitalistic and a socialistic model? If we, for example, take into account the many discussions going on about the uniqueness of Japanese culture

115

and the ramifications of these in the continuing controversy about the "Asian awareness" of the Japanese, one wonders whether cultural differences—and development models—within Asia itself are after all not bigger than the alleged differences between East and West.

And finally, the main theme of this chapter is the role of Christianity in Eastern Asia: What sort of Christianity are we really talking about? Are we talking about the influence of Christianity in terms of its ideational contents, or in terms of its organizational strength? Is it Christianity as adopted by a (small) number of Asians, or Christianity as perceived by those (the majority) who do not confess it as their own faith?

The overwhelming complexity of the problems can only mean that our answers will necessarily be partial and tentative. As a student of Eastern religion, and particularly of Japanese religion, I feel my own perspective to be extremely limited. Yet, I hope that the following pages will be an appropriate, if small, contribution to this fascinating issue.

Types of Christian Presence in Asia

Statistics about the numerical strength of the Christian churches in Asia teach us that the results of Christian missionary endeavors have been far from spectacular, with the remarkable exception of South Korea, where the Christian churches, and especially Protestant denominations and sects, have succeeded in attracting a considerable number of adherents and are still growing at a fast pace.[4] But it goes without saying that in discussing Christian influences on the cultures of East Asia, Christianity cannot be discussed simply in terms of its numerical strength. In order to acquire a correct understanding of it, one has to view Christianity in the overall framework of each country's religiosity, that is, the way the people themselves look at and adhere to religion. It is in this sense that we can distinguish at least four different types of Christianity or ways by which Christianity has been adopted in the countries of East Asia.

The first type of Christianity consists of the relatively small group of people in the different countries who explicitly belong to a church, i.e., who are registered as Christian believers in one of the many churches to be found in Asia, whether churches "imported" from the West or so-called "indigenous churches." These people are church-affiliated believers, whether because of a personal commitment to Christian faith, because of being born in a Christian family, or for other reasons. It is this group, who are Christians in the very strict sense of the word, that is the prime referent establishing the public image of Christianity—and also, to a certain extent, of Western culture in general—in those countries. As far as institutional membership is concerned then, in spite of years of strenuous missionary efforts, Christianity remains in most countries a minority group and, with the exception of South Korea, it looks very much as if no major change in this situation will occur in the near future. To what extent this first, core type of Christianity has served and continues to serve as a kind of natural bridge between values which originated in the West (including the work ethic) and the values of the respective Asian countries is a question that still has to be answered.

Surveys on the belief patterns of the people, however, often offer a slightly different picture of the number of Christians. In response to a question about what religion they believe in, a number of people in the various countries who do not explicitly belong to a particular Christian church invariably answer "Christianity."[5] This indicates that besides the formal Christians of the first type, there is a group of people in Asia—the number of which differs from country to country—who call themselves Christians although they have not been baptized and, apparently, do not want to be. These "self-styled" Christians esteem the person of Christ and, in many cases, seem particularly to esteem the ethical ideals of Christianity, but they refuse to commit themselves to a specific Christian church. In other words, they seem to make a distinction between Christ, Christianity, and the Christian churches, raising the question to what extent the churches in East Asia really represent in the mind of the people the Message of Christ. Anyhow, the existence of these "sympathizers" proves that the institutional form of Christianity does not necessarily exhaust a religious mentality that can in one way or another be called Christian, and, more generally, that religious affiliation bears for many people other connotations than it has historically in the West.

The influence of Christianity, however, reaches still further than these first two types—church members and self-styled Christians. Although exact numbers evidently are not available, one can assert that a relatively high percentage of the total population of the various countries have, or have had, a direct and fairly long-term contact with Christianity, particularly through the vast Christian educational network and through welfare and other institutions.[6] What is remarkable in this respect is that many, if not most, of those contacts are *voluntary* responses on the part of the people to an invitation extended to them by the Christian churches. When, for example, parents send their children to a Christian school, this constitutes an *active* gesture on their part which can be interpreted as being in itself the expression of a friendly and expectant attitude, if not toward Christianity as such, then at least toward the ideals that Christianity stands for and toward the influence that Christianity as an institution is supposed to exert. In a certain sense, then, we can label these people's actions the third type of Christian adoption in Asia.

There is finally a fourth type of Christianity, or Christian influence, in East Asia—admittedly, Christianity in a very broad sense. It is Christianity as one element, not only of the religious consciousness of those who had a direct contact with it, but—more broadly—of the cultures and societies of East Asia themselves and of the people socialized in them. We touch here upon the core of the question we are concerned with. First, if cultural values have an influence upon the establishment and structure of "development models"— and it seems we can hardly deny some degree of influence—then we have to ask to what extent ethico-religious values are also implied in these, both in the West and the East. Second, since it is difficult to imagine a situation in which a country can in fact restrict the meaning and realities of intercultural contacts, i.e., modernization, to mere technology and bureaucracy while keeping its own culture completely pure and undefiled,[7] we have to ask to what extent Christian values have entered the cultures of Asia together with modernization. Indeed, if we focus on the East Asian development model, we see that it differs from the Western capitalistic and socialistic models not so much because it is Asian, in the sense of having preserved a pure form, but because Asian culture (or cultures) has become a *mixture* of various elements, including Christian-related elements that were brought in by intercultural contact as was the modernization process. The ultimate problem, then, is to find out the relative weight of those elements, how they relate to each other, how they are structured, and so forth. In a sense the question becomes: What kind of "inculturation" of Christianity does the East Asian development model exhibit?

In East Asia, Japan is still the only country that, after years of holding up the ideal of "catching up with the West and passing it," has reached the stage in which it can indeed rightly claim, in many respects, to have attained just that goal. At the same time, Japan is not only the East Asian country with the lowest percentage of church-affiliated Christians but also, in the eyes of many observers, the least religious, even considering the influence of the Eastern religious traditions themselves. Leaving open the question to what extent the "Japanese model" can really be exported to the other countries of Asia, Japan might serve as a kind of paradigm for much of what is happening in that part of the world. Therefore, a look at the role of religion and of the "inculturation" of Christianity in Japan can give us valuable clues for a better understanding of the Asian situation as a whole.

The Japanese Model of "Inculturation"

It has always been a moot question whether Japan is really the most irreligious country in the world, as it is often said to be. It certainly remains a fact that, according to most surveys, up to two-thirds of the total population claim to have no religious beliefs.[8] On the other hand, at least half of the alleged "unbelievers" may readily affirm that religion is important in life, and they do not exclude the possibility that at some time they themselves may need it and, if so, will make use of it in order to be happy. In a word, religion—like most other values—is evaluated primarily in a pragmatic or utilitarian way, and the salvation it promises is mainly interpreted in this-worldly terms, as being the benefit of a material or psychological nature, with specific time limits. What this means is that in Japan, religious values—at least in the sense of values related to specific religious institutions—are not regarded as ends in themselves, but rather as means for attaining ends that somehow belong to another dimension. In other words, we might have to look elsewhere for finding the core values sustaining Japanese society and culture.

Japanese religiosity (and/or irreligiosity) is part of and subordinated to the general characteristic of Japanese culture often expressed by the term *wa*, or "harmony."[9] *Wa* has to be distinguished from "unity" as it presupposes and finds its ultimate justification in the existence of pluralism. Indeed, while the Japanese boast a homogeneity of race and culture, this homogeneity in fact finds expression in a mosaic of seemingly conflicting elements on every level of Japan's social system. The wide range of differentiated institutions on the level of social structure, as well as the plurality of cultural values, both indigenous and imported, with their correlate in the personality structure of the Japanese, attest to a diversification with endless possibilities of further development. Again, however, these various elements coact and interact in such a way that their relative independence does not seem to harm too much the inner balance of the respective levels or the harmony of the social system as a whole.

The problem Japan has always faced was *how* to preserve its cultural identity while continuously absorbing new, and sometimes conflicting, alien values. It has done this in various ways. One method, in the realm of ideas, has been to positively evaluate the existence of this plurality as being superior to unity, and to give a sacred aureole to the balance, or *wa*, of the diverse elements.[10] Another, more practical, method—related very closely though to the sacrality of the *wa*—has been to cope with the influx and impact of alien values by invoking the revered principle of what can be called "selective adoption and adaptation." Especially worthy of notice is the way this adaptation has taken place traditionally, which I would like to call the method of "compartmentalization." This method can best be illustrated and expressed by referring to another Japanese concept, namely that of *bun*, meaning "part," "share," or "segment."[11] In other words, all incoming values have been reduced to the status of a *bun*, i.e., assigned a proper place, a proper compartment, so that the balance and order of the whole (*wa*) are not only maintained but even strengthened. The concept of *bun* indeed implies that each value, put into a compartment, is to be considered not as an integer, but only as part or fraction of the whole, the subordination to which lends to that value its proper worth and identity. It further implies that all the different *bun* or values are interdependent and contribute to the overarching value of *wa* which keeps the whole together by acknowledging the (limited) role and claims of each and by not overstepping the assigned boundaries.

Indeed, perhaps the most striking example of this pattern is the plurality in Japan of ethico-religious values and the more or less harmonious way they are related, or are made to relate, to each other. Admittedly, in the course of Japan's religious history, the different traditions—Shinto, Buddhism, Confucianism, and later Christianity—were not always strictly kept apart but often blended into a more or less amorphous amalgam to which no label of Shinto, Confucianism, or Buddhism (or Christianity in some cases, like that of the so-called "clandestine Christians" of the Tokugawa Period) could be attached. It also happened that the harmony was broken and that the celebrated tolerance of the various religions towards each other gave way to bloody interfactional and intra-factional strife, a fact sometimes overlooked by all too zealous Western admirers of things Oriental. Yet, throughout all these vicissitudes and notwithstanding numerous cases of amalgamation, Japanese society gradually developed into a patterned structure in which the various religious traditions and the institutions that express and represent them have preserved a relatively high degree of self-identity, each of them occupying a specific *bun* or compartment in the whole of Japanese religiosity which can be distinguished from the others.

Concretely, what has the preservation of this relative self-identity meant? In other words, what are the boundaries that have defined the *bun* in which the different religious traditions of Japan have performed their role? Westerners, inclined to think of religion primarily in terms of ideational elements and doctrinal orthodoxy, will point out immediately that on this level no clear boundaries are to be discerned. Indeed, besides the case of a few Buddhist sects which have always shown a certain apprehension about the "syncretistic" faith-structure of their adherents and have tried to propagate a "pure" faith, most Japanese religions display a remarkable tolerance and flexibility in matters of doctrine. But this precisely gives us a clue for discerning the boundaries of the *bun* and, at the same time, for deepening our insight into the structure of Japanese religiosity and of Japanese culture in general. For the Japanese, as for so many other peoples, religion does not lie primarily in adherence to particular, rationalized beliefs, but in the acting out of religious feelings and aspirations in a wide spectrum of rituals which accompany man's life from birth to death and, still further, in his afterlife, in unison with the recurring and always developing rhythm of the seasons. It is here that the different religious traditions have met the people, not so much through the imposition of differentiated doctrines that are supposed to distinguish their *bun* from that of the others, but rather through specializing in rituals and other activities answering the specific needs of their clientele.

We see this pattern of assigning a proper *bun* to the different religious traditions so that the harmony, or *wa*, of the whole is maintained and strengthened being reflected in the practical religious behavior of the Japanese people. It can certainly be called syncretistic, but this syncretism is patterned. Most Japanese do not care very much for doctrinal subtleties and put "gods" and "buddhas" on the same line. Yet, on the other hand, without any rational justification people seem to have a kind of intuitive feeling which leads them to ask for religious benefits from the various religious institutions according to more or less well-defined patterns. For example—always exceptions excepted—nuptial blessing will seldom be asked from a Buddhist priest, but the latter will be called in when a death occurs in the family. Of course, this well-known "simultaneous adherence" of the Japanese to different religions—roughly speaking, Shinto for rituals of life and of the local community and Buddhism for rituals of death and of the family or household—is, for Western eyes in particular, a contradictory phenomenon. In fact, however, the Japanese are not "simultaneously" adhering to or believing in different religions. Ruth Benedict, an authoritative scholar on Japan, has pointed out that, in contrast to the integrated behavior of Westerners and other people, the Japanese have a flair for swinging from one behavior to another according to the situation without much psychic cost.[12] Thus the division in *bun* does not only exist on the level of social institutions but also, in a certain sense, inside the personality structure of the Japanese people. There is a compartment, or *bun*, for Buddhism, one for Shinto, and one for many other religious traditions, even if this might not be consciously acknowledged. Each is given its proper share, and in this way the harmony and balance of the whole are guaranteed. Inside one *bun*, the commitment is complete to the extent that even the distinction between subject and object might become blurred. But once matters are settled in this specific area, e.g., a Buddhist funeral, one puts an end to this activity (in Japanese, *kejime o ɪsukeru*) and can easily switch to another one for a different purpose, e.g., a Shinto birth celebration, without being aware of any contradiction in beliefs. As long as the different *bun* do not infringe too much upon each other, a balanced psychic life is possible, and the harmony in the life of the individual contributes to the harmony of the Japanese nation as a whole.

It should be obvious that what I have called the fourth type of Christianity is, at least in the case of Japan, precisely Christianity insofar as it has been adopted and adapted in that country according to the principle outlined above. Needless to say, I do not mean Christianity as it has been accepted by those who became formal members of a Christian church but Christianity as seen and experienced by the average, non-Christian people and as one of the elements that help shape the fabric of Japanese society and culture in general.

I mentioned already how religion in Japan is not so much a belief in well-defined doctrines as a matter of participating in rites which are supposed to confer immediate benefits of a material and/or psychological nature. In this sense, like most other values, religion is appraised primarily for the pragmatic worth it has in the everyday life of the people, and since Christianity seems to possess this worth, it is consequently also evaluated as such. In other words, Christianity (in Japan) has gradually been allotted a specific *bun* in the totality of Japanese religiosity, and to illustrate this we have to look first for rituals connected with Christianity that have been "adopted and adapted" by the average Japanese.

The pattern is rather clear, especially in the so-called "annual cycle of observances." Here Christianity has been given a complete monopoly-*bun* with the celebration of Christmas. Christmas, or better Christmas Eve, has become one of the annual events in which the majority of the Japanese participate in one or the other way. Admittedly, the relation of this celebration to Christ and to Christianity as a "religion" is extremely slight and, in many cases, even completely absent. Yet, this fact might be proof of the Japanization of Christianity, a process Buddhism and other religious traditions have undergone.

In the "life cycle observances," or "rites of passage," the pattern is not yet so pronounced, but it certainly exists. As mentioned above, birth rites have usually been conducted according to Shinto norms and death rites are mostly Buddhist. Another important "passage" in life is marriage, and it is here that Christianity again comes into the picture and is given a share or *bun*. Although at present most wedding ceremonies are performed in Shinto shrines, many non-Christians prefer a "church wedding." In fact, Shinto wedding ceremonies also are a relatively new phenomenon. Before the introduction of Christianity in Japan, marriages were traditionally performed in the household without the assistance of any religious functionary, and it can therefore be said that this *bun* was still open and unoccupied. This is now a "contested" *bun* among the religions, and Christianity is considered a very strong rival indeed in the competition.

The role of Christmas in the annual cycle of events and, to a certain extent, of Christian wedding ceremonies in the life cycle of the Japanese indicates that Christianity has been adopted and adapted in a way that is very much Japanese. Christianity becomes part of a bigger whole and is one of the many elements which together constitute "Japanese religiosity," or, in broader terms, Japanese culture and society. The role of these rituals implies further that Christianity should acknowledge the place, for example, of Shinto on initiation rites and of Buddhism on mortuary rites. Christianity is allowed to exert full efforts in propagating Christmas celebrations and in the competition for trying to perform wedding ceremonies, but it should not step beyond these boundaries and try to conquer the other *bun* traditionally assigned to other religious traditions. For this, indeed, would jeopardize the *wa*, which is precisely built upon the acknowledgment of each tradition's proper *bun*. In other ways, Christianity should be satisfied with being "inculturated" in this way and with being adopted and adapted according to the same principle on the level of the individual person, i.e., as one *bun* among the many others which together shape the personal identity of the Japanese and which can be invoked according to circumstances. Christianity, therefore, should not try to claim the total allegiance of the person, but rather it should cater to specific needs at specific occasions and be tolerant of the person's switching to other *bun*, occupied by other religious traditions, for other specific needs at other specific occasions. In other words, on this personal level Christianity, by keeping its proper place, should contribute to the self-identity of the people, which is based upon the harmony and balance between the different *bun* in the personality structure of the Japanese. And here we can already add that this higher value of harmony or *wa*—also often called the value of "Japaneseness"— seems to be the ultimate locus of sacrality. It has been called the "religion of Japaneseness," or *nihonkyō*, since the most sacred value for many Japanese seems to consist in contributing to the *wa* of the community to which they belong, and through these smaller communities to the sacred dignity of the Japanese nation itself.

In short, Christianity of this fourth type is a form of Christianity that has become "Japanized," not so much through the efforts of the church-affiliated Christians, but primarily through the particularizing and relativizing genius of the average Japanese who has adopted and adapted Christianity to the balanced pattern of so many different *bun*, in the service of the sacred value of the *wa* of Japan, as an element of both personal and social identity. Judging, then, from within an understanding of Japanese culture and religiosity, Christianity has thus become an "inculturated" religion, almost on a par with Shinto and Buddhism. But whether the fact that Christianity has become an element of Japanese religious culture really constitutes a "Christian influence" on that culture is a question which I assume most Christians (especially of the "first type") would not want to answer in the affirmative.

A Few Problem Areas

I am aware that the above description does not offer a direct answer to the question of the role Christianity has played in the establishment and maintenance of an East Asian and, more specifically, a Japanese development model. Many important questions remain. To see the role of religion, including Christianity, primarily in terms of their "ritual usefulness in a division-of-labor pattern" does not mean, of course, that they have been completely devoid of ideational content with a correlated influence on the thought patterns and ethical behavior of the people with respect to, among other things, modernization. However, what I would like to stress again is that even in the realm of ideas and ethics there exists a strong tendency to apply a similar principle of "compartmentalization." If, for example, we speak about the "concept of divine reality" of the Japanese, it looks as if with many, if not most, Japanese this itself has a multilayered structure, consisting of various and apparently contradictory concepts that are "activated" according to the situation in which people find themselves. Again, what is important here is the ability to switch from one concept to another and precisely by doing so to preserve a kind of harmonious balance between the different concepts. It is again this balance, or *wa*, which constitutes the most basic value, the ultimate focus of identity which bears a sacred character and to which all other values have to be subordinated.

But maybe we still have to take a further step and, although this might be a rather "wild" argument, apply the "compartmentalization method" to the modernization process. The relation between modernization, Westernization, and Christian values is certainly a complex one. The *wakon-yōsai* theory (usually translated as "Japanese spirit and Western technique"), which is commonly invoked when dealing with this subject, used to be interpreted as the adoption by Japan of Western techniques distinguished and separated from their cultural (Western) and religious (Christian) roots, thus making it possible to preserve Japan's cultural identity. However, insofar as the "compartmentalization method" can also be applied in this case, we might not need to solve the question of the extent to which it was possible to introduce Western technique without necessarily also taking in Westernization and Christian values. Regardless of whether Westernization and Christian values accompanied modernization, the whole process of modernization can be considered as having been adopted and adapted according to the "compartmentalization method." This would mean that modernization (or the development model) does not characterize the whole of Japanese society and culture but is only one (although very big) *bun* that contributes to the *wa* of the whole. In other words, the specific characteristic of the Japanese development model itself might be found in the fact that it is only a "means" to a goal that lies elsewhere, not only in the sense that modern technique is "used" to promote the *wa* of Japan but also in the sense that it is limited to some areas. If Westernization and Christian values necessarily accompany modernization, this is after all not too big a problem, since the whole modernization process is relegated to a subordinate role. At least this seems to be how many Japanese "ideally" look at modernization: as something that is needed for Japan to "catch up with and overcome" the West (or to become "Number One"), but also as something that could be discarded if it should no longer prove to be valuable.

One of our problems, of course, is whether the way Japan dealt with the establishment and maintenance of its development model can also be applied to other countries of Asia under discussion. Is the "compartmentalization method" something specifically Japanese, or something Asian? Or, is it even an exponent of something that goes beyond those limits? Before probing this question, let me once more turn to Japan.

In describing the four types of Christianity—or four different models of Christian influence—that can be found in Japan and particularly in my observations on Japanese religiosity and culture in general, I have implicitly taken the stance that the basic principles underlying Japanese culture and society have not undergone radical changes. In other words, built into my argument is the suggestion that, since the encounter between Japan and the West in the nineteenth century which resulted in the establishment of a Japanese development model, Japan has indeed succeeded in preserving its cultural identity relatively intact and that Western—and consequently also Christian—influences have been mainly relegated to their own compartment, subordinated to the sacred *wa* of the Japanese nation, so that Japan has changed the adopted Western (and Christian) values by adapting and conforming them to the patterns of their particular traditional culture more than Western (and Christian) values have changed Japan. Of course, the question is not that simple. It may no longer suffice to look at the current Japanese development model as the result of an ongoing modernization process, prepared for by certain traditional Japanese values that have existed from time immemorial and then have been brought into the open through the introduction of foreign ideas and techniques over the past 150 years. Some stirrings are now apparent which could well herald the advent—for the first time in Japanese history—of changes of a more radical nature. One aspect of this problem that we cannot disregard is the impact of internationalization. Growing internationalization certainly does have the effect of giving the individual a greater freedom vis-à-vis constraints of the surrounding society and culture and of loosening the traditional power of the community. Keeping this in mind, I would like to return once again to this community aspect from a somewhat different perspective.

Japan's New Communities

In the preceding pages I have stressed the overarching power of belonging to the community of the Japanese nation as a whole—the "religion of Japaneseness" centered on the *wa*. This assertion should now be further clarified by adding that this wider belonging has been concretized in a strong sense of belonging to the sub-units of society which have traditionally been predominately the local rice-growing agricultural communities.[13] It is not surprising that the advent of industrial society is often lamented as having brought in its wake the demise of those traditional communities and, consequently, the very values that sustained them. But is this really so?

Nobody can deny that, aside from some surviving "pockets" of traditional agricultural society, Japan has indeed become a modern, industrialized nation. But this does not necessarily mean the loss of all of the basic principles upon which Japanese culture has been built. The efforts to "accommodate" or "compartmentalize" the impact of modernization seem to have been fairly successful, although the increasing emphasis lately on preserving Japan's traditional heritage might signify that, for the first time, Japan's cultural identity is indeed undergoing unprecedented stress.

If we focus now on the sub-units of society, the communities, we can hopefully throw new light on this question. I have to return in this context to pre-industrial Japanese society and discuss a characteristic which I have not directly mentioned but which is very closely related to our general problem. This characteristic is nothing else than the value of work in common—particularly in the cultivation of rice—for sustaining the life and harmony of the community and the religious implications it bears.

Traditional religiosity was centered upon the (non-rationalized) idea of fertility and life-power in which the whole community participated and to the enhancement of which it contributed by each member's fulfilling his or her own role as one ring or link in both the vertical chain of ancestors and descendants and in the horizontal chain of fellow rice-producers. All members of the community were united in the sacredness of the whole cosmos, which comprised not only the gods and buddhas and the "family of the living and the dead," but also animals and natural phenomena such as plants and trees, not to mention objects that in Western eyes are considered inanimate.

One term which aptly describes this religious mentality is *musubi*, or "power of becoming and growth that links all together." *Musubi* refers to the life-power and fertility mentioned above and to the necessity of common labor in order to co-create it and to enhance it.[14] It was this *musubi*-faith which defined to a great extent the spiritual outlook of the people living in the traditional agricultural communities and which gave rise to the gradual establishment of a specific religious system called *Shintō*, or "way of the *kami* (deities)." But what is important in this respect is that, even if an organized Shinto religion gradually came into existence, the real carriers of the *musubi*-faith remained the people themselves and where a professional priesthood developed, it mainly functioned as a kind of "service agency" for the local community. The community offered specific symbols and rituals needed for the times when the people—and not the priests—decided to take a rest from their rice-growing activities for celebrating the life-power in which they participated through their common labor. This pattern—which is in fact the same pattern of "compartmentalized" or "apportioned harmony" described above—was so strong that even a newly introduced religion like Buddhism somehow had to accommodate itself to it and become on a par with others, one of the elements sharing in the maintenance and enhancement of the community's life-power, or *musubi*, so that *wa* prevailed.

If, then, we attribute a central significance to *musubi*, the life-power of the community primarily sustained by work in common, it is evident that at least in this respect not very much seems to have changed in the transition from an agricultural to an industrial society. Admittedly, if we think in terms of an opposition between fertility and productivity as Westerners tend to do, i.e., between cooperation in the continuity of life-power through the natural process and the production of inanimate objects in industrial plants, the transition has indeed involved quite a radical break. Yet, also in this respect there seems to exist within the psyche of the people a tendency, if not of completely disregarding this opposition, then at least of softening it so that the transition from fertility to productivity can be made with relative ease. In other words, the ethos that sustained the rice-growing labor can be transferred to labor in an industrial context without too much psychic cost, and in this sense it is hard to believe that Japan's present economic success is based only upon the influence of a work ethic of foreign origin.[15] Although, as we will see in a moment, the danger of too much generalizing is certainly not to be ignored, present-day Japanese seem, for the most part, to find satisfaction in their work, whatever concrete form this might take. To stress too much the degrading aspect of industrial productivity because it is only the manufacturing of inanimate objects might betray a (typically Western?) biased way of thinking which as such cannot be immediately applied to Japan.

Yet, we have to probe a little deeper and seek elements, besides the natural human joy of giving birth to things, that create and sustain people's satisfaction in their work. One such element is indeed the (traditional) feeling of community. One can feel pride in what one produces only if a feeling of responsibility accompanies this production. Lest I be misunderstood, I have no intention whatsoever to idealize the plight of workers in Japanese plants nor to idealize laborers in the agricultural society. But one of the reasons for Japan's success in the economic field is certainly the fact that many, if not most, Japanese workers have (or better, are given) a sense of pride that all that they produce is something of themselves, something for which they themselves are responsible. And this sense of pride and responsibility is precisely given by nurturing and strengthening their consciousness of belonging to a community, the factory or company being the community of production.

Japan's traditional communities have largely broken down. And while in many cases this has naturally caused psychic unrest, one result has been a sort of reorganization of the social structure around other, new forms of community. Some people have benefited from the breakdown by establishing a strong individual personality (and the role of Christian ideas in this respect, indirect as it might be, has to be taken into account). But a majority has gradually flocked to places where their latent *musubi*-faith is nurtured and further sustained by a fellowship reminiscent of the old days when they formed together with other fellow human beings and the whole universe what was considered one big cosmic family.

The role performed in this respect by the many companies (*kaisha* or *kigyō*) cannot be denied. Of course, this does not mean that every single Japanese who no longer belongs to a traditional community has now become a member of a company-community, or that the latter is in all aspects, except for the type of labor, a complete replica of the former. Yet, the similarities are too many to be taken lightly. Especially among those who belong to a company which promises them lifelong employment, a kind of company-faith can be found which in many ways resembles the faith of the people in traditional society with its intrinsic relationship to the integration of the community and the importance of work in common. But what is still more remarkable is that the specifically religious form by which this faith is expressed also resembles very much the old pattern. Also in the companies of today the sacredness of work can only be maintained by regular periods of rest and, particularly, by celebrations that glorify the work ethic and strengthen the communal bonds between the workers and management needed for this work ethic.

In recent years it is increasingly becoming evident that in the companies one has recourse to the divine to symbolize the integration of the community and the labor done within it. The main actors are indeed again the people themselves—or, at least, they are made to think this way by the bosses of the new "company-villages"—but they need a kind of service-station which provides them with symbols and rituals for expressing this. The primary service-station in former times was the local Shinto shrine. More and more Japanese companies have started to imitate this pattern and to hold Shinto rituals at regular intervals. In some instances the companies have "infiltrated" the existing local shrines and it is no longer an exception to see that traditional festivals have become an affair sponsored by business enterprises rather than by the local population. But especially worthy of notice is that many companies presently have their own festivals, and in quite a few cases have established their own Shinto shrines.[16]

However, it is not only Shinto that fulfills the role of a service-station for the new communities. The pattern of each religion being allotted its own *bun* or share in the maintenance of the *wa* is also repeated here. Established Buddhism is, of course, after Shinto the first in the running, and its contribution is seemingly most appreciated in April, the season when hordes of "freshmen" are to be initiated in the companies. Reports are on the increase of companies which offer their new recruits a Zen meditation session, often at a Zen training hall set up in the company itself. They openly state that the purpose is "to deepen human relationships and to teach proper etiquette and strict adherence to company rules through common attendance at those sessions." Of course, this is not to nurture or strengthen Buddhist faith and belonging, but through Buddhism to nurture and strengthen a loyal *musubi*-faith in and to the company-community.

Since all this is still a relatively recent phenomenon and, consequently, the process of allotting shares to the various religions is, as yet, not completely finished we might venture to say that even Christianity can still be considered a contending candidate in the race for an "appropriate" *bun*. In the mind of many Japanese, Christianity possesses excellent credentials of high morality and of "international feelings," and, as I hear, there are not a few instances where these have already been tapped and mobilized for enhancing the morale of business enterprises in our internationalizing world. It could very well be that in this present age of internationalization Christianity will be increasingly invited to contribute its proper share to the *musubi*-faith, particularly in those fields, and that "pep talks" by Christian ministers for company employees on those subjects—for this is the concrete form that the Christian "share" sometimes seems to take—will be more and more in demand. In a word, the future of the religions, including Christianity, is very much guaranteed, under the condition that they are again willing to acquiesce in their traditionally played role—although now perhaps in a somewhat different pattern of the "division of labor"—of being subordinated to the broader but real, living faith of the Japanese. This living faith is no other than working together for the enhancement of life-power and the harmonious development of the community, i.e., the company, and ultimately the Japanese nation. And again we have to ask the question whether Christianity can content itself with seeing its influence on contemporary Japanese society and culture being channeled in this direction, as one competing influence among the many that serve the sacredness of the Japanese nation.

The spirit of *wa*, *musubi*-faith, community-belonging, and religion of Japaneseness—these and other terms are all different ways for expressing the basic ethos that underlies Japanese culture and society and also, in my opinion, Japan's "development model." All other values are welcome insofar as they contribute to this basic ethos in their proper, limited way. The strength of Japan's development model lies in this basic ethos, which I have called religion in a broad sense but which others would describe as "secular." Religious (and ethical) values in the strict sense are given a limited role in it and in this way subordinated to it.

Christianity is also given such a limited and subordinate role, and while it has become "inculturated" by the Japanese primarily in terms of its "ritual usefulness," Christian ethical ideals—seen in the minds of most Japanese as based upon individualism—are accepted only insofar as they can be "used" for promoting the basic ethos and insofar as they do not disturb it by making total claims over the individual persons or over society as a whole.

Let me add that there are not a few observers of the Japanese scene who predict that sooner or later Japan will start "suffering" from the "individualistic disease" that affects Western culture.[17] After all, some contend, the Western-capitalistic model of development was also built upon the mobilization of non-individualistic manpower, adroitly used by a few "individualists." *L'histoire se répète*. Japan was only lucky to be able to join the race— also of ideas—a little later than the West. And what about the other countries of Asia and the world?

Is an Application to Other East Asian Countries Possible?

I have dwelt at length on the case of Japan, keeping in mind the question to what extent Japan's development model can be applied to the other countries of East Asia and particularly to the so-called Four Little Dragons. The greater number of church-affiliated Christians in these countries, especially in South Korea, would suggest that their role, and consequently also that of Christian ideas in general, are much more important, although I fear that, again, we have no concrete yardsticks to measure this. Of course, a similar question should also be asked with respect to the influence of the traditional ethico-religious values of those countries, and it is in this context that most would mention Confucianism. To put it very briefly, there might be *at present* a kind of "affinity" between Confucian ethical values and the work ethic that sustains development. But we still have to face the question of why there has been such a great difference—certainly in terms of time—between the development of Japan and that of the other countries, all of which belong to the Confucian world although in different degrees. Maybe Weber was not completely wrong when he stated that Asian cultures and religious traditions were deeply uncongenial to modernization, at least when we focus on Confucianism, insofar as Confucianism was not a strong incentive in giving rise to modernization. The argument that Japan was by far the first to modernize because it was the least influenced by Confucian values cannot be dismissed lightly.[18]

All this does not exclude the possibility that some elements of Confucianism (as of Christianity) can be used for maintaining a development model that arose because of other main factors. Could it also be that in the case of the Four Little Dragons one factor, if not the main factor is a kind of basic ethos which is neither typically Confucian nor Christian nor belonging to any other specific religion, but which "uses" all of them, also by allotting to each of them a proper "share" in which it is more or less contained? It is precisely here that we have to consider the role of folk culture, including folk religios-

ity, as a powerful element in this basic ethos. Folk culture is basically communitarian, and it allows for the coexistence of seemingly contradictory
values. The pragmatism and activism of folk culture and folk religiosity are,
therefore, of extreme importance in explaining development models. As I see
it, folk religiosity might not contain within itself the power needed for giving
rise to modernization. On the other hand, not only is it less an obstacle to
modernization than is usually thought, it also positively promotes it once the
process of modernization has started. In contrast with powerful religions or
ideologies, which are more prone to foster explicit and clear ideas about the
pros and cons of modernization and consequently can easily act as brakes,
folk religiosity possesses a practical this-worldliness and does not care too
much about "contradictions" between its own irrational aspects and the rationality of modernization. Thus, if mobilized it offers a substratum which
generates hard work for a common goal—necessary ingredients for modernization and development. If, in the long run, the work force in those countries
also becomes more aware of the existence of other values, particularly as a
result of growing intercultural encounters, and as a result of "overstimula-
tion," starts having difficulties in coping with the new situation and is no
longer able to arrange the incoming values without mutual contradiction, then
we could very well have a crisis in the offing. The question is how long people
can be mobilized for a common goal without becoming too individualistic.[19]

In conclusion I would like to add the following comment. The problem of
the linkage between modernity and individualism also has to be considered in
East Asia. Individualism is certainly at the roots of Western development. But
is it not in the first place the individualism of a few who were able to muster
the work power of the masses, who themselves were much less individualistic? In a sense, modernity might be digging its own grave since it gradually
inculcates individualism in all who participate in it, and individualism is not
exactly a strong force in maintaining a work ethic. In East Asia, the concrete
form which the whole process takes might differ from the Western model, but
its present success also seems to be largely due to the individualism of a few
who have been able to mobilize the work power of the community-feeling
masses. Yet, to what extent is the non-individualistic version of capitalist modernity in East Asia really different from, say, Western capitalistic modernity
in its initial stage? And will it remain so?

In the West, Christianity had an affinity to both the individualists, who
were the agents of modernization, and to the masses, who lent it their manpower, and it played therefore a bivalent role. In the East, Christianity's role
is much more one-sided and indirect. Because it comes from the outside and
requires in most cases a "personal" conversion, it is usually evaluated only in
terms of (Western) individualism, i.e., in a form in which the elements opposite to the "communitarian ethos" of the East tend to be abstracted and pre-

sented in an exaggerated form.[20] Insofar as the agents of modernization in East Asia are also more or less "individualists," I suspect that the Christian values which are intertwined with Westernization and modernization also exert a certain influence upon them, whether they are conscious of this or not. But a Christian ethos has as yet scarcely reached the masses (except perhaps in Korea). If it does, it probably will be mainly in terms of its emphasis on individualism. But since this is a factor with the potential for undermining the traditional communitarian ethos, it is understandable that many Asians are rather afraid of it and try to limit its influence to well-defined compartments that, hopefully, do not overflow into other spheres of life. How long will they be able to do this since today so many other alien values must compete with each other to get a place on the market of ideas?

Notes

1. Edwin O. Reischauer, "Introduction" to Stuart D.B. Picken, *Christianity and Japan: Meeting-Conflict-Hope* (New York: Kodansha International Ltd., 1983), p. 6.
2. One author who explicitly mentions Christianity in this respect is Peter L. Berger. See his "Secularity: West and East," in *Cultural Identity and Modernization in Asian Countries* (Tokyo: Institute for Japanese Culture and Classics, Kokugakuin University, 1983), pp. 36, 44.
3. Recently, several symposia have been held in Japan dealing with this and similar topics. Besides the one sponsored by the Institute for Japanese Culture and Classics of Kokugakuin University in Tokyo (see *Cultural Identity and Modernization in Asian Countries*, op. cit.) I could mention: Professors World Peace Academy, *Emerging Asia: The Role of Japan* (Tokyo: Riverfield, Inc., 1981); and Hiroshi Mannari and Harumi Befu, eds., *The Challenge of Japan's Internationalization* (Tokyo: Kodansha International and Kwansei Gakuin University, 1983).
4. Statistics can be found in David B. Barrett, ed., *World Christian Encyclopedia* (Oxford University Press, 1982). We should, of course, not forget that there is indeed a Christian nation in East Asia, namely the Philippines. What the role of Christianity has been and still is in that country with respect to the problem of development is worth pursuing but cannot be taken up here.
5. In Japan, for example, roughly one percent of the population professes affiliation to Christian churches, while another one percent call themselves Christians but are not members of any specific church. The *World Christian Encyclopedia* (op. cit.) also mentions this second type of Christians in its statistics.
6. In Japan, for example, up to 20 percent seem to have such direct relationship. See James P. Colligan, ed., *The Image of Christianity in Japan* (Tokyo: Sophia University, 1980), pp. 78–79.
7. This problem will be taken up more in detail in the following pages. I might already refer in this context to the work of Robert N. Bellah with regard to the modernization process of Japan, *Tokugawa Religion* (Glencoe, IL: Free Press, 1957).
8. The most recent survey is the one conducted by NHK (Japan Broadcasting Corporation) and published as NHK Hōsō-seron-chōsa-kyoku, ed., *Nihonjin no shūkyō-ishiki* [The Religious Consciousness of the Japanese] (Tokyo, 1984).

9. As a counterbalance against overemphasizing the element of harmony in Japanese culture, several recent studies point out the existence of conflict. See, e.g., Ellis S. Kraus et al., eds., *Conflict in Japan* (Honolulu: University of Hawaii Press, 1984).

10. I have dealt with this subject in more detail in my *Wa to bun no kōzō* [The Structure of Apportioned Harmony] (Tokyo, 1981). See also my "Japanese Religiosity in an Age of Internationalization," in *Japanese Journal of Religious Studies* 5:2–3, 1978, pp. 87–106.

11. I have taken this concept from Takie Sugiyama Lebra, *Japanese Patterns of Behavior* (Honolulu: The University Press of Hawaii, 1976), pp. 67–69, where it is applied to the position of Japanese individuals in the organic whole of a social group or society as such.

12. Ruth Benedict, *The Chrysanthemum and the Sword* (Tokyo: Charles E. Tuttle, 1954), pp. 195–227.

13. In this respect, the work of Nakane Chie is an excellent reference, especially her *Tate-shakai no rikigaku* [The Dynamics of the Vertical Society] (Tokyo: Kodansha, 1978).

14. See Honda Sōichirō, *Nippon Shintō nyūmon* [Introduction to Japanese Shinto] (Tokyo, 1985), passim.

15. It goes without saying that the problem of the roots of Japan's work ethic is an extremely complex one and should not be explained exclusively in terms of the Shinto-derived concept of *musubi*. Also the contributions of Confucianism and Buddhist thought have to be duly acknowledged. See, e.g., Robert N. Bellah, *Tokugawa Religion*, op. cit. I do think, however, that the basic Shinto tradition in fact exerted the greatest influence and that this point has not been sufficiently stressed in most treatises on this problem.

16. A wealth of data about this phenomenon is found in Honda Sōichirō, *Nippon Shintō nyūmon*, op. cit., and in a regular column in the official newspaper of the Japanese Association of Shinto Shrines, the *Jinja shinpō*, published during 1984.

17. See, e.g., Robert N. Bellah, "Cultural Identity and Modernization," in *Cultural Identity and Modernization*, op. cit., pp. 16–27.

18. Gregory Clark stresses this point in "Japan as a Model for Development," in Professors World Peace Academy, *Emerging Asia*, op. cit., pp. 95–105.

19. I leave open the question about the extent to which the "compartmentalization method" I described above is related not only to folk religiosity but also to a characteristic of human beings in general, and of modern people in particular, as pointed out by certain psychologists such as Robert J. Lifton and James Hillman who speak about "Protean man" and a "polycentric or polytheistic psychology."

20. This point has been forcefully expounded by Suzuki Norihisa in his essay on Christianity in Hori Ichirō et al., eds., *Japanese Religion* (Tokyo: Kodansha International, 1972), pp. 71–87. I have dealt with the same problem in my "In Search of a Church with a Japanese Face: A Delayed Endeavor," in *The Japan Missionary Bulletin* 37, 1983, pp. 113–18.

7

The Applicability of Asian Family Values to Other Sociocultural Settings

Siu-lun Wong

The Family and Economic Development

"Familism" and economic development are antipathetic.[1] This view has gained such currency that it appears almost as a self-evident truth. The adverse economic effects of the family, as listed by Clark Kerr and his associates, are well-known:

> It provides shelter and food for all its members, regardless of their individual contributions, so that the indigent and the indolent alike are cared for in a sort of "social security" system. Working members are expected to pool their earnings for the benefit of everyone; individual saving is discouraged. The behaviour and careers (including marriage) of its members are the close concern of the elders. Family loyalty and obligations take precedence over other loyalties and obligations. Thus, the extended family tends to dilute individual incentives to work, save, and invest.[2]

In the specific case of the Chinese family, Max Weber has set the tone by highlighting the "sib fetters of the economy."[3] The Chinese "sib" relationship, in Weber's eyes, was the embodiment of the strong force of traditionalism that blocked rationalization. It weakened "work discipline," thwarted the "free market selection of labour," and inhibited the emergence of the impersonal form of "business confidence" and "universal trust."[4] The power of the sib, according to Weber, was backed by the Chinese religious ethic centering on piety which could only create a "community of blood." On the other hand, the Protestant ethic, which was oriented towards a supramundane god, had the strength to shatter the fetters of the sib and create "the superior community of faith" with its far-reaching economic ramifications.[5] Harping on Weber's theme of rationalization, Marion Levy also identifies the traditional Chinese family, "a highly particularistic structure," as a major obstacle to industrialization. "It enormously complicates the operation of modern enterprise in China in two major ways," he writes; "The first is the problem of employment, where particularism injects the element of nepotism on a large scale. The second is the problem of maintaining relations outside a given organization itself, the purchase or sale of goods, services, and so on."[6]

Such a negative evaluation of the family largely accords with the self-diagnosis of the modernizing Chinese elites. Whatever their political persuasions, these elites shared the conviction that the Chinese family must be reformed before modernization could proceed. This conviction was clearly expressed in successive attempts at legislating for family change. The dominant aim of the Civil Code promulgated in 1931 by the government of the Republic of China was "to turn China into a real State . . . and to enable the citizens to make use of their personal abilities to the best interest of their country." In order to attain that goal, the chairman of the Civil Codification Commission declared that "it was imperative that the excessive grip of the old family tie over the individuals should be loosened."[7] Two decades later, the government of the People's Republic of China promulgated a new Marriage Law soon after it took power. According to C.K. Yang, "[the] reason for the Communist policy of reshaping the traditional family seems plain. The Communist regime is bent on building an industrial society on the socialistic pattern, and it is fully aware of the incompatibility between such a society and the kinship-oriented structure."[8]

Kinship and the Chinese Business Firm

The obvious implication of the above diagnosis is that traditional Chinese family values should be discarded, or at least neutralized, for the sake of economic growth. But this prescription has apparently not been adopted in the capitalistic Chinese communities in the postwar era, and yet they prosper. This anomaly seems to suggest that the negative economic effects of family values have been overblown. A close examination of the various economic manifestations of these values in Hong Kong leads me to think that this is the case.

Kinship does not play an important role in regulating the external business transactions of Hong Kong Chinese enterprises. There is little evidence that a dualistic business ethic is prevalent or that honesty and trust are found only within the kin group while sharp practices reign without. In the cotton-spinning industry, which represents the large-scale, capital-intensive sector of Hong Kong's economy, intermarriages among the mill owners' families have been rare, there have been few interlocking directorships established on the basis of kinship, and though clan associations existed in the colony, their impact on business activities has been tenuous at best. The textile industrialists have tended to have their social status confirmed by their clan associations, but not achieved through them.[9] In the multitude of small industrial firms in Hong Kong, a similar pattern is found. Of the 415 establishments surveyed in 1978, only 4 percent of them relied on loans from relatives as a major source of funding to start their businesses; these firms were involved in an intricate and volatile network of subcontracting that did not seem to be mediated by kinship links.[10]

The inter-firm economic order, so it appears, is secured largely on non-kin solidarities. Several factors contributed to the weak role of the family in this sphere. In the first place, forging business alliances through a conscious marriage strategy is hardly practicable with the decline of the custom of arranged marriages and the inability of Chinese family heads to disinherit their children for disobedience. Second, the intensity of kinship reciprocity tends to limit economic options. Therefore it is invoked sparingly only when it suits one's own ends. Such considerations are vividly shown in Deglopper's description of commercial dealings in a community in Taiwan:

> Retailers are expected to give close kinsmen a lower price, but the kinsman is also expected to buy without a lot of quibbling. . . . One old lady carefully avoided shopping at the mixed goods shop run by her sister's son because she would feel obligated to buy once she went in. If she wanted a blue thing and all they had were red ones, she would have to take a red one. So she went to the shop of a non-kinsman where she could carefully look for something that exactly suited her taste, walk out if she didn't find it, and bargain fiercely if she did.[11]

Finally, kinship bonds are intrinsically restrictive and not easily amenable to extensions. Economic groupings constructed on a kinship basis will necessarily be confined in scope. In Chinese economic conduct the crucial distinction is not that of kin and non-kin, but personal and impersonal.[12]

The Chinese tend to personalize their economic relations. Shared characteristics, including real or fictive kinship, regional origin, educational background, etc., often provide convenient bases for cooperation to be initiated. Where such commonalities are lacking, intermediaries are usually brought in as guarantors or brokers to set up the necessary personal linkages. During the 1950s the Hong Kong and Shanghai Bank, for example, had enlisted the service of a Shanghainese with banking experience to mediate between its predominantly British managers and the cotton-spinning community consisting mostly of entrepreneurs from the Shanghai region.[13] With the operation of such an "informal adviser" who knew the spinners personally, it was said that these textile industrialists were able to start from scratch with bank loans granted practically on an unsecured basis.[14] Such particularistic ties are highly elastic. While the kin circle is finite and bound, the personalized economic network used by the Chinese can reach widely. It is in this sense that I think Liang Shu-ming is right to characterize Chinese society as organized on the basis of social bonds rather than on the basis of kinship; family ties only serve as the nucleus from which a Chinese can spin a web of ever-widening social circles.[15]

The influence of the family is much more strongly felt in the internal organization of Hong Kong Chinese enterprises than in their external dealings. Such an influence manifests itself, in various combinations, as paternalistic managerial ideology and practice, nepotistic employment, and family ownership. Let us consider paternalistic management first. Joe Endland and John Rear found that "authoritarianism is a strong trait among virtually all Hong Kong employers."[16] My research on the cotton spinners has shown them to be industrial patriarchs who exercised tight control, shunned the delegation of power, conferred welfare benefits on their employees as favors, acted as moral custodians of their subordinates, opposed protective labor legislation, and disapproved of trade union activities.[17] Such a managerial approach is shaped by both cultural as well as economic forces. The metaphor of the family provides a form of ready-made cultural rhetoric to legitimize managerial authority. Patron-client relationships are further cultivated to cope with problems of loyalty and to contain the centrifugal tendency of subordinates to set up on their own and become rival competitors. Economically, for industries such as spinning and weaving which require a stable work force to deal with regular business cycles, benevolent paternalism is one of the means to attract and retain workers, the majority of whom (63 percent of a sample of 1,000 workers) are found to believe that "the employer of a firm should look after the interests of his workers like the head of a large family."[18] This form of Chinese paternalism does not seem to be incompatible with industrial efficiency. As a prominent Hong Kong entrepreneur points out,

> In a Western industrial society, paternalism is frowned upon; in Hong Kong it has been an instrument for industrial success and social equilibrium in a period of great social upheaval. Here again it is worth noting that in 1968, out of a total of about 170 million industrial man-days, only 8,432 man-days were lost through disputes.[19]

The relative industrial tranquility obviously has many causes, but it is highly probable that the existence of patron-client relations within enterprises has a part to play in dampening the growth of class consciousness among workers. Labor discontent is expressed more often in individual acts such as absenteeism and resignations rather than in collective forms of bargaining and strikes. But does paternalism foster dependency among the subordinates and stifle initiatives? I would think not, as there are indications that the demand for obedience from the employees is largely a matter of form. The emphasis is on outward deference to one's superiors in the organization. Eye contact, for instance, has been found to be avoided by Chinese employees with their chief executive during board meetings.[20] Dissenting views and personal opinions may be advanced by executives, and are sometimes even demanded of them, but they must be made at the appropriate moment so as not to undermine the authority of superiors in public. Such an orientation seems to support Gary Hamilton's view that Chinese patriarchalism as a principle of traditional domination is different from its Western counterpart. According to Hamilton, the core value of the former is *xiao* (filial piety) which involves "obedience" and the "institutionalization of roles," while the guiding idea of the latter is *patria potesta* which means "power" and the "institutionalization of jurisdictions." Therefore in Chinese patriarchalism, "[loyalty] to the father and to emperor was not personal loyalty, but rather was a part of one's own role, was depersonalized, and resembled the type of loyalty known as allegiance— which is loyalty to symbols and philosophic principles."[21]

Nepotism, the preferential employment of one's relatives, can be found in probably about half of the Hong Kong Chinese firms.[22] But this bald generalization requires several qualifications. First, relatives as employees make up just a tiny fraction of the personnel in nepotistic companies unless they are very small. Second, such relatives are predominantly members of the employers' families (*jia*) rather than their wider kin group. Third, there are active as well as passive forms of nepotism. As a rule, Chinese industrialists in Hong Kong tend to appoint family members to key positions in their enterprises, but they take on kinsmen outside of the *jia* rather reluctantly. They might well be thinking of the latter category of relatives when many of them told researchers that they were against nepotistic practices.[23] Passive nepotism is not likely to overburden the firm because most Chinese will only ask their kinsmen for jobs as a last resort. Beyond the family, a Chinese has few specific economic claims on his kinsmen.[24] After the division of the family estate, even brothers are not obligated to provide financial help to one another. Therefore, to ask for a job from a kinsman is to incur a social debt, and one has to accept whatever is offered without complaint.[25] Active nepotism, on the other hand, is often practiced on rational economic grounds. For small firms, family members and other relatives provide reliable and cheap labor. They may be expected to work harder for less pay. For example, only 67 percent of small Hong Kong factories with relatives in their workforce are found to give full pay to their kinsmen-employees on a par with ordinary workers.[26] This may have contributed to their resilience and competitiveness particularly in times of recession. Owners of large firms put their sons or other *jia* members in responsible positions mainly to prevent the dissipation of family property and the loss of business profits to outsiders. Espy's data on a small sample of such firms suggests that the inclusion of family members in management probably has little harmful effect on the performance of the company. Growth rate of the enterprise and the employment of family members are found not to be correlated.[27] The major reason is probably because Hong Kong Chinese industrialists usually take meticulous care to equip their family members for responsible positions through formal education as well as on-the-job training. Therefore, these kinsmen are seldom substandard employees with inferior ability.

Active nepotism as found in many Hong Kong Chinese enterprises is thus very much a derivative phenomenon of the family mode of ownership. Taking 50 percent shareholding or more as the measure of possession, nearly 60 percent of the small-scale factories and at least half of the cotton-spinning mills surveyed in 1978 were discovered to be held by individual proprietors and their families.[28] When industrial capital is held by the family as a unit, what effects will this have on the enterprises? Will they tend to remain small and conservative, ever wary of intervention from the outside and reluctant to tap external financial sources?[29]

The behavior of Chinese family firms is of course affected by the general economic climate. They might be expected to display more vigor in times of prosperity and to act more cautiously during economic downturns. But equally important is the way in which Chinese families are formed and evolved. They have a number of features with close bearings on their conduct as units of industrial ownership.[30] One feature is the principle of patrilineal descent so that relatively more discreet and enduring corporate kinship units can be constituted for the management of economic resources. Another is the rule of equal inheritance among male heirs, and a third is the process of family division which occurs in several stages. In general, the first asset to be divided is the right to the profits derived from the family estate. It is then the turn for the right of utilization and the right of tranferral of the *jia* property respectively. Demands for the division of profit rights can be made by the heirs after their marriage. For the division of utilization and transferral rights, they have to wait till the retirement or death of the family head. Whether these demands are pressed depends very much on the nature of the family property. When the property takes the form of industrial assets which often involve economies of scale, team work, business reputation, and financial borrowings, it is generally in the interest of the heirs to defer the physical fragmentation of the *jia* estate.

With these features in mind, I think we can have a better understanding of the Chinese family firm by positing four significant phases in its development, as shown schematically in Table 7.1, with a plus sign indicating unity and a minus sign representing division.

These phases tend to coincide with generational shifts inside the *jia*, so the profit, management, and estate of the family enterprise are progressively fragmented.

During the emergent phase, the pater-entrepreneur is usually involved in a venture with several partners. He uses his family savings as the capital share, and the well-being of his *jia* provides the main spur to his business activities. A Chinese family head is in some ways only a trustee of the *jia* property, which ultimately belongs to his children. But a distinction should be made between *jia* property that is inherited and property that is acquired by the pater-entrepreneur himself.[31] The latter carries with it greater freedom of maneuver, social recognition and esteem, as well as gratitude from his offspring. In a religious sense, the pater-entrepreneur's "salvation" or immortality also depends on the continuation and glorification of his family line. All of these are powerful incentives for his endeavor to create an endowment.

Once the pater-entrepreneur is successful in capturing the majority shares of the partnership or in accumulating enough capital from that venture to set up on his own, the family enterprise can be said to enter the second phase, centralization. As he acquires the estate himself, he has the authority to make use of the assets as he sees fit. Before the division of the *jia* estate, he need not obtain the consent of his sons in the investment of family funds.[32] Decision-making power is thus highly centralized in the hands of the pater-entrepreneur. This highly personalized style of leadership has two major implications for capital formation. The possibility for profits to be retained and reinvested is much enhanced. Besides reinvestment, funds can also be freely transferred from one line of business to another for lateral expansion and mutual sustenance. Capital is mobile within the family group of enterprises because it belongs to an essentially unified *jia* budget. Managerially, the style

TABLE 7.1
The Development of the Chinese Family Firm

Phases	ASPECTS OF FAMILY FIRM		
	Estate	Management	Profit
I Emergent	+	+	+
II Centralized	+	+	−
III Segmented	+	−	−
IV Disintegrative	−	−	−

+ = unity
− = division

of leadership involves a low degree of delegation of authority as well as a reluctance of the pater-entrepreneur to abdicate power. Retirement from the family business will remove the very basis on which his social status in the wider community is built. A super-annuated family head is also powerless to contain the centrifugal tendency among his heirs.

But ultimately he has to relinquish control as he cannot live forever. It is then that the family firm will enter its third phase, gradual segmentation. Centralization is no longer possible mainly because the heirs as brothers are jural equals. In their socialization, younger siblings have not been brought up to submit to their elder brothers.[33] But for reasons mentioned above, it is not very likely for them to divide up the family estate. The tensions arising from sibling rivalry are usually contained in two ways. The first method is the institution of elaborate controls to check the power of whoever becomes the chief executive. Formal contracts are sometimes drawn up among brothers to specify how company profits should be distributed and utilized.[34] The second means is to agree on different spheres of responsibilities among the brothers. This approach, to give maximum independence to participating brothers, means a proliferation of departments, factory plants, or subsidiary companies within the family concern. Outwardly, there tends to be physical expansion; internally, centralized decision making becomes untenable and strong personal leadership declines. The mutual watchfulness among brothers in a segmented family firm is very similar to the relationship among partners during the emergent phase. The same opportunity for the asymmetrical growth in shareholding is present because of the continuing practice of conferring "red" shares to top executives who succeed in leading the enterprise to prosperity. In some cases, therefore, a brother in a segmented family firm may manage to build up a majority stake, and the enterprise is taken over by his *fang*. The firm will then reenter the centralized phase.

If this does not happen and the brothers remain in partnership until it is their turn to yield to their own offspring, then the family enterprise will pass into the final phase, disintegration. When the sons of the brothers in turn succeed to power, the number of members in the family economy has greatly increased so that discord over the running of the enterprise is likely to multiply. In addition, the economic considerations against the sale of family shares is less inhibitive. The value of individual shareholding has become much smaller due to the subdivision, and this reduces the attraction of the regular income derived from the shares. Moreover, since it is unlikely that brothers will have identical numbers of children, inheritance by the third generation will create unequal ownership among the shareholders. Brothers may still cooperate on a more or less equal footing as owners, but cousins with unbalanced portions of shares have less reason to do so. Those in a weaker bargaining position may decide to break off the economic ties to the family enterprise, especially when they are brought up with little emotional attachment to it. Family members as shareholders will then be more concerned with immediate, tangible benefits than long-term business prospects. From this stage onwards, the family firm will be crisis-ridden.

Thus in a developmental perspective, the Chinese family firm behaves differently in successive stages of its life cycle. It is not intrinsically conservative or lethargic. Relative to its Japanese counterpart, it is less durable. But compared to families constructed on the principle of bilineal descent, it is not short-lived, particularly as it can avoid disintegration by shedding the alienated branches and reentering the centralized phase. Even if the firm disintegrates, the dispersed family units can quickly spawn new enterprises of their own. The competitive strengths of the Chinese family firms are considerable: there exists a much stronger measure of trust among *jia* members than among unrelated business partners; consensus is easier to attain; and the need for mutual accountability is reduced. These factors enable family firms to be more adaptable in their operations. They can make quick decisions during rapidly changing circumstances and maintain greater secrecy by committing less to written records. As a result, they are particularly well-suited to survive and flourish in situations where a high level of risk is involved, such as in an unstable political environment, a fluctuating industrial sector, or a newly created line of business.

"Entrepreneurial Familism" in Hong Kong

There are reasonably solid empirical grounds to conclude that family values as found in postwar Hong Kong are on the whole not antipathetic to economic development. Though the grounds are less secure, I would nevertheless like to take the argument a step further and propose that there exists in Hong Kong an economically dynamic ethos of "entrepreneurial familism."[35] This ethos involves the *jia* as the basic unit of economic competition. The family provides the impetus for innovation and the support for risk-taking. Entrepreneurial familism is by no means confined to the rich sector of the population in the form of family firms; it permeates the whole society. Where there is little physical capital to be deployed, heads of less well-off families still marshall the limited *jia* resources and try to cultivate human capital for collective advancement. In her study of 28 middle- and working-class families in Hong Kong, Janet Salaff finds that all of the working daughters contributed the major portions of their income to the budgets of their families. Once these families had acquired the basic material necessities, such as adequate quarters and essential consumer durables, "more resources were invariably channeled into the education of [their] younger sons and daughters. There were greater sex differences in educational opportunities within poorer families. Sons of [these families] were always encouraged to continue to secondary school even if their exam scores did not merit government financial support, whereas stricter conditions were imposed on the daughters' advancement." She sums up the situation in this way: "Each family thus aspired to improve its position in life by means of combining the income of wage-earning members."[36]

Entrepreneurial familism in Hong Kong entails a peculiar style of economic organization with three distinguishing characteristics. The first is a high degree of centralization in decision making, together with a low level of formalization of organizational structure.[37] Even for family firms in the segmented stage, the concentration of decision-making power is retained in individual business segments.

This pattern is closely related to the second feature, the existence of an internal centrifugal force. Among Hong Kong owners and workers alike, autonomy is valued and self-employment is preferred. The common ideal is to become one's own boss. A small Hong Kong industrialist has been reported to say that "a Shanghainese at forty who has not yet made himself owner of a firm is a failure, a good-for-nothing."[38] The cotton spinners who were large employers also held a similar view. Nearly two-thirds of those I interviewed chose the option of becoming the owner-manager of a smaller firm rather than the senior executive of a larger corporation if both alternatives were available to them early in their career.[39] Such an outlook is partly engendered by the Chinese family system which recognizes brothers as independent and equal claimants of the *jia* estate. Most Chinese males can look forward to the day when they will have their own portion of the family estate and become a separate family head. But the preference for self-employment, it seems, is also shaped by the longstanding Chinese cultural assumption that men are "naturally equal," meaning that they possess common attributes at birth.[40] Social inequalities appear, according to most classical Chinese philosophers, because some people can better realize their potentials through their own efforts, especially by means of education. This conception of man buttressed the traditional Chinese system of social stratification where a strictly hierarchical structure coexisted with an ideology upholding the virtue of bettering oneself and the reward of social advancement.[41] The resultant popular desire to strike out on one's own tends to deprive Chinese owners of dependable executives. As the loyalty of subordinates cannot be taken for granted, employers typically rely on paternalistic practices, tight supervision, and minimal delegation of authority as a means of coping with the situation. Executives, on their part, dislike subjugation and tend not to regard management as a career. The consequence is an abundant supply of entrepreneurs with an acute shortage of dedicated managers.

The last characteristic of the Chinese style of economic organization induced by entrepreneurial familism is the fluidity of the economic hierarchy.

As the *jia* is an ephemeral entity that dies with each generation, family firms seldom endure. They are regularly in flux. In addition, enterprises are unlikely to join in collusion because entrepreneurial independence is jealously guarded. As a result, there is a rarity of oligopolistic groupings that will deny entry to new competitors and block social mobility in the business realm.[42] With few institutional barriers to upward and downward movements along the social ladder, family fortunes rise and fall in quick succession. To borrow Hugh Baker's imagery, the social and economic order appears "like a seething cauldron, with families bubbling to the top only to burst and sink back to the bottom."[43] In Chinese entrepreneurial familism, the main problem is not with economic inertia. It is rather the danger of "excessive" competition.

Chinese entrepreneurial familism has its own competitive strengths as well as weaknesses, and it has its own share of problems. But most of these problems are not insurmountable. The internal centrifugal force, for instance, has led to the evolution of a system of subcontracting, under which the production process is broken up into multiple independent parts. This enhances Hong Kong industry's flexibility and responsiveness to external market fluctuations. Furthermore, these problems are not the ones commonly attributed to the Chinese family for dragging the feet of industrial development. What transpires in Hong Kong is apparently the very opposite of the assertion by Kerr et al. cited earlier that "the extended family tends to dilute individual incentives to work, save, and invest." How is this state of affairs to be explained? It could be argued that Chinese familism has undergone a metamorphosis so that the Hong Kong variant is qualitatively different from the original as it existed in the Chinese mainland. But different in what sense? Hong Kong familism might be different in and of itself, or it might interact differently as part of a new, reconstituted configuration.

Because of social change, it is to be expected that familism as found in Hong Kong and in traditional China will not be identical. It would not take long for us to find out that arranged marriages have faded, neo-local residence is favored, and the circle of eligible heirs to family estates has been enlarged to include daughters as well. But other features remain which enable us to recognize the unmistakable Chineseness of the pattern of family life in Hong Kong. For old and young alike, family solidarity is still regarded as of paramount importance; descent is still traced patrilineally; ancestor worship is still going strong; and filial piety is still widely observed as far as the financial support due to one's parents is concerned.[44] Therefore, the "core" features of the Chinese family are preserved in Hong Kong while "[peripheral] adjustments have been made to accommodate to the effects of industrialization and transnational penetration."[45] Such an adaptability of the *jia* is probably not a new phenomenon. Recent studies are beginning to unveil the plasticity of the

Chinese family even in traditional times to suit diverse economic needs.[46] It is more reasonable for us to assume the existence of a common and stable stock of Chinese cultural principles relating to the family which is "capable of generating a much greater range of creative organizational responses to changing historical and environmental circumstances."[47] Equally, the entrepreneurial flair of the *jia* may not be a novelty. In his study of the traditional Chinese lineages, Maurice Freedman has arrived at a superior model of the Chinese social system which challenges the conventional one upheld by Francis Hsu. The difference, as Freedman puts it, is as follows:

> For Hsu the lineage and the family look like relatively closed and comfortable worlds beyond the frontiers of which individuals are nervous to tread. Peace, harmony, and security prevail within; outside there is danger. In fact, on my showing, competition and conflict are inherent at all levels of the social system; brother contends with brother, segment with segment, lineage with lineage, the lineage with the state. But there is also harmony because each contender must be united against its opponents—war without and peace within. I hate my brother but I am united with him against other families. The members of a lineage struggle among themselves for scarce resources of land and honour, but they stand shoulder to shoulder when they are confronted by another lineage. Harmony and conflict are not mutually exclusive; on the contrary, they imply each other.[48]

Substituting "trust and suspicion" for "harmony and conflict" in the last sentence of the quotation, and we begin to see why Weber and other scholars have missed the mark by hitting at the Chinese "sib fetters."

In internal makeup, the family in Hong Kong is not genetically different from its traditional Chinese counterpart. But the same cannot be said of the external sociopolitical milieu. The social configuration of Hong Kong differs from that of the Chinese mainland in two critical ways: it is a small social entity and it is governed by a colonial administration. In these respects, Hong Kong resembles Singapore and Taiwan, both of which bear the imprints of colonialism and are modest in territorial scale. Because of these two factors, the role of the state is rather special in these peripheral Chinese communities. On the one hand, the state tends not to act as the magnet for the best local talents as it is less accessible and prestigious. On the other hand, the problem of coordination and integration with which the state has to grapple is far less formidable than that found on the Chinese mainland. The significance of the state in economic development is well-recognized by Weber and Levy. But both of them perceive the state-family relationship in traditional China in terms of a struggle between the forces of universalism and particularism. "The rationalism of the bureaucracy," wrote Weber, "was confronted with a resolute and traditionalistic power [i.e., the sib]."[49] Therefore Levy pins his hope of modernization on the Chinese state:

China can achieve a level of industrialization comparable with that of the highly industrialized western nations. In order to accomplish this quickly, one of the best available techniques would be the renovation of the institutionalization of universalism in the national government, and the establishment and operation of the major heavy industrial installations by the national government. There is a long tradition of universalism in this sphere. Its change to accord with the demands of the new technology should therefore be relatively easy.[50]

In his more recent writings, Levy further argues that for the late-comers to modernization, there is a mandatory trend towards centralization and a concurrent weakening of the family as the "last unit of decentralization of control."[51] Yet in the postwar economic race among various Chinese communities, it is mainland China which follows Levy's prescriptions most closely but still lags behind. Levy has betted on the wrong horse, I think, partly because of the analytical glasses that he has been wearing. His vision has been distorted by the too sharply drawn dichotomy of universalism and particularism, so that he misread the economic potential of the Chinese family. My hypothesis of entrepreneurial familism suggests that the Chinese family is and was an economically active force. In the past, it was checked probably by a state preoccupied with the task of integration and a peculiar ecological and economic environment that constituted a "high level equilibrium trap."[52] Once such external contraints are removed, Chinese familism will fuel the motor of development.

The Applicability of Entrepreneurial Familism Outside China

Is Chinese entrepreneurial familism applicable to other sociocultural settings? The answer depends on whether we have in mind an East Asian model for emulation or for heuristic purposes. Since Chinese familism is sustained by a particular cultural stock, it is unrealistic to expect it to be duplicated elsewhere and embraced by other peoples. But I believe several useful lessons can be learned from a proper appreciation of the role of family values in the developmental experiences of the peripheral Chinese communities.

The first general lesson pertains to the overseas Chinese. As bearers of entrepreneurial familism, Chinese immigrants are usually economic assets to countries where private enterprise is valued. Given a reasonably congenial environment, they may be expected to seek out economic opportunities by themselves and to look after their own welfare. They are necessarily "clannish" at the initial stage of settlement and will take time to be assimilated into the host societies. Until their cultural characteristics are gradually changed, they will continue to consider the interests of the family prior to those of the community and the nation. If these qualities of the overseas Chinese can be accepted as they are, they will inject an element of dynamism into capitalistic economies.

But if these qualities are frowned upon, and they are obliged to abandon their cultural heritage, then their economic worth will be greatly decreased. Many of the justifications for discriminatory state policies towards the overseas Chinese in Southeast Asia can hardly stand up to close scrutiny. For example, the Chinese there are often regarded by the host governments as exerting a stranglehold on the economies by monopolizing various economic sectors. But as the above analysis shows, this is unlikely to happen, owing to the existence of an internally centrifugal force. Therefore, policies designed to foster "native" entrepreneurship at the expense of the Chinese settlers often prove to be counterproductive. Economic dislocations usually result as the native entrepreneurs are not forthcoming, while Chinese initiatives are stifled.[53] The assumption that the Chinese are disloyal to their countries of residence and will serve as the "fifth column" of their motherland is also probably false. Chinese immigrants are seldom politically ambitious because they are familistic before they are nationalistic.

The second general lesson pertains to social engineering in developing countries. It should not be taken for granted that the family or other "traditional" social institutions are necessarily incompatible with modern technology. Before the economic potential of these social institutions has been accurately assessed, it may be less harmful for the various developing states to restrain their reforming zeal. The costly experiment made by the government of the People's Republic of China should be instructive. It had made a draconian effort to break the Chinese family as a unit of production by creating the commune and other socialistic organizations. The consequent economic paralysis has compelled it to retrace its steps recently with the so-called responsibility system which in effect restores most of the productive functions to the family.

The last lesson pertains to the question of historical transitions to industrialism. Not being well-equipped to tackle this problem, I shall confine myself to some preliminary observations. Various studies have indicated that "family capitalism" was an early stage of industrial development in many European countries.[54] Should we expect this historical pattern to recur in the Chinese case? Is Chinese entrepreneurial familism a transitory phenomenon destined for extinction when capitalism matures? My tentative answer is no. For a start, family enterprises have proved to be far more resilient than expected even in the West.[55] But more importantly, the preindustrial European societies and traditional Chinese society might be typologically distinct. In discussing how modern Western society came into being, Talcott Parsons and Neil Smelser have made much use of the idea of differentiation. They suggest that European feudalism represented a special "fusion" of political and kinship functions in which the state was fused with politically privileged aristocratic "lineages." Early capitalism emerged with a loosening of such a fusion.

"Lineages" had risen from below, deriving their power from the ownership of land and then of capital. They, in turn, established another fusion, that of kinship and property. But Parsons and Smelser believe "that the kinship-property combination typical of classical capitalism was, in the nature of the case, a temporary and unstable one. Both economic and political differentiation were destined, unless social development stopped altogether, to proceed toward 'bureaucratization,' toward differentiation between economy and polity and between ownership and control, finally toward further differentiation of kinship as part of the pattern maintenance system, i.e., no longer as a functionally undifferentiated status group."[56] Parsons and Smelser are trying to sketch what they perceive to be the inner logic of the evolution of Western feudalism. But traditional China, since its unification under an imperial structure, had not been feudal. There had not been a fusion of the polity and kinship. Instead, there had existed in imperial China a "proto-bureaucratic" state which was involved in a delicate balance of power with local, semiautonomous kinship groupings. Therefore, it is not very likely that the European experience of capitalistic development will be replicated in China. And this brings me to the reason why so far I have only referred to Chinese familism and not to the Japanese or Korean equivalents. Lack of expertise aside, I tend to agree with Levy that the social arrangement existent in late traditional China was radically dissimilar to that found in Meiji Japan, and thus their divergent patterns of modernization.[57] Their geographical proximity and purportedly common Confucian heritage should not detract us from their fundamental difference in social structure.

On the level of values, there are probably sufficient similarities among Chinese, Japanese, and Korean families for us to refer to East Asian familism. But on the level of structures and configurations, their roles in economic development might be distinctive enough to warrant individual treatment.

Notes

1. Besides the participants in the symposium, "In Search of an East Asian Development Model," sponsored by the Carnegie Council on Ethics and International Affairs (formerly the Council on Religion and International Affairs) in New York City, I would like to thank Professor Raymond Apthorpe and Dr. Thomas W.P. Wong for their comments on an earlier draft of this paper.
2. C. Kerr, J.T. Dunlop, F. Harbison, and C.A. Myers, *Industrialism and Industrial Man* (Harmondsworth: Pelican Books, 1973), p. 94.
3. Max Weber, *The Religion of China: Confucianism and Taoism* (New York: The Free Press, 1951), p. 95.
4. Ibid., pp. 95, 237.
5. Ibid., p. 237.
6. M.J. Levy, Jr., *The Family Revolution in Modern China* (Cambridge: Harvard University Press, 1949), p. 354.

7. Quoted in H.D.R. Baker, *Chinese Family and Kinship* (London: Macmillan, 1979), p. 179.
8. C.K. Yang, *The Chinese Family in the Communist Revolution* (Cambridge: The MIT Press, 1959), p. 19.
9. S.L. Wong, "Industrial Entrepreneurship and Ethnicity: A Study of the Cotton Spinners of Hong Kong," unpublished Ph.D. dissertation, Oxford University, 1979, pp. 304–7.
10. V.F.S. Sit, S.L. Wong, and T.S. Kiang, *Small Scale Industry in a Laissez-Faire Economy: A Hong Kong Case Study* (Hong Kong: Centre of Asian Studies, University of Hong Kong, 1979), pp. 337, 339–49.
11. D.R. Deglopper, "Doing Business in Lukang," in W. Willmott, ed., *Economic Organization in Chinese Society* (Stanford: Stanford University Press, 1972), p. 319.
12. M. Freedman, *Chinese Family and Marriage in Singapore* (London: Her Majesty's Stationery Office, 1957), p. 88.
13. S.L. Wong, "Industrial Entrepreneurship and Ethnicity," op. cit., pp. 138–39.
14. See Y.C. Jao, *Banking and Currency in Hong Kong: A Study of Postwar Financial Development* (London: Macmillan, 1974), p. 216.
15. S.M. Liang, (*The Essence of Chinese Culture*) (Taipei: Zhengzhong Bookstore, 1963 [1949]), pp. 78–95. See also X.T. Fei, (*Rural China*) (Shanghai: The Observers Society, 1947), pp. 22–30.
16. J. England and J. Rear, *Industrial Relations and Law in Hong Kong* (Hong Kong: Oxford University Press, 1981), p. 94.
17. S.L. Wong, "Industrial Entrepreneurship and Ethnicity," op. cit., pp. 161–72.
18. H.A. Turner et al., *The Last Colony: But Whose? A Study of the Labour Movement, Labour Market and Labour Relations in Hong Kong* (Cambridge: Cambridge University Press, 1980), p. 198.
19. S.N. Chau, "Family Management in Hong Kong," *Hong Kong Manager* 6, 1970, p. 21.
20. R.H. Silin, *Leadership and Values: The Organization of Large Scale Taiwanese Enterprises* (Cambridge: Harvard University Press, 1976), p. 66.
21. G.G. Hamilton, "Patriarchalism in Imperial China and Western Europe: A Revision of Weber's Sociology of Domination," *Theory and Society* 13, 1984, p. 418.
22. V.F.S. Sit, S.L. Wong, and T.S. Kiang, *Small Scale Industry in a Laissez-Faire Economy*, op. cit., p. 353; J.L. Epsy, "The Strategy of Chinese Industrial Enterprise in Hong Kong," unpublished D.B.A. dissertation, Harvard University, 1970, p. 174; and S.L. Wong, "Industrial Entrepreneurship and Ethnicity," op. cit., p. 274.
23. See, for example, A.Y.C. King and P.J.L. Man, "The Role of the Small Factory in Economic Development: The Case of Hong Kong," occasional paper (Hong Kong: Social Research Centre, The Chinese University of Hong Kong, 1974), pp. 41–42; and S.K. Lau, "Employment Relations in Hong Kong: Traditional or Modern?" in T. Liu, R.P.L. Lee, and V. Simons, eds., *Hong Kong: Economic, Social and Political Studies in Development* (New York: M.E. Sharpe, 1979), pp. 71–72.
24. M. Freedman, "The Family in China, Past and Present," in G.W. Skinner, ed., *The Study of Chinese Societies: Essays by Maurice Freedman* (Stanford: Stanford University Press, 1979), p. 243.
25. See A.H. Smith, *Village Life in China* (New York: Fleming H. Revell Co.,

1899), p. 328; and D.R. Deglopper, "Doing Business in Lukang," op. cit., p. 318. For cases of disgruntled kinsmen-employees, see S. Rosen, *Mei Foo Sun Chuen: Middle-Class Chinese Families in Transition* (Taipei: Orient Cultural Service, 1976), p. 197.

26. V.F.S. Sit, S.L. Wong, and T.S. Kiang, *Small Scale Industry in a Laissez-Faire Economy*, op. cit., p. 355. For a similar finding in Singapore, see S.Y. Lee, "Business Elites in Singapore," in P.S.J. Chen and H. Evers, eds., *Studies in ASEAN Sociology: Urban Society and Social Change* (Singapore: Chopman Enterprises, 1978), p. 39.

27. J.L. Epsy, "The Strategy of Chinese Industrial Enterprise in Hong Kong," op. cit., p. 174.

28. V.F.S. Sit, S.L. Wong, and T.S. Kiang, *Small Scale Industry in a Laissez-Faire Economy*, op. cit., p. 337; and S.L. Wong, "Industrial Entrepreneurship and Ethnicity," op. cit., p. 287.

29. See D.S. Landes, "French Business and the Business Man: A Social and Cultural Analysis," in H.G.J. Aitkins, ed., *Explorations in Enterprise* (Cambridge: Harvard University Press, 1967), pp. 185–97.

30. For a more extended analysis of the Chinese family firm, see S.L. Wong, "The Chinese Family Firm: A Model," *British Journal of Sociology* 36:1, 1985, pp. 58–72.

31. See Lung-sheng Sung, "Property and Family Division," in E.M. Ahern and H. Gates, ed., *The Anthropology of Taiwanese Society* (Stanford: Stanford University Press, 1981), pp. 361–78.

32. S. Shiga, "Family Property and the Law of Inheritance in Traditional China," in D.C. Baxbaum, ed., *Chinese Family Law and Social Change* (Seattle: University of Washington Press, 1978), pp. 128–33.

33. M. Wolf, "Child Training and the Chinese Family," in M. Freedman, ed., *Family and Kinship in Chinese Society* (Stanford: Stanford University Press, 1970), p. 53.

34. For samples of such contracts, see Economic Research Institute of the Shanghai Academy of Social Sciences, *Heng Feng Schachang di Fasheng Fazhan he gaizo (The Establishment, Development and Transformation of the Heng Feng Cotton Spinning Mill)* (Shanghai: Shanghai People's Press, 1958), p. 35; and Shanghai Economic Research Institute of the Chinese Academy of Sciences, and Economic Research Institute of the Shanghai Academy of Social Sciences, *Nanyang Xiongdi Yancao Gongsi Shiliao (Historical Materials on the Nangang Brothers Tobacco Company)* (Shanghai: Shanghai People's Press, 1958), pp. 11–12.

35. S.K. Lau uses the term "utilitarian familism" to account for Hong Kong's political stability which is not quite the same as the term "entrepreneurial familism." See S.K. Lau, *Society and Politics in Hong Kong* (Hong Kong: The Chinese University Press, 1982), pp. 67–85.

36. J. Salaff, *Working Daughters of Hong Kong: Filial Piety or Power in the Family?* (Cambridge: Cambridge University Press, 1981), pp. 263–65.

37. See G. Hofstede, *Culture's Consequences: International Difference in Work-Related Values* (Beverly Hills: Sage Publications, 1980), pp. 314–19; R.P.L. Lee, "Organizational Size, Structural Differentiation and the Men at the Top," occasional paper (Hong Kong: Social Research Centre, The Chinese University of Hong Kong, 1972); and S.G. Redding and G.L. Hicks, "Culture, Causation and Chinese Management," Mong Kwok Ping Management Data Bank Working Paper (Hong Kong: Department of Management Studies, University of Hong Kong, 1983), p. 8.

38. A.Y.C. King and D.H.K. Leung, "The Chinese Touch in Small Industrial Organizations," occasional paper (Hong Kong: Social Research Centre, The Chinese University of Hong Kong, 1975), p. 34. See also J.A. Young, "Interpersonal Networks and Economic Behaviour in a Chinese Market Town," unpublished Ph.D. dissertation, Stanford University, 1971, p. 195.
39. S.L. Wong, "Industrial Entrepreneurship and Ethnicity," op. cit., pp. 206–10.
40. D.J. Munro, *The Conception of Man in Early China* (Stanford: Stanford University Press, 1969), pp. 1–22.
41. See T.T. Chu, "Chinese Class Structure and Its Ideology," in J.K. Fairbank, ed., *Chinese Thought and Institutions* (Chicago: University of Chicago Press, 1957); and P.T. Ho, *The Ladder of Success in Imperial China: Aspects of Social Mobility, 1368–1911* (New York: Columbia University Press, 1962), pp. 1–91.
42. See S.L. Wong, "Industrial Entrepreneurship and Ethnicity," op. cit., p. 205; and H. Kahn, *World Economic Development: 1979 and Beyond* (Boulder, CO: Westview Press, 1979), p. 381.
43. H.D.R. Baker, *Chinese Family and Kinship*, op. cit., p. 133.
44. On family solidarity, see S. Millar, *The Biosocial Survey in Hong Kong* (Canberra: Centre of Resources and Environmental Studies, Australian National University, 1979), p. 150; R.L. Moore, "Modernization and Westernization in Hong Kong: Patterns of Culture Change in an Urban Setting," unpublished Ph.D. dissertation, University of California, 1981, p. 237; and S.K. Lau, *Society and Politics in Hong Kong*, op. cit., p. 74. On ancestor worship, see J.T. Myers, "Traditional Chinese Religious Practices in an Urban-Industrial Setting: The Example of Kwun Tong," in A.Y.C. King and R.P.L. Lee, eds., *Social Life and Development in Hong Kong* (Hong Kong: The Chinese University Press, 1981), p. 279. On filial piety, see D.C. Chaney and D.B.L. Podmore, *Young Adults in Hong Kong: Attitudes in a Modernizing Society* (Hong Kong: Centre of Asian Studies, University of Hong Kong (Hong Kong, 1973), p. 60; and C.F. Ikels, "Urbanization and Modernization: The Impact on Aging in Hong Kong," unpublished Ph.D. dissertation, University of Hawaii, 1978, p. 143.
45. J. Salaff, *Working Daughters of Hong Kong*, op. cit., p. 271.
46. See for example, M.L. Cohen, "Developmental Process in the Chinese Domestic Group," in M. Freedman, ed., *Family and Kinship in Chinese Society*, op. cit., pp. 21–36; and A.P. Wolf and C.S. Huang, *Marriage and Adoption in China, 1845–1945* (Stanford: Stanford University Press, 1980).
47. P.S. Sangren, "Traditional Chinese Corporation: Beyond Kinship," *The Journal of East Asian Studies* 43:3, 1984, p. 411.
48. M. Freedman, *Chinese Lineage and Society: Fukien and Kwangtung* (London: The University of London, The Athlone Press, 1971), pp. 158–59.
49. M. Weber, *The Religion of China*, op. cit., p. 95.
50. M.J. Levy, Jr., *The Family Revolution in Modern China*, op. cit., p. 361.
51. M.J. Levy, Jr., *Modernization: Latecomers and Survivers* (New York: Basic Books, 1972), p. 24.
52. M. Elvin, *The Pattern of the Chinese Past: A Social and Economic Interpretation* (Stanford: Stanford University Press, 1973), pp. 298–316; and M. Elvin, "Why China Failed to Create an Endogenous Industrial Capitalism: A Critique of Max Weber's Explanation," *Theory and Society* 13, 1984, pp. 379–91.
53. For a concise appraisal of the contemporary economic role of the Chinese in Southeast Asia, see Yuan-li Wu, "Chinese Entrepreneurs in Southeast Asia," *American Economic Review* 73:2, 1983, pp. 112–17.
54. See, for example, J.A. Schumpeter, *Capitalism, Socialism and Democracy*, 5th

ed. (London: George Allen and Unwin, 1976), pp. 156–63; H.J. Habakkuk, "Family Structure and Economic Change in Nineteenth-Century Europe," *Journal of Economic History* 15, 1955, pp. 1–12; C.P. Kindleberger, *Economic Growth in France and Britain, 1851–1950* (Cambridge: Harvard University Press, 1964), pp. 115–34; and D. Bell, *The End of Ideology* (New York: The Free Press, 1962), pp. 39–45.

55. See, for example, A. Francis, "Families, Firms and Finance Capital: The Development of U.K. Industrial Firms with Particular Reference to Their Ownership and Control," *Sociology* 14:1, 1980, pp. 2–27; and M. Lisle-Williams, "Beyond the Market: The Survival of Family Capitalism in the English Merchant Banks," *British Journal of Sociology* 35:2, 1984, pp. 241–71.

56. T. Parsons and N.J. Smelser, *Economy and Society: A Study in the Integration of Economic and Social Theory* (London: Routledge and Kegan Paul, 1956), p. 289.

57. See M.J. Levy, Jr., "Contrasting Factors in the Modernization of China and Japan," in S. Kuznets, W.E. Moore, and J.J. Spengler, eds., *Economic Growth: Brazil, India, Japan* (Durham, NC: Duke University Press, 1955), pp. 496–536.

PART IV
INDIVIDUAL SOCIETIES

8

The Distinctive Features of Japanese Development: Basic Cultural Patterns and Politico-Economic Processes

Iwao Munakata

This study is an attempt to search the distinctive feature of Japanese modernization since the Meiji period. The term modernization is used to mean a complex process of social change which is brought about mainly by political and economic developments toward nation-building. This study does not presuppose that modernization is an intrinsically desirable goal for human life. Rather, it is viewed as a traditional pattern of social change which often involves serious paradoxes and fundamental ambivalences.

The basic methodology employed in this study is an interpretative cultural approach. The basic cultural patterns of Japan provide the central focus, and they will be viewed within a paradigm of comparative world views, in order to interpret the results of this study within a wider comparative perspective on modernization. This interpretative cultural approach does not, however, presuppose a mono-causational approach to development in terms of cultural values and norms; it is supplemented by a multi-causational approach which includes the functions of political and economic causes.

The Basic Cultural Patterns, Symbolic Immanentism, and Four Social Entities in Japan

The Basic Cultural Patterns

The conventional methods of describing the basic cultural patterns of Japan have been to trace them back to Confucianism, Buddhism, Shinto, or other ethical teachings. Since these studies rely mainly on written documents, the

155

cultural practices of the common people have not been directly studied. This study is instead based on field studies of the basic cultural values and norms shared by the common people in traditional sectors of Japanese society in their everyday lives.[1]

My theoretical concern here focuses on the discovery of the distinctive features of Japanese modernization within a holistic, comparative perspective, and, therefore, the characteristics of the basic cultural patterns of Japan will be explained through a paradigm of comparative world views. In this study, structural types of world views are conceptualized on the level of a "basic cultural type" or a "cultural archetype."[2] Elsewhere I have conceptualized five hypothetical types of world views which may be classified together into two basic categories—immanentistic world views and transcendental world views. Within this framework, the Japanese world view is classified as a "symbolic immanentistic type," which is structured primarily upon non-figurative symbols dispersed within nature and without human fabrications. Non-figurative, natural symbols function as vehicles mediating the "sacred" which is assumed to be residing beyond this worldly dimension. People feel the "breath of the sacred" through the expressive symbols dispersed in the surrounding natural phenomenon. These aesthetically perceived natural phenomena create deep resonance between the human spirit and the symbolic images of nature. Within this world view, shared intersubjective values proliferate in the subconscious of the people. The kinship structures perform important religious functions as symbolic vehicles. And the continuity of inseparable human souls extends through their particular links and continues into the world beyond.

In this world view, the endogenous culture can be understood as being composed of two basic symbolic strata—that of the relations between man and nature and that of the relations between man and man. The ultimate religious question is answered through the meaningful structure designed within these dual relational patterns. The first stratum involves the inseparable relation between nature and man and carries a basic religious meaning. Nature is the transmitter of "ultimacy." People working within the aesthetically embracing natural environment tend to share a cooperative religious sensibility, which in the subconscious becomes an intersubjective basis for their world view. Natural scenery is filled with aesthetically and religiously meaningful symbols but it is qualitatively incompatible with the scenery of industrial towns. The second stratum of this immanentistic world view is centered on interpersonal relations. The patterns for these relations are contained within the first stratum, within man's relations to nature.

The inseparable continuity of the human soul possesses an important existential premise in providing an answer to religious inquiry. The continuity of human existence in this world, however, is not restricted to this-worldly relations. "Continuity relations" extend to the souls of the deceased and even to every living object in nature. Relations with the souls of the deceased continue until the date of the "toburai-age," the final memorial service for the dead. The dual cyclical patterns of the flow of souls of the living and dead are recognized in Japanese tradition as belief in the transmigration of souls in accordance with the Indian Buddhist tradition. However, according to Japanese belief patterns, the transmigration of souls is not believed to possess an individualistic substance; 33 or 50 years after death, the soul is assimilated into the great body of souls within nature.[3]

In a world view where the intersubjective understanding of the human soul's nonindividualistic nature is shared, it is consciously or unconsciously presupposed that the individual human being does not exist eternally. Obviously, desolateness and sorrow are experienced when confronting separation by death, however, it is inevitably accepted that human beings are destined to return to nature. Accordingly, the interpersonal relations in the second stratum continue until the re-fusion of souls with nature, at which time the relation precedes from this secondary relation to the primary relation between nature and man.

Symbolic Immanentism

In this study the value patterns of symbolic immanentism are used as "ideal-types" of the endogeneous culture to provide a basic interpretative orientation on an analysis of Japanese development. Although the actual developmental process has often deviated from them, these ideal-type concepts are useful for our interpretative approach. These value patterns have originated from the nature-man relations and the man-man relations and have been shared and transmitted by the common people in their everyday life.

The value sensibilities that support these value patterns are "feelings of life originating from nature" (*shizen seimei kan*), "feelings of an aesthetically symbolized eternity" (*biteki eien kan*), "feelings of a fusion of man with nature by the emptying of human ego" (*shizen gōitsu kan*), and "feelings of symbolic continuity among all living things including human beings" (*renzoku kyosei kan*).[4] They are values which are phenomenological expressions of the pure a priori value sensibilities in the natural and social environment. On the level of social interactions, these intersubjective value sensibilities appear in three normative patterns: continuity, cooperation, and equality.

The first normative pattern, continuity, is primarily a development nurtured by the kinship structure. The concept of continuity encompasses the total range of human existence from birth to the return to nature-death. This value sensibility regarding the existence of the self is accepted unconsciously. As an exemplary definition, it may be said that in this world view no fundamental distinction between the self and others exists. Accordingly, no absolute separation and confrontation in interpersonal relations exists in the subconscious.

The normative pattern of cooperation can be established under circumstances where people require mutual assistance to attain a specific goal. Cooperative relations are supported by the same normative patterns which exist in continuity relations. However, there is a tendency for the values expressed in cooperative actions to be oriented more toward specific goals and to be relatively short-term.

The third normative pattern, equality, springs from the ideal-type world view based on symbolic immanentism. It is assumed that all human beings, born of and returning to "motherly" nature, are fundamentally equal despite their divergent roles in daily life.

As we have noted, these three normative patterns are nothing but "ideal-typical" conceptual constructs. In the actual social process, the combination of these norms tends to function in highly flexible patterns. For instance, the norm of cooperation might increase group solidarity, but it also encourages inter-group conflict. When a stratified power structure is established by a ruling group, the normative pattern of equality will be segmented within particular social groups. Furthermore, the natural value sensibilities could be ideologically manipulated by the ruling-elite for their political purpose. In spite of all these possibilities of deviance from the ideal-typical patterns, the deep-rooted resilience of the basic cultural orientation makes these ideal-type norms an important aspect of our interpretative cultural approach to Japanese development.

Four Social Entities

In order to apply the aforementioned normative patterns to the interpretative cultural approach to Japanese development, the four types of social entities must be differentiated. The social entities are categorized as: primary, secondary, functional, and ideological. The primary social entity consists of various kinship organizations, such as extended or nuclear families. The secondary social entity is found in various traditional communities, such as a village which is centered around a shrine to the ancestors of Honke (the head family) of the village. Those entities of the third type, called here "functional social entities," perform specific social functions, such as economic, medical, and educational ones. The fourth, ideological social entity, refers to the national political system. The cultural functions of the symbolic immanentistic world view in the process of Japanese development will be seen to be relatively different in each of these four social entities.

Transferability of Endogeneous Cultural Values

From the point of view of an interpretative cultural approach, another important concept is the transferability of endogeneous cultural values. The term "transferability" means that a person may move from one organizational structure to others by carrying within his personality certain internalized values, perception patterns, and modes of behavior which have been preserved within a symbolic immanentistic variety of cultural worlds. For instance, when a person, in the process of modernization, moves from his rural community to an urban industrial plant, he tends to perceive and to identify this new social environment as if it were fundamentally similar to the place he left. The industrial plant is not conceived as being an entirely different social environment from his past social entities. The modernized industrial plant tends to be consciously or often unconsciously perceived by the incoming workers from the rural areas as a "primary or secondary social entity.". Therefore, the principles of a modernized bureaucracy, such as rational, impersonal, and contractually delimited role-performance, are not compatible with the expectation of these workers.

Although there are fundamental differences in the cultural and intellectual heritage, the philosophical basis of the concept of an immanentist world view and the transferability of a person's perceptually structured reality can be traced back partly to the early phenomenological study of Franz Brentano (1838–1917). The symbolic structures of immanentistic world view can be viewed as meaningful constructions of "intentional objects."[5] The word "intentional" as used by Brentano is synonymous with "immanent" and stands in contrast to "transcendent."[6] The amplification of these conceptual usages may suggest that the symbolic immanentistic world view is constructed by perceptive responses to the existing natural world without any direct transcendental interventions. The "intentional" relations to the world are symbolically formed by using immanent objects. Man-nature relations and man-man relations are central symbolic vehicles in the formulation of a world view. In contrast to the transcendental world view, the possibility of transferability is much higher in a symbolic immanentist world view. There is no need for "conversion" in the transfer from one world to another within a symbolic immanentist world.

The concept of transferability can be divided into two levels: "natural transferability" and "ideological transferability." The former can be seen within the primary and secondary social entities where the value patterns of symbolic immanentism will be spontaneously transmitted intergenerationally over time. In the early phase of modernization, many new "functional social entities" developed, such as industrial and commercial organizations. Large-scale population inflows from rural areas into these new functional social entities occurred. These population movements take a form of natural transferability. Without any particular "indoctrination" by entrepreneurs, the new employees of the corporation tend to identify their work organizations as a social entity which carries within it composite elements of symbolic immanentism.

The patterns of ideological transferability can be found in the early phase of Japanese political development since the middle of the nineteenth century. In contrast to natural transferability, ideological transferability occurs through deliberate political education. After the Meiji Restoration in 1868, the new government leaders devoted their efforts to the national compulsory educational system in order to implant in the minds of the people the new image of the family-state under the authority of the emperor. This ideology was called *kokutai-no-hongi* (the fundamental principle of nation). Although as early as the seventh century a centralized government had been established, the real political authority had been often entrusted to various political and military leaders. When the restoration of political power from the Tokugawa feudal ruler to the emperor Meiji took place in 1867, it became imperative that the new government leaders again engage in thorough political education. The concept of ideological transferability is the process of deliberate construction and propagation of new national ideology by the new ruling group. In this process certain basic value elements of symbolic immanentism are eliminated and are replaced by new ideological elements such as a politicized mythology. Instilling a new ideology through political education leads to the legitimatization of the power structure.

The primary and secondary social entities have been structured by giving symbolic meaning to particular blood relations found within a particular area of land. In the transfer process of culture to a "functional social entity," such as an industrial corporation, the land tie is left behind. Symbolic blood relations are partially transformed and carried over into the new work-places.

In the economic arena the patterns of natural transferability are seen to be the predominant feature of value transfer. In this process the transferable quality of the value components in the symbolic immanentism play latent but important functions. We may be able to say that one of the distinctive features of Japanese development could be found in the patterns of the upward diffusion process of the basic endogenous cultural values. In the political arena, the striking feature of the transferability pattern is the active and deliberate roles played by the political leaders to construct a new ideology and propagate it among the people. In an "ideological social entity," a nation-state, the symbolic functions of the kinship structure and the land ties were ideologically magnified by the politicized mythology of the family-state.

Although it is indispensable to view Japanese development through the interpretative cultural approach, it is also quite obvious that the process of Japanese modernization could not be explained simply by focusing on the transferability of basic cultural patterns. The roles of political, economic, and military leaders, and their accompanying groups, also had important functions in bringing the latent cultural potentials into play in the process of national development. Further, it is important to pay close attention to the legacy of the Tokugawa feudal system which had ruled Japan for 264 years through its highly centralized system of government. The direct impact of the powerful Western nations was another situational cause which contributed to mobilizing the deeply static Tokugawa society into becoming a modernized industrial nation.

The early phase of Japanese modernization occurred within a comparatively short period of time. The rapid transformations of the traditional feudal system into a modernized nation proceeded without involving the process of "individualization" of the people through breaking out of the cohesive traditional culture. By the functions of "natural" and "ideological transferability," Japan was modernized without destroying basic archetype cultural values.

Symbolic Features of Political and Economic Development Since Meiji Era

In order to describe the distinctive characteristics of Japanese development within a broader historical and cultural perspective, the following three historical episodes will be summarized: the transfer of political power from the Tokugawa feudal government to the Meiji government; the Meiji Constitution as the central symbol of new national integration; and the development of an absolutist ideology and the way toward the authoritarian state. In addition, the ongoing transformation of the political system and current economic development will be discussed.

The Transfer of Political Power from the Tokugawa Feudal Government to the Meiji Government

Since the middle of the eighteenth century, the Tokugawa feudal system began to show signs of disintegration. The political path toward the restoration of imperial rule in 1868 was a complex process filled with dramatic individual political personalities. Tokugawa Keiki, the last shogun of the feudal government, was confronted simultaneously with two different political pressures. First, he faced the uncompromising demands of Chōshū and Satsuma feudal clans to transfer his political power to the new imperial regime. Second, there was consistent pressure from the Western nations to open the country to foreign trade after more than 200 years of isolation. Although limited in scale, several bloody wars were fought by the stubborn conservative feudal groups against the revolutionary troops. Political bargaining and compromises were made, and the transfer of political power was finally carried out. The spread of the local conflicts into a fatal nationwide disaster was narrowly avoided.

During the turmoil in 1867, Tokugawa Keiki had to contend with an extremely precarious political situation. First of all, he had to persuade his faithful, but indignant vassals to accept his determination to transfer his ruling power to the new regime.

On October 12, 1867, two days before the restoration of imperial rule, Keiki spoke in earnest of his policy, which was based on his religious convictions, to a large assembly of the feudal lords.[7] It was a long, persuasive speech. He started by saying that his government had lost the political power necessary to effectively control all the feudal clans, and that his government could not effectively cope with the difficult problems deriving from newly developed diplomatic relations with the Western nations. Then, after officially confirming the traditional legitimacy of imperial rule, he mentioned to his lords that the political power once entrusted to the Tokugawa family should not be "privatized" by his kin group. Rather, it had to be returned to the emperor in order to restore national unity, which was the most important issue at the time of national crisis. During his highly political speech, Keiki confessed his belief that the will of the ancestral souls of the past Tokugawa family vehemently supported his determination.

Analyzing Keiki's long and complex statement is a difficult and time-consuming task. But what can be drawn from it at first glance is the fact that his speech contains a prudent and carefully sorted out political judgment. But, his address comprises a personal religious view which could be traced back to the value patterns and social norms that had been firmly preserved within the traditional primary social entity.

On October 14, 1867, after receiving overwhelming support from his subjects, Tokugawa Keiki succeeded in freeing himself from the complicated political burden: the prolonged ruling power of the Tokugawa family was finally returned to the Emperor Meiji. In spite of the complex political drama, the basic cultural value patterns were unchanged. Ideological challenges and counter-challenges were not exchanged among the participants. On the contrary, the traditional cultural values and the political mythology were reconfirmed and reinforced through the political actors' performances. Therefore, the transfer of political power in the Meiji restoration could not be viewed simply as a revolution caused only by the power struggles in the "secular" political arena. In the inseparable diffusions and dynamics of political as well as religio-cultural elements in the crisis-bound situation, we get a glance of the distinctive feature of Japanese development.

The Meiji Constitution as the Central Symbol
of the New National Unification

The Meiji Constitution represents a basic symbolic feature of the political system of post-feudal Japan. After Iwakura returned from a study tour of Europe, an imperial edict was issued on September 7, 1875, to order the preparation of a new constitution. After long and fervent preparation, the Meiji Constitution was finally promulgated on February 11, 1889. In 1881, in the first stage of the framing of the constitution, Ōkuma Shigenobu, one of the leading political figures in the Meiji government, proposed a constitutional model based on the British parliamentary monarchy. However, his proposal was bitterly opposed by Iwakura and Itō as a plan incompatible with Japanese tradition. In 1882, the government mission for the study of constitutional systems in European countries was organized by Itō Hirobumi, Itō Miyoji, Iwakura Tomomi, and others. They visited Bismarck in Germany and met the constitutional scholars Rudolf von Gneist and Albert Mosse. In Austria, Itō called on Lorenz von Stein, professor of law at Vienna University. Stein explained the political institutions in England, France, and Germany. Itō was deeply impressed by his wide knowledge and moderate view.[8] Upon returning from his tour, Itō and Iwakura began to study with Inoue Kowashi, Itō's closest adviser in the framing of the constitution, on the fundamental principle for the constitutional government in Japan. They decided to use the parliamentary monarchy of the Prussian model. But their central problem was to find a way to incorporate the historical peculiarities of Japan into a constitutional framework of a parliamentary monarchy. In 1878, Hermann Roesler, a German scholar in the fields of economic science and law, was hired by the Japanese government as a legal adviser and became a collaborator of Itō and Inoue. As a trusted adviser, Roesler played an important role in the shaping of the final version of the Constitution.[9] Roesler's proposals were generally accepted by Itō and Inoue, although they disagreed with him on one fundamental point.[10] This concerned Article I of the constitution; an article that finally read: ''The Empire of Japan shall be reigned over and governed by a line of Emperors unbroken for ages eternal.'' A similar expression will also be found in the first paragraph of the Preamble of the constitution: ''Having, by virtue of the glories of our Ancestors, ascended the Throne of a lineal succession unbroken for ages eternal. . . . The rights of sovereignty of the State, we have inherited from our Ancestors, and we shall bequeath them to our descendants.''

This article contains "religious" elements that are rooted in the tradition of ancestral worship and have been primarily preserved and transmitted through the functions of the primary and secondary social entities. However, the new mythological wording was added to make sacred the origin of the line of emperors. As we have noted, in the primary social entity the ancestor's souls were believed to return again to the "great spiritual entity" 33 or 50 years after death. Then, the individuality of human souls was supposed to disappear. The line of kinship fused into an invisible spiritual universe which was felt to exist within nature. However, in order to make sacred and preserve the monopolistic sovereignty in the line of emperors, the particularistic mythological explanation was employed to respond to the political needs of the Meiji government. The traditional structural elements and value patterns of the primary and secondary social entities were partially transferred into the constitution, but at the same time, the new ideological elements, derived from a politicized folk mythology, were added to it to establish the firm legitimacy of the imperial rule. This religio-political system was later called the Kokutai ideology. The literal translation of Kokutai is "body of the nation," which means the entire structure of the nation or "national entity." They conceived that the Kokutai ideology was the only culturally adaptable principle for the unification of the Japanese nation. Article I of the Meiji Constitution was a concrete expression of this ideology.

On June 18, 1888, Itō Hirobumi made a speech in the Privy Council on the fundamental idea underlying the Meiji Constitution. He emphasized the following points: (1) the indispensable function of the religio-political ethos which could provide the integrative core for the whole national political system; (2) the fact that, in European countries, traditional religion had played an important role in integrating the national system; (3) the fact that, in Japan, the function of religion had traditionally been too weak to unite the nation— Buddhism had flourished once in the past, but had already declined, and Shinto had been transmitting the ancestors' moral teachings, but was too weak to provide a source of national unity; and (4) the fact that only the traditional authority of the Imperial House could generate the ethos for the national unification of Japan.[11]

An analysis of the Meiji Constitution suggests a pattern to the distinctive features of Japanese development. As Itō had emphasized, the Meiji leaders were sensitive enough to recognize the necessity of mobilizing the basic cultural values shared among the common people in their everyday lives. They paid close attention to the function of the primary and secondary social entities as potential political resources. However, they also attempted a political modification of the folk mythology to construct a national ideology. In the process of framing the Meiji Constitution and programming of the national educational system to "evangelize" the Kokutai ideology, we see an example of the functions of "ideological transferability." The Kokutai ideology was a complex product synchronistically constructed by archetype cultural values and politically amplified folk mythology. Thus, there exists some parallelism between the symbolic structures of the primary and secondary social entities and the ideologically constructed nation-state under the Meiji government. The new national ideology as exemplified in the Meiji Constitution functioned positively to unify the new nation in a relatively short period of time in defense against the pressures exerted by the Western nations.

However, the political manipulation of the "sacred" symbolic structure soon produced an ideologically self-enclosed political culture. The politicization of the mythology eventually resulted in the formation of an absolutistic nation. We may perhaps be able to say that if the Diet and the political parties were able to function properly by taking advantage of rights and power guaranteed by the Meiji Constitution, the political tragedy of the 1930s could have been avoided. However, since the political culture of the nation was changing so rapidly within such a short period of time, active participation of the common people in the new national political process might have been extremely difficult. The Meiji Constitution was a remarkable product of a joint effort by German scholars and the Meiji political leaders. The main legal structure of the Meiji Constitution, however, was not framed through the direct political experience of the Japanese people, but was a model of parliamentary monarchy urgently imported from the West. The historical development of Japan shows that various political uprisings and movements derived from the endogenous cultural roots were in fact much more powerful, especially in the period of national crisis, than the mere functions of the political parties and the Diet, which were based on the imported constitutional structure.

*The Development of an Absolutist Ideology
and the Way Toward an Authoritarian State*

Although the political reorganization by the Meiji leaders was an emergency countermeasure in the face of a national and international crisis, the greater part of their immediate political objectives were achieved. These were the unification of the nation, the preservation of political independence, the peaceful settlement of the unequal treaty, and the encouragement for the development of basic industries.

In 1869, the new social ranks composed of *Kazoku* (peerage), *Shizoku* (samurai descendant) and *Heimin* (commoner) were proposed. The plan for the vocational assistance for samurai descendants was proposed by Iwakura in 1881.[12] In order to stabilize the new political order, his plan was to create a new middle class of samurai descendants. The policy of recruiting the well-trained bureaucrats from the ex-samurai group in the feudal government was actively promoted by Itō and Inoue. They also proposed the open peerage system. On July 7, 1884, the Peerage Ordinance, which created five ranks—prince, marquis, count, viscount, and baron—was promulgated. Many former *daimyo* in the fuedal government, ex-samurai bureaucrats and commoners of special merit, were conferred the ranks of peerage. Following the gradual reinstatement of his public status, the former shogun, Tokugawa Keiki, was conferred the highest rank, prince, in June 1902.[13]

In spite of the successful transfer of governing power, the establishment of the new political regime, and the achievements of the initial political purposes, the Meiji government soon confronted difficult political dilemmas. The first difficulty was derived from the legal structure of the Meiji Constitution. The role of the mythology-based "sacred" sovereignty of the emperor was a highly ambiguous one in the constitutional power structure. In the constitution, the emperor's divine power was not unlimited. His judgment had always to be countersigned by a cabinet minister. The government was in fact operated according to the views of the cabinet.

In the Meiji Constitution, the cabinet system was instituted as a transcendent cabinet which was responsible only to the emperor.[14] Consequently, under this constitutional system political leaders were able to enforce their policies in the name of the emperor's unbridled authority.

The danger of this dualistic political system was that the symbolic authority frequently became the object of political maneuvers by various interest groups. Under this "sacred" political authority, political power is likely to be monopolized by a prestigious group which closely encircles the emperor. Any political movements among the people which challenge the vested interests of the ruling group will easily be suppressed. The inevitable political stagnation will invite more radical political reactions from unsatisfied groups.

Furthermore, the emperor's special prerogatives on the supreme command of the military in the constitution opened a channel for the military to intervene directly in national politics. The emperor's command over the army and navy depended solely upon his personal sanction and was beyond the advisory authority of the ministers. Since the emperor did not usually exercise decision-making power, the advice rendered directly by the military was consequently accepted. Thus, the military had a constitutionally guaranteed channel to influence national policy.

A second dilemma was derived from a broader social basis. Once the military took over political hegemony of national politics in the 1930s, Japan was transformed into an absolutistic military state. Although the historical study on the rise of the military cannot be pursued here, the following point falls along the line of our main theoretical concerns.

One of the latent social causes which invited the rise of the military in national politics can be found in the establishment of the new prestigious group after the Meiji Restoration. Many political leaders who were once lower-class samurai in the local feudal clans were raised to the peerage along with many former *daimyo* and the newly rising industrialists. Thus, the new political establishment began to take shape soon after the restoration. Although the reformative policies of the Meiji government encouraged the rapid development of basic industries, many farmers, especially peasants, were left behind. The land and tax reform enforced by the Meiji government since 1875 imposed a heavy burden on the peasants. Already in 1876, several peasant riots had been recorded and protest movements had spread into Gumma and Saitama prefectures during 1882–86. The gradual marching of the military into the center of national politics was a complex phenomenon, but widespread political indignation among the discriminated peasants provided a ground for the military to intervene into the power structure of the prestigious ruling group. When the military took over political control of the nation, the provisions of the original Meiji Constitution that would have spurred democratic development were gradually discarded. [15] The nationalist philosophers and the military leaders together formed the mythological root of the Meiji Constitution.

Looking back at the history of Japanese development, we can see that the transfer of political power from the Tokugawa feudal government to the Meiji government was successfully executed, and that in the early developmental phase, the Meiji government achieved its main political objects.

The construction of the new ''ideological social entity,'' the unified nation-state, by the Meiji leaders was accomplished through the infusion of the folk mythology into the parliamentary monarchy of the Western model. However, the latent structural dilemma which was inherent in the Meiji political system was gradually manifested in the course of later historical development. When the original structure of ''ideological social entity'' in the form of the Meiji parliamentary monarchy was transformed into ''absolute constitutional monarchy'' by mixing within it a ''sacred'' political dogma, the whole political establishment was ideologically ''frozen,'' and the national political entity was transformed into an absolute, inviolable, ''sacred'' entity.

With the intensification of national ideological control, the autonomous functions of the primary, secondary, and functional social entities were largely controlled by the authoritarian government. Under the national policy of mobilizing all these social entities toward the nationalistic movement, many of them conformed to or actively supported the government policy. However, it would be an oversimplification to visualize whole social entities as being completely infused in this absolutist ideological control. Many people who were living in the primary and secondary social entities had several secret ways to evade and resist the authoritarian military controls during this period. Generally speaking, however, the function of the political system, consisting of the primary, secondary, and functional social entities existing within the symbolic immanentistic culture, indicated a high conformity to the absolutist ideological control of the national goverment during the period of the political crisis. The "ideological social entity," as concretized in the Meiji political system, which was the product of the mixture of the traditional basic culture, the folk mythology, and the Western parliamentary monarchy, exhibited highly ambivalent functions in the course of national development. In the early phase of development this system contributed remarkably to the unification of the Meiji nation-state, but in the later phase, the same system also contributed to the development of the authoritarian power structure in the form of the "sacred" absolutistic monarchy.

The Transformation of the Political System and New Economic Developments Since 1945

August 1945 marked a historic turning point in the history of the Japanese political system. The surrender of Japan required the government to transform the political structure, which had been designed by the Meiji political leaders and had been later tranformed by the nationalistic philosophers and the military into an absolutist military regime. The Meiji restoration was not a revolution against despotism and a stratified society, as the revolutions of seventeenth-century Europe had been. It was an emergency political reorganization executed by a small political group to overcome a national crisis. The ideology behind the Meiji Constitution, which identified the new nation-state as a large political family, originated from the value patterns traditionally preserved by the family and the community. A new mythological interpretation was added to legitimize the new imperial authority. When the value patterns of the primary and secondary social entities had been intentionally transferred by the Meiji leaders into the new political system, these endogenous value patterns were selectively "ideologized" in order to make them functionally adaptable to the new ideological social entity, the Meiji nation-state.

In the process of "ideologization," these value-patterns were transferred "upward" toward the power center and, after being sanctioned by a national mythology, were propagated "downward" to the people through various channels of political education. By taking these double-transfer processes, the ideological social entity was established in the form of a parliamentary monarchy.

The basis for governmental reform since 1945 was laid in the Potsdam Declaration which called for the abolition of militarism and ultranationalism, disarmament and demilitarization, the strengthening of democratic processes in governmental, economic, and social institutions, and the encouragement and support of liberal political tendencies in Japan.[16] The new constitution was enacted, and it transformed Japan into a representative parliamentary democracy, characterized by the supremacy of the legislature over the executive. The ultimate authority of the state is vested in the people. The status of the emperor was defined in Chapter I as a legal organ of the state, subject to the constitution: ''The emperor shall be the symbol of the State and of the unity of the people, deriving his position from the will of the people with whom resides sovereign power.'' Article 4 of this chapter defines the extent of the emperor's authority: ''he shall not have powers related to government.'' The power and influence of a military establishment were destroyed by Chapter 2, which renounces war and prohibits armed forces.

Through the revision of the Meiji Constitution, the mythological elements and sacred authority of the emperor were removed from the national political system. The principle of the separation of politics from religion was also achieved. The ideological shield of the sacred emperor system was removed, and the once-sacred political institutions were transformed into a secular system.

It is noteworthy that in spite of all these radical changes in the central power structure, the basic culture and institutions remained largely unchanged. Following our previous conceptual models, we are able to say that the ideological social entity was almost completely dismantled by the demilitarization policy of the Allied Forces, but the cultural feature of the primary, secondary, and functional social entities by and large remained without substantial change. This fact may well suggest that economic development in the postwar period could be analyzed by our previous approach, which was based on the principle of natural transferability of the basic cultural values into the functional social entity, which includes industrial corporations.

The natural transferability, as we have noted, means that certain internalized values, perceptions, and behavioral norms may be carried over along with the movement of a person from one social organization to another. In contrast to ideological transferability, natural transferability occurs along with social mobility without any particular intention of transmitting a person's values, perceptions, or behavioral norms.

From the point of view of the conceptual model of ''social character,'' I have used a type of personality participating in the natural transferability as the ''latent immanentist type.''[17] ''Latent'' is used to mean that, although the external lifestyle is in large measure modernized, the traditional symbolic immanentist culture is retained in a latent form. The latent immanentist type receives his childhood socialization experiences in the immanentist religious culture. The social environment of his adult years, however, is constituted not only by the world of farming and fishing villages, but also by the world of the city. The work group to which he belongs is a modernized, bureaucratic organization. Culturally speaking, these people possess a dual social character. These latent-immanentist-type employees adapt themselves to roles in the high-technology plant organizations, but at the same time, preserve traditional values and sentiments. Their work performances in Japanese industrial organizations are indicative of how deeply noted traditional culture is in the area of human relations.

As the result of the widespread "inflow functions" of natural transferability, many Japanese industrial corporations have adopted important cultural characteristics which had been traditionally preserved among the primary and secondary social entities. The "upward inflow" of the basic cultural values through the channel of natural transferability has produced several unique organizational patterns within industrial corporations. First of all, employment tends not to be considered as a purely contractual affair; instead, recruitment of an employee to an enterprise is considered more like "adopting" a new member into a family. Traditionally, the Japanese family was never limited to blood relationships alone. The social custom of adoption was practiced extensively to strengthen the family organization. This pattern of adoption seems to be continuing as an underlying custom of employment in many Japanese enterprises.[18]

Second, many employees tend to identify their enterprise as an extension of primary or secondary social entities such as the family or village community. As a natural response to employees' expectations, the lifetime employment system and a long-range comprehensive training program were instituted to create a member well adapted to an enterprise. Third, the manager is expected to perform his role within the familial atmosphere of the enterprise. The manager is not usually recruited from outside, but has grown within the enterprise. The important qualification of the manager is not to command his employees through top-down leadership, but to create consensus among them. He is expected by his employees to play the role of a good communicator. Furthermore, the manager is expected to be sensitive and to understand his employees' feelings, expectations, and intentions—if possible, even without relying upon verbal communication.[19]

All these organizational patterns, however, do not mean that relations between employees and managers in Japanese enterprises have always been peaceful and harmonious. There have been frequent disagreements, just as there are among the members of a family. In fact, many industries experienced bitter labor-management confrontations in the 1950s. During these politically turbulent years, labor-union movements were often linked with political strife. Japan's enterprise-based unions have developed out of this historical background. Since an enterprise-based union consists only of employees of the particular company, the union members are aware that improvements in employees' living standards are dependent on the prosperity of the company to which they belong. The structure of this enterprise-based union is also compatible with the principle of the enterprise-family.

An important characteristic of the dynamic functions of value transferability is that some original structural elements in the primary and secondary entities are taken out in the value-transfer process, and new organizational patterns are added in their place in the functional social entity. In the process of the value transfer from the rural family and village community to industrial corporations, the particularistic land and blood ties are eliminated.

The transferred values are recrystalized into new organizational patterns within industrial organizations. The lifetime-employment system, seniority-based wage system, enterprise-based unions, Japanese-style quality-control circle, and the suggestion system are examples of the recrystalization of endogenous cultural values into new organizational patterns in industrial corporations. The quality-control system originated primarily in the United States as a means of statistically oriented quality control. When it was introduced into Japan, its function was gradually transformed; Japanese-style quality-control circles were developed for the overall improvement of both the work process and the results. The suggestion system (*Teian Seido*) also yields important results. Various original ideas of individual employees are implemented through this system into corporate management.[20] Also, the "no-layoff" policy is another reflection of the deeply culture-bound nature of many Japanese enterprises.[21]

Structurally speaking, there are many differences among industrial organizations in Japan. However, there seems to exist some important underlying similarities. These distinctive features of the Japanese industrial system are the result of the transfer of the basic cultural patterns.

The institutionalization of modern industrial corporations in Japan has been promoted without a concomitant process of functional differentiation. Therefore, many corporations, like social organizations, contain within them various diffused institutional components, and cannot be viewed as "rationally" structured to attain the maximization of capital profits. Furthermore, some industrial corporations, like a functionally diffused social system, may transform from a functional social entity to an ideological social entity of a specific variety. There are several empirical facts which suggest the possibility of this complex transformation. For instance, one of the leading automobile corporations, Toyota, founded a shrine, *Hōkō-Jinja*, in the site of the plant in Toyota City on November 3, 1938. This shrine was dedicated to the purpose of inviting the guardian deities from the two main shrines. One is the famous Atsuta-shrine in Nagoya, which, according to ancient mythology, enshrined one of three sacred objects of worship in the Shinto tradition, the sacred sword called *Kusanagi-no-Tsurugi*. Another deity was invited from the Nangu-shrine in the Gifu prefecture, which enshrined the deity of iron. The annual company festival has been held on November 3, and all the souls of deceased former employees of Toyota are also enshrined on this day. In the annual festival of 1985, altogether 2,135 souls were enshrined. There are many other Japanese commercial and industrial corporations which have a company shrine like Toyota's. Taken together, these characteristics indicate that many corporations in contemporary Japan are functioning as highly inclusive sociocultural entities. Therefore, the introspective understanding of the meaningful functions performed by these corporative organizations must be viewed through the interpretative culture approach.

The Distinctive Features of Japanese Development

The distinctive features of Japanese development must be looked at within a broader sociocultural perspective. Preparatory to undertaking this comparative approach, I have drawn a paradigm of comparative world view and have categorically allocated the basic characteristics of the Japanese world view within this paradigmatic schema.

An important contribution to the patterns of sociocultural dynamics is found in the works of Max Weber. His well-known essay, entitled *"Die protestatische Ethik und der Geist des Kapitalismus,"* was a classic on the development of modern capitalism. From the point of view of the encompassing paradigm of comparative world view, his work can be classified as a study concerning sociocultural dynamics in the transcendental cultural world. When he wrote that "one of the fundamental elements of the spirit of modern capitalism . . . was born from Christian asceticism" and "the social activity of the Christian in the world is solely activity in majorem gloriam Dei. . . . This character is hence shared by labour in a calling which serves the mundane life of the community,"[22] he was obviously describing the causal relevance of the religious beliefs of Calvinism and other Protestant sects to the development of modern industrialism. According to the paradigm, a world view, in Weber's essay, belongs specifically to the category of incarnated transcendentalism.

As we have noted, the predominant characteristics of the Japanese world view was defined as a variety of symbolic immanentism.[23] Therefore, the patterns of the causal relevance of Japanese development must be looked at within this basic cultural world.

Many studies have been conducted on the history of thought and culture in Japan based on the written materials of Buddhism, Confucianism, and Shinto scholars, which have clarified several streams of intellectual thought toward modernity.[24] However, the cultural values shared among the common people in their everyday lives have not been sufficiently reflected in these studies. As we have noted, the value patterns preserved traditionally among the primary and secondary social entities are empirically important in understanding Japanese development. In the above-mentioned essay, Max Weber studied the value patterns expressed in Calvinism, Pietism, Methodism, and the Baptist sects. However, the value patterns shared among the common people in Japan are not traceable to written teachings. Only through direct, intensive field research can these "invisible values" be discovered and conceptualized.

Generally speaking, we may be able to say that the patterns of fluctuation in the value patterns in the basic culture of the Christian West have been fundamentally different from those which have been found in immanentistic cultural worlds like Japan. Western Christian culture has had a "transcendental reference point,"[25] although the history of European culture has indicated long-range cyclical fluctuations of basic value orientations.[26] Compared with these Western patterns, the history of basic cultural value orientations in Japan has shown a stable pattern. On the basis of this macroscopic observation of cultural change, the former may be called a "self-activating culture under a transcendental God" and the latter an "order-maintaining culture within a deified Nature." The basic relational structures on which immanentistic culture was constructed are fundamentally composed of the two patterns: man-nature relations and man-man relations. These relational structures support a system that has been traditionally grounded on an "invisible archetype value." In contrast to Western transcendentalism, this archetype value could be characterized as an a priori value orientation toward "preservation and development of organic social entities."

Within this cultural universe, the existential meaning of "self" is consciously identified, or often unconsciously taken for granted, with a particular role or range of roles in these social entities. The ethical responsibility of a person is to succeed in various roles and to work as much as he can for the development of a committed social entity. The meaning of life and death tend also to be given within this inclusive cultural framework.

In a stable, traditional community, individuals are expected to work through the ascribed roles for the preservation and development of primary and secondary social entities such as the family, an extended kin group, or the village community. In the daily lives of the rural agricultural or fishery communities, the two principal norms in interpersonal and intergroup— cooperation and competition—have been practiced interchangeably. When the villagers see that an external threat to their everyday lives is imminent, competitive relations among the villagers change quickly into cooperative relations against the external challenge. The interchange of these two norms functions on various social levels ranging from inter-village relations to international relations.

Another important, but often invisible, social norm shared among the common people has been the principle of equality. The origin of this norm derives from their "religious self-awareness" that all human beings are born from and return to the same "motherly" nature. Beyond all these norms there exists a fundamental norm of continuity. In the immanentistic world view, the deified nature-world is supposed to exist eternally. Among the common people in Japan, eschatological cultural perceptions have not been accepted. Each person is born as a mutable being and returns soon by melting into nature, the "sacred" eternal continuum. Consequently, the norm of continuity presupposes as a self-evident fact nonindividualistic selfhood. These religiously sanctioned social entities may be crystalized into various forms. The social entities derived from the symbolic immanentistic culture are highly inclusive bodies composed by the complex of this-worldly and other-worldly symbolic vehicles, including natural and fabricated objects as well as patterns of human interconnections.

The concept of value transferability is important in clarifying the dynamics of functional structures of the sociocultural system based primarily on symbolic immanentism. The distinctive features of Japanese development could be partially explained by the functions of value transferability. In the area of economic development, the employees' identification of the industrial organization as a new family or village community has been an essential condition for Japanese-style development. Here, the natural transferability has performed a crucial function: the culturally defined cognitive and motivational elements are transmitted into the enterprise by a personality, which carries a transferable perceptive image on various social realities.

In industrial enterprises, the role of managers is important for integrating the organizations, which is done by defining the enterprise as a culturally meaningful system to newly "adopted" employees. The managers usually set up well-prepared in-house educational programs, some of which include intensive training in foreign languages or even in the practice of contemplation in Zen temples. There has been no proclamation by Japanese employees about their work commitments, as in the case of Calvinist entrepreneurs as explained by Max Weber.[27] Rather they carry within them culturally internalized values and act accordingly in their work-places. This is not to say that Japanese workers are not concerned with monetary compensation or promotion within an enterprise. It is obvious, however, that the Japanese worker's commitment to his work cannot be fully understood without clarifying his deep tradition-based, cultural commitments.

In the area of political development, modern Japanese history has exhibited some intrinsic functional dilemmas. The social organizations, which are structured upon the symbolic immanentistic culture, are fundamentally segmental in their characteristics. The segmental diversifications of social entities are derived from the fact that their symbolic vehicles are primarily constituted by particularistic objects such as a local natural environment or specific interpersonal relations. Therefore, there has been an inevitable limitation on the "spacial range" of the organizations.

The ideological anguish among the Meiji political leaders was well expressed by Itō's speech in the Privy Council in June 1888. They desperately wanted a mythology that could integrate segmented and diversified political entities into a unified national system. During the long Tokugawa era, several Confucian scholars, such as Yamazaki Ansai, Hayashi Razan, and Muro Kyūsō, tried to legitimize the feudal establishment by employing the teachings of Chu Hsi (*Shushigaku*). However, their ideological positions for the feudal political establishment were challenged by other scholars of early Confucianism (*Kogaku*), such as Yamaga Sokō, Itō Jinsai, and Ogyū Sorai, and also by scholars of the early Shinto-oriented School of National Studies (*Kokugaku*), such as Kamono Mabuchi, Motoori Norinaga, and Hirata Atsutane. The shrewd political performances of the feudal government in manipulating the restless clans by a divide-and-rule policy was indicative of the fact that the feudal government could not establish effective ideological control over the clans and had to depend largely on tactical power games.

The concept of ideological transferability was used to describe the distinctive features of Japanese political development. The Meiji political leaders attempted to deliberately set up the "mythologized political ethos" to achieve national unification. The disputes between Itō, Inoue, and Roesler on the indispensability of Article I of the Meiji Constitution reflect how desperately the Japanese political leaders intended to use supra-political values for the legitimization of the power structure of the Meiji government. The transfer of political power from the Tokugawa feudal government to the Meiji government was successfully carried out. From the overall cultural point of view, this transfer of power can be viewed as an example of the transition of basic norms from competition to cooperation under threatening external pressures exerted upon the national political process by Western nations.

As stated above, the introduction of mythology into the national political arena might have been considered an "indispensable" option by the Meiji political leaders. However, the manipulation of the sacred into secular national politics sowed the seed of a serious dilemma: When the military took over political control in the 1930s, the sacred sovereignty of the emperor was used by the military and ultranational ideologists as a foundation of the absolutist nation.

From the aspect of the interpretive cultural approach, the history of Japanese development seems to indicate that the symbolic immanentistic culture was, on the whole, positively functional to economic development. However, in the area of the political development, the system has been confronted with serious functional difficulties and dilemmas. The emperor system, which had been institutionalized by the Meiji leaders, was able to unify the country, but for the further development of the political system Japan had to pass through difficult and disastrous steps toward modernization.

Finally, some recent tendencies and unanticipated social consequences of economic developments in Japan should be mentioned briefly. As a result of rapid industrialization, several important syndromes of social disintegration have become apparent. Increases in divorce, suicide (among all age groups), and social violence are striking. Urbanization and industrialization have interrupted and suspended the functions of socialization processes, which in the past transmitted the endogenous culture. The march of Japanese cultural disintegration appears to be slow but insidious. It is still difficult to predict whether this widespread structural change accompanying the destruction of symbol systems may result in the complete exhaustion of the latent cultural reservoir.

Considerable ambivalence is built into the behavior of people who are deprived of the support of their traditional culture and who have yet to grasp a new world view which includes a religious dimension. There may be some who nostalgically long for a return to traditional, immanentist, religious culture, but the difficulties of maintaining the symbolic world of the past are considerable.

Notes

1. See Munakata Iwao, "Worldview and the Concept of Self among Japanese Fishermen in the Shiranui Inland Sea Area," research paper, Series A-48 (Tokyo: Institute of International Relations for Advanced Studies on Peace and Development in Asia, Sophia University, 1984).
2. The concept of archetypes was defined and used by C.G. Jung. According to Jung, "The concept of the archetype, which is an indispensable correlate of the idea of the collective unconscious, indicates the existence of definite forms in the psyche which seem to be present always and everywhere. Mythological research calls them "motifs," . . . and in the field of comparative religion they have been defined . . . as "categories of the imagination." Jung also said that "the archetype in itself is empty and purely formal, nothing but a *facultas praeformandi*, a possibility of representation which is given a priori."

   Jung's concept of the archetype is particularly useful in interpreting and conceptualizing the structural types from the symbolic immanentistic world view. C.G. Jung, *The Archetypes and the Collective Unconscious*, R.F.C. Hull, trans. Bollingen Series XX, The Collected Works of C.G. Jung (Princeton: Princeton University Press, 1977), vol. 9, part I, pp. 42, 79.
3. Yanagida Kunio, "*Senzo no Hanashi*," in *Teihon Yanagida Kunio Shū* (Tōkyō: Chikuma Shobō, 1962), vol. 10, p. 106.
4. Munakata Iwao, "*Minamata no Naiteki Sekai no Kōzō to Henyō* (The Structure and Change in the Inner World of Minamata)," in Daikichi Irokawa, ed., *Minamata no Keiji (The Revelation of Minamata)* (Tōkyō: Chikuma Shobō, 1983), vol. 1, pp. 91–154.
5. Franz Brentano, *The Origin of our Knowledge of Right and Wrong* (London: Routledge and Kegan Paul, 1969), pp. 14, 16.
6. Herbert Spiegelberg, *The Context of the Phenomenological Movement* (The Hague: Martinus Nijhoff, 1981), pp. 14, 29.

7. Shibuzawa Eiichi, *Tokugawa Keiki Kō Den (The Life of Prince Tokugawa Keiki)* (Tōkyō: Ryumonsha, 1917), pp. 79–84.
8. Kaneko Kentarō, ed., *Itō Hirobumi Den (The Life of Itō Hirobumi)* (Tokyo: Tōseisha, 1940), pp. 285, 317.
9. Johannes Siemes, *Hermann Roesler and the Making of the Meiji State* (Tokyo: Sophia University, 1968), pp. 13–14.
10. Inada Masatsugu, *Meiji Kempō seiritsu shi (The History of the Framing of the Meiji Constitution)* (Tokyo: Yuhikaku, 1962), p. 248.
11. Shimizu Shin, *Teikoku Kempo Seitei Kaigi (The Council for the Enactment of Imperial Constitution)* (Tokyo: Iwanami, 1940), pp. 87–89.
12. Tokutomi Iichirō, *Iwakura Tomomi kō (Prince Iwakura Tomomi)* (Tōkyō: Minyūsha, 1932), pp. 266–68.
13. Shibuzawa Eiichi, *Tokugawa Keiki Kō Den*, op. cit., p. 402.
14. Although the cabinet system was instituted as the transcendent cabinet according to Roesler's suggestion, he did not realize that the Japanese leaders did not constitute an aristocracy. There still existed strong factionalism among the Meiji leaders based on their previous feudal clan system. See Joseph Pittau, *Political Thought in Early Meiji Japan* (Cambridge Massachusetts: Harvard University Press, 1969), p. 191.
15. Article XXVIII of the Meiji Constitution granted freedom of religious belief to Japanese subjects. This article presupposes that "the constitutional liberties of a people would not be complete and would lack their proper foundation without the constitutional freedom of religious belief." The Kokutai ideology prevented the actuation of the value of the Meiji Constitution.
16. Government Section, Supreme Commander for Allied Powers, *Political Reorientation of Japan, September 1945 to September 1948* (Washington, D.C.: U.S. Government Printing Office, 1949), p. 89.
17. Munakata Iwao, "Ambivalent Effects of Modernization on Traditional Folk Religion," *Japanese Journal of Religious Studies* 3:2–3, June–September, 1976, p. 114.
18. Gene Gregory, *The Logic of Japanese Enterprise* (Tokyo: Institute of Comparative Culture, Sophia University, 1982), p. 39.
19. Nakane Chie, *Japanese Society* (London: Penguin Books, 1973), p. 63.
20. Kawamata Katsuji, Chairman, Nissan Motor Co., claimed that "At Nissan Motor in 1980 approximately 1.3 million suggestions were submitted by employees, or about 24 suggestions per worker, which I interpret as a sign of vitality and concern for the company's prosperity among the entire work force." Kawamat Katsuji, "*Labor-Management Relations in Japan*," speech given at Nihon Seisansei Honbu (Japan Productivity Center), August 8, 1981 (Tokyo: Nissan Motor Co., 1981), p. 7.
21. On the "no-layoff" policy, the management of Nissan explains its view as follows: "As demand for the company's product increases when the business cycle turns up, instead of hiring more employees, the workers' overtime hours are increased. When demand decreases as the business cycle turns downward, overtime is cut. But the layoff of redundant labor . . . is not acceptable. Because of the "no-layoff policy," the overtime work of labor serves as the adjustment valve. . . . Consequently, the average overtime of the Japanese worker is inevitably longer. . . . When the company is confronted with a prolonged recession or structural depression, the salaries and various compensations of the top management and managers are first cut before the wages of the workers are reduced. If these measures are inadequate to cope with the situation, redundant labor is reas-

signed to other jobs. But if redundancy still persists, voluntary retirement is sought; and finally as a last resort, employees may be fired.'' Kawamata Katsuji, "Labor-Management Relations in Japan," op. cit., p. 4.

22. Max Weber, *"Die protestantische Ethik und der Geist des Kapitalismus,"* in *Gesammelte Aufsätze zur Religionssoziologie* (Tübingen: Verlag von J.C.B. Mohr, 1947), pp. 100, 202. (Also, Max Weber, *The Protestant Ethic and the Spirit of Capitalism,* Talcott Parsons, trans. (New York: Charles Scribner's Sons, 1952), pp. 108, 180.

23. Several Japanese scholars have expressed an interest in a transcendental god. Kaibara Ekiken, a Confucian scholar, used the concept of *Ten* (Heaven), and Hirata Atsutane, a Shinto scholar, wrote about an image of a creator God as *Ame no Minakanonushi no Mikoto.*

24. Maruyama Masao, *Nihon Seiji Shisōshi Kenky (The Study of Political Thought in Japan)* (Tokyo: University of Tokyo Press, 1952).

25. Talcott Parsons, *The Structure of Social Action* (Glencoe, IL: The Free Press, 1949), p. 552.

26. Pitirim A. Sorokin studies the patterns of fluctuation of the "cultural supersystem" in Western history. He considers the oscillation of ideational, idealistic, and sensate culture as the fundamental dymanics of Western transcendental culture; see Pitirim A. Sorokin, *Social and Cultural Dynamics* (New York: American Book Co., 1962), vol. 4, pp. 587–620.

27. Max Weber, *"Die protestantische Ethik,"* op. cit., pp. 87–128 (English translation, pp. 98–128).

9

The Distinctive Features of Taiwan's Development

Rong-I Wu

Economic development of underdeveloped countries is a very complicated process. Many books and articles have been published on this subject. However, there are still more questions than answers. And, the economic performance of the developing countries during the past thirty years has not shown a satisfactory result either in the increase in per-capita income or in growth rates. As a consequence, the gap of per-capita GNP (gross national product) between developing countries and the industrial market economies has been widening. Table 1 shows that while per-capita GNP of low-income and middle-income economies in 1982 were only $280 and $1,520 respectively, per-capita GNP of industrial market economies was as high as $11,070 in the same year.[1] The average economic growth rate of low-income economies in the years 1960-82 was 3 percent per annum, which was lower than that of industrial market economies. The economic growth rate of middle-income economies was a little higher, registering 3.6 percent per annum during the same period.

Among middle-income economies, the Republic of China on Taiwan (ROC), the Republic of Korea (ROK), Hong Kong, and Singapore—the so-called four dragons—had much higher economic growth rates than either developing or industrial market economies. Their remarkable performance in economic development has attracted worldwide attention. Since these four countries have historically faced different economic conditions, they may have different features of development. However, this chapter will be limited to examining the distinctive features of development in Taiwan.

179

TABLE 9.1
Selected Economic Indicators

	GNP PER CAPITA	
Country	1982 (U.S.$)	Average Annual Growth Rate 1960–82 (%)
Low-income countries	280	3.0
Middle-income countries	1,520	3.6
High-income oil exporters	14,820	5.6
Industrial market economies	11,070	3.3
Japan	10,080	6.1
Republic of Korea	1,910	6.6
Republic of China	2,554	6.7
Hong Kong	5,340	7.0
Singapore	5,910	7.4

Sources:
For Taiwan: *Taiwan Statistical Data Book 1984.*
For others: World Bank, *World Development Report 1984.*

Taiwan's Economic Development:
Rapid Growth and Structural Change

High Growth Rates

Economic development in Taiwan has been rapid during the past three decades. Using average annual growth rates of GNP per capita as an indicator, Taiwan's growth rate was 6.2 percent during 1952–84. This growth rate is quite high as compared with the other countries, as shown in Table 9.1. If we take into consideration only the 1962-84 period, per-capita GNP in Taiwan grew at 7 percent per annum (see Table 9.2). With a 7 percent growth rate, GNP per capita can be expected to double in ten years and quadruple in twenty years. Indeed, GNP per capita in Taiwan increased from $151 in 1961 to $3,067 in 1984. Although GNP per capita in Taiwan was still less than one-third that of the United States in 1984, it was higher than those of most non–oil exporting developing countries.

Structural Change

Another criterion used to gauge a country's economic development is the rapidity of structural change, particularly in the agricultural and industrial sectors. The share of agriculture in GDP (gross domestic product) decreases as an

TABLE 9.2
Growth in Per-Capita GNP in Taiwan, 1952–84

Period	Average Annual Increase in Per-Capita GNP (%)
1952–61	4.4
1962–70	7.1
1971–80	7.6
1981–84	5.1
1962–84	7.0
1952–84	6.2

Source:
Statistical Abstract of National Income in Taiwan Area, Republic of China (1951–1984), Directorate-General of Budget, Accounting and Statistics, Executive Yuan, March 1985.

economy continues to grow. From Table 9.3, we can see that the share of the agricultural sector in GDP declined from 32.4 percent in 1951 to only 6.5 percent in 1984, while the share of the industrial sector in GDP increased from 23.9 percent to 50.6 percent during the same period. The service sector maintained almost the same share. In other words, the declining importance of agriculture was almost matched by the increasing weight of the industry. The contribution of manufacturing is undoubtedly the most important factor in this sector. After three decades of rapid development, Taiwan has been transformed from a primarily agricultural economy to a primarily industrial one.

However, the decreasing importance of agriculture in the national economy does not imply that agricultural development has been stagnant. Actually, average agricultural product increased 2.5 percent per annum in the period 1962–84, which is quite high by any standard. While many underdeveloped countries encountered the bottleneck of development due to slow growth in agriculture, economic development in Taiwan was very rapid because the performance in the agricultural sector has been remarkable.

Rice and sugarcane have been and still are the two main agricultural products in Taiwan, where rice is the staple food. Before 1965, with a high annual population growth rate of more than 3 percent, rapid increase of rice production was essential. Moreover, rice was the second largest single export product, second only to sugar before 1960.[2] In contrast to many developing countries whose food imports absorb a portion of foreign exchange which could be used to import capital goods for industrial development, agriculture in Taiwan not only provided food to feed the rapidly growing population, but also was a source of exports earning a large sum of foreign exchange.

Another important agricultural product which has played a crucial role in the early stage of Taiwan's economic development is sugarcane. Sugar was

TABLE 9.3
The Structure and Growth of GDP in Taiwan, 1951–84

SECTOR	STRUCTURE (%)					Total 1951–84	AVERAGE ANNUAL GROWTH RATE (%)			Total 1962–84
	1951	1961	1971	1981	1984		1962–71	1972–81	1982–84	
Agriculture	32.4	27.6	13.1	7.4	6.5	−25.9	3.8	1.6	1.2	2.5
Industry	23.9	29.5	43.5	50.2	50.6	+26.7	15.2	11.1	7.3	12.4
Manufacturing	17.3	21.8	35.9	40.2	41.2	+23.9	16.9	11.2	8.5	13.3
Services	43.7	42.9	43.4	42.4	42.9	−0.8	9.6	8.7	7.3	8.9
Total	100.0	100.0	100.0	100.0	100.0	—	10.2	9.0	6.9	9.2

Source:
Statistical Abstract of National Income in Taiwan Area, Republic of China (1951–1984), Directorate-General of Budget, Accounting and Statistics, Executive Yuan, March 1985.

the most important export product before 1965. The share of sugar in total exports exceeded 50 percent before 1960 and continued to account for 24 percent in total exports in the period 1961–65. It is evident that sugar exports provided an important source for foreign exchange, which is indispensable for the import of machinery and equipment during the early period of industrialization.

Nevertheless, Taiwan's rapid economic growth was mainly a result of the rapid expansion of the industrial sector. From 1962 to 1984, growth in the industrial sector reached 12.4 percent per annum. If only the manufacturing sector is considered, the average annual growth rate was as high as 13.3 percent. The main factor behind this rapid industrial expansion was the export-oriented strategy of industrialization, which will be investigated further in the following section.

The growth in the service sector was also very fast during 1962–84, registering 8.9 percent per annum, close to that of the rate of GDP. This is the reason why the share of the service sector in GDP can be maintained at a stable level.

High Dependency on Foreign Trade

A simple method of measuring the dependence of an economy on foreign trade is to look at the ratios of export to GNP, imports to GNP, or exports plus imports to GNP. According to these measurements, the foreign dependence of Taiwan's economy increased very fast. Table 9.4 shows that the ratio of exports to GNP (X/GNP) rose from 10.2 percent in 1951 to 57.6 percent in 1984, and that the ratio of imports to GNP (M/GNP) rose from 15.0 percent to 45.4 percent during the same period. Putting these two items together, the ratio of foreign trade to GNP (X + M/GNP) rose from 25.2 percent in 1951 to

TABLE 9.4
The Ratio of Exports and Imports to GNP in Taiwan, 1951–84

Year	Ratio of Exports to GNP (X/GNP) (%)	Ratio of Imports to GNP (M/GNP) (%)	Ratio of Foreign Trade to GNP (X + M/GNP) (%)
1951	10.2	15.0	25.2
1961	13.8	21.0	34.8
1971	35.0	32.5	67.5
1981	52.5	50.4	102.9
1984	57.6	45.4	103.0

Source:
Statistical Abstract of National Income in Taiwan Area, Republic of China (1951–1984), Directorate-General of Budget, Accounting and Statistics, Executive Yuan, March 1985.

103 percent in 1984. The higher growth in trade than in production is undoubtedly the main reason behind this dependence. Due to the limitation of the domestic market in Taiwan, the international market has become both the main destination of Taiwan's products and the guarantor of rapid industrial growth. Therefore, Taiwan's economic development is a typical example of "trade-led" growth. In fact, trade can be considered the "engine of growth" in Taiwan.

Both exports and imports sustained high growth during the past three decades, though exports grew faster than imports (see Table 9.5). From 1952 to 1984, exports grew 15.1 percent per annum, while imports grew 12.5 percent. In a developing country like Taiwan, there is a relative shortage in capital and technology while labor is quite plentiful. How Taiwan exports expanded so fast during the period under study is crucial to understanding the real context of Taiwan's development. We will deal with this problem in the next section.

Another feature in merchandise trade is the significant structural change in commodities exports (see Table 9.6). In the early 1950s, crude and processed agricultural products accounted for about 90 percent of total exports. In particular, the share of sugar and rice in total exports was as high as 73 percent in the period 1952–55, while industrial products accounted for less than 10 percent of total exports in the same period. In other words, Taiwan was a primary-product exporting country during the 1950s.

The government adopted several important measures in the late 1950s and early 1960s which are considered vital to the rapid growth of exports and consequently to industrial development. Import-substitution industrialization became the predominant characteristic after the 1960s. The most important measures were probably those enacted in the 1950s to cure hyper-inflation.

TABLE 9.5
Growth Rate of Exports and Imports
in Taiwan, 1952–82
GROWTH RATE PER ANNUM
(%)

Period	Exports	Imports
1952–62	9.4	8.9
1962–71	22.7	17.9
1972–81	13.9	12.1
1982–84	12.1	6.2
1952–84	15.1	12.5

Source:
Statistical Abstract of National Income in Taiwan Area, Republic of China (1951–1984), Directorate-General of Budget, Accounting and Statistics, Executive Yuan, March 1985.

TABLE 9.6
The Structure of Exports in Taiwan, 1952–83

Product	PERCENTAGE OF TOTAL EXPORTS			
	1952–55	1961–65	1971–75	1981–83
Crude Agricultural Products	19.6	16.7	5.9	2.0
Rice	14.6	5.8	0.1	0.3
Banana	3.7	6.2	0.7	0.1
Processed Agricultural Products	71.1	39.3	10.3	5.4
Sugar	58.6	24.0	3.9	0.4
Canned food	3.0	8.1	3.2	0.8
Tea	6.1	2.5	0.4	0.1
Industrial Products	9.3	44.1	83.8	92.6
Textile products	1.2	15.8	30.0	21.2
Electrical machinery & apparatus	0.1	1.5	16.4	18.5
Plastic articles	0	0	5.1	7.0
Metal manufactures	0.5	0.9	2.3	4.9
Machinery	0.2	0.9	3.3	3.9
Wood products	0.7	1.8	3.7	3.6
Total exports	100.0	100.0	100.0	100.0

Source:
Taiwan Statistical Data Book 1984.

Prices in Taiwan rose at an annual five-fold rate from 1946 to 1948 and then accelerated to approximately thirty-fold in the first half of 1949. Normal economic activities were almost impossible under such circumstances. The ROC government effected several measures in order to stabilize the economic situation. Monetary reform, which was put into effect on June 15, 1949, devalued the currency at a rate of forty-thousand old Taiwan currency to one New Taiwan dollar. In addition, a policy of high interest rates was introduced in March 1950.[3] The interest rate on new deposits was as high as 7 percent per month, which, if compounded, would amount to 125 percent per year. The high interest rates were very effective: the inflation rate decreased rapidly and has remained stable since then; and urban consumer prices rose 8.7 percent annually from 1953 to 1962 and 2.9 percent from 1963 to 1972, which was important to and very helpful for export expansion.

The second most important measure was the devaluation of the New Taiwan dollar (NT$). The effective exchange rate for exports of private enterprises was maintained at NT$14.73–15.55 to one U.S. dollar from April 1951 to March 1954. By July 1958, the N.T. dollar had gradually devaluated to NT$36.08–39.78 to US$1.00. The effective rate of NT$40.00 to US$1.00 established by market forces was then fixed as the new official rate.[4]

The third important measure decisive to Taiwan's rapid export expansion was the adoption of tax rebates on exports in 1951 in order to facilitate their importation of a particular kind of fiber from Japan for the making of straw hats. The finished product would then be exported to the same country. Later, this system was extended gradually to other commodities, and by July 1954, it covered all export goods. At first, custom duties were the only tax that was refundable. The scope of tax rebates was later extended to cover the commodity tax, defense surtax, and other taxes. The value of tax rebates increased rapidly, reducing costs for exporters and improving the international competitiveness of Taiwan's products. Therefore, tax rebates provided a direct incentive to promote exports.

Distinctive Features of Development in Taiwan

The above section illustrated that rapid growth, structural change, and export-oriented industrialization may be considered the distinctive features of Taiwan's development. There are, however, some other features which are apparent when one delves deeper into the study of the rapid development of Taiwan, particularly the agricultural and industrial sectors.

Quick Acceptance by Farmers of New Varieties of Seed

Although the share of agriculture in GDP decreased rapidly during the period under study and amounted to only 6.5 percent in 1984, agricultural products still grew 2.5 percent annually from 1962 to 1984. How is such sustaining growth in agriculture to be explained?

The main characteristic of Taiwan's agriculture is the large number of small-scale farm families, who cultivate an area of land around one hectare per family. The percentage of full ownership and part ownership in the agricultural population has been quite high, particularly after land reform in the 1950s. Tenants accounted for less than 20 percent of the agricultural population after 1954 and only 6 percent in 1982–83. Therefore, farmers are very sensitive to the profitability of farm management. Since agricultural commercialization is very high, farmers face market competition and are naturally profit-oriented.

There are several important factors which can be used to explain the increase in agricultural productivity, of which a vital factor is the introduction of new seed varieties.

Whether farmers adopt the new seed varieties is a very complicated matter, but it seems clear that a quick response by the farmers to the introduction of new varieties will undoubtedly provide for agricultural development. Since sugarcane and rice are the two most important agricultural products in Taiwan, we will use the introduction of new sugarcane and rice varieties in Taiwan to study the degree of farmers' response to incentives and opportunities.

Recent studies support the idea that peasant farmers do act rationally and are responsive to economic incentives and opportunities.[5] Evidence from many underdeveloped countries shows that under proper conditions, small farmers are responsive to incentives and opportunities and will make radical changes in what and how they produce. Lack of innovation in agriculture is usually due not to poor motivation or fear of change per se but to inadequate or unprofitable opportunities.[6] A study of mine on the factors of the technology diffusion in Taiwan's agriculture also found that farmers are responsive to incentives.[7]

The most important characteristic of Taiwan's agricultural sector is probably the small area of land cultivated by each farm laborer; therefore, raising land productivity became the critical factor in agricultural development. In fact, the sustaining increase in land productivity of two major crops—rice and sugarcane—provided an important explanation for the remarkable agricultural development of Taiwan.

As the statistics in Table 9.7 show, the yield per hectare of rice and sugarcane increased rapidly from 1946 to 1980. Yields of rice increased from 1,603 kilograms per hectare (kg/ha) in the years 1946–50, to 3,439 kg/ha in the years 1976–80. Sugarcane yields also rose significantly, from 37,929 kg/ha to 83,406 kg/ha during the same period. The causes of such rapid growth in land productivity are varied, and can be examined from two perspectives: the response of farmers to economic incentives; and the availability of opportunities such as an increase in the supply of new varieties and the development of new or improved methods of farming and other inputs such as fertilizer and irrigation facilities.

How do we know that farmers are responsive to economic incentives? We can use the rate of acceptance of new seed varieties as a rough indicator of the strength of farmers' responsiveness to profitability. If farmers behave ration-

TABLE 9.7
Yields of Rice and Sugarcane in Taiwan, 1946–80
FIVE-YEAR AVERAGE YIELDS PER HECTARE (KG/HA)

Period	Rice	Sugarcane
1946–50	1,603	37,929
1951–55	2,065	62,489
1956–60	2,391	73,622
1961–65	2,805	74,131
1966–70	3,079	78,002
1971–75	3,157	81,903
1976–80	3,439	83,406

Source:
Industry of Free China, various issues.

ally, the rate at which farmers accept a new technique depends on, among other things, the magnitude of the profit to be realized from the changeover. This hypothesis is based, first, on the general observation that the larger the stimulus, the faster the reaction to it, and second, on the fact that in an uncertain environment it takes a shorter time to find out if a difference exists, and if it does, if that difference is large.[8] Using the percentage of planted area of new varieties as a percentage of total area of cultivation to represent the rate of acceptance of new varieties indicates the rates of acceptance of new sugarcane and rice varieties. The rate of acceptance of sugarcane NCO 310 grew from 1.3 percent in 1952–53 to 91.5 percent in 1956–57, and in terms of area, the planting of NCO 310 increased from 1,412 nectares (ha.) to 86,150 ha. within four years.[9] The number of cane farmers rose from 2,796 to 142,519; that is, about 140,000 new farm families accepted this new sugarcane variety within four years (see Table 9.8). It is estimated that 72,914 more farm families accepted the new varieties in 1952–53; 8,346 in 1953–54; 31,322 in 1954–55; and 27,141 in 1955–56. Of course, how these 72,914 farmers obtained information about the new varieties and how such a large supply of cane seed was supplied to the cane farmers in one year is also very important. The rate at which farmers shifted to NCO 310 depends, among other things, upon the profitability of such a shift. The difference of yields per hectare between new and old varieties may be considered as a rough criterion of profitability of new varieties. The yields per hectare of NCO 310 was 22.7 percent higher than non–NCO 310 in 1952–53 and 20.2 percent higher in 1953–54. This may represent the relative superiority of a new variety to that of the old and consequently explain the reason for the high rate of acceptance.

Availability of new varieties and improved seeds are, of course, also indispensible. As a rule, crop varieties degenerate in quality after a certain period of planting. Therefore, research and development in agriculture are necessary to develop new varieties of good quality with strong resistance to disease. Table 9.9 shows that yields per hectare of dominated varieties increased rapidly, from 28,000 kilograms/hectare (kg/ha) in the period 1902–06, to 48,000 kg/ha in the years 1947–50, and further to 89,000 kg/ha in the years 1968–70. We find a similar trend in rice varieties. Since small-scale farm families dominated the agricultural sector in Taiwan, research and development on high-yield varieties can only be undertaken by the government. Research and development requires large expenditures which farmers can not afford. Taiwan had a quite strong agricultural research institution to undertake various kinds of agricultural research and experimentation. Undoubtedly, for the wide diffusion of new technology released by the Agricultural Research Institute, it is crucial that institutions are organized so as to make available to the majority of farmers complementary inputs and services including fertilizers, water, credit, marketing, and education.

TABLE 9.8
Rate of Diffusion for Sugarcane Variety NCO 310 Among Taiwanese Farmers, 1951–61

Crop Year	Total Cane Planted Area (a) (Ha.)	NCO 310 Planted Area (b) (Ha.)	Rate of Acceptance $(c = \frac{b}{a})$ (%)	Number of Cane Farmer	Estimated Cane Farmers Planted NCO 310	Yearly Increase
1951–52	95,703	79	0.1	179,322	179	–
1952–53	108,522	1,412	1.3	215,065	2,796	2,617
1953–54	93,150	39,869	42.8	176,893	75,710	72,914
1954–55	76,311	52,084	68.3	123,069	84,056	8,346
1955–56	87,642	71,534	81.6	141,395	115,378	31,322
1956–57	94,109	86,150	91.5	155,759	142,519	27,141
1958–59	97,836	92,043	94.1	157,994	148,672	6,153
1959–60	96,241	90,801	94.3	154,565	145,755	–2,917
1960–61	93,523	85,035	90.9	147,478	134,057	–11,698

Source:
Taiwan Sugar Corporation, *Taiwan Sugar Statistics*, 1975.

TABLE 9.9
Changes in Sugarcane Varieties in Taiwan

Major Sugarcane Varieties	Period of Dominance	Area Cultivated as a Percentage of Total	Yields (kg/ha)
Bamboo cane	1902–06	97.0	28,000
Rose bamboo	1910–17	94.7	29,000
Slender Java variety POJ 161	1922–26	84.1	42,500
Bulky Java variety POJ 2725	1930–35	78.4	66,500
Taiwan local varieties F 108	1947–50	52.5	48,000
NCO 310	1955–63	90.0	75,000
F 146	1868–70	42.0	89,000

Sources:
Taiwan Sugar Corporation, *Sugar Industry Handbook*, vol. 2, 1952, p. 253;
Taiwan Sugar Corporation, *Taiwan Sugar Statistics*, 1975.

Fast Response of Firms to the International Market

Using the same reasoning as in agriculture, we will examine the response of the private firms to economic incentives, which is crucial to development in the industrial sector. It seems unnecessary to discuss whether profit-seeking firms are responsive to economic incentives. Nevertheless, it is important to note that profit-seeking firms do not necessarily achieve the same results due to the competition their products face in the international market and the fluctuation of supply conditions.

The previous analysis indicated that the growth rate of commodity exports of Taiwan was so high (i.e., 15.1 percent per annum in the period 1952–84) that few countries in the world could compare. However, just as the introduction of high-yield seed varieties and their quick acceptance by farmers are the distinctive features for the growth of the agricultural sector, rapid expansion and the change in composition of export products in response to the world market can be considered as distinctive features in the industrial sector. In order to face the strong competition in the world market, profit-seeking firms need to make large and quick adjustments. The rapid increase in the share of industrial products in total exports provides a vivid example of the increasing competitiveness of industrial products. The significant changes in the commodity composition of industrial products also indicate the result of adjustment.

Since the world market is open to all countries, commodities which can be sold in the international market must be competitive. Thus, the growth rate of

exports in Taiwan can be considered a reflection of the improvement in competitiveness. Likewise, a negative growth rate indicates a decline in commodity competitiveness. The statistics in Table 9.10 indicate the average annual
growth rate of 61 major commodity exports in the years 1972–84. These major commodities accounted for 52.5 percent of the total exports in 1984. With
the exception of seven commodities, all commodities increased their volume
(in quantity) of exports in the period 1972–84. The most interesting fact observed from the statistics is the remarkably high growth rate. For example,
eighteen commodities had average annual growth rates of 15–30 percent for
more than one decade, and twelve commodities had average annual growth
rates of over 50 percent in the same period.

In an economy where the unemployment rate is low (the average rate was
1.05 percent in Taiwan from 1972 to 1983), capital is limited and rapid expansion of exports in certain commodities implies that factors of production
such as labor and capital were invested or reallocated from other uses to the
production of export commodities. The very high growth rate of exports indicates that the process of reallocation has been swift. In addition, the fact that
the process of rapid reallocation continued for more than one decade implies
that, in a country dominated by small-scale firms which employ labor-
intensive technology, many new producers were entering the market. This is
only possible if technology is simple and easy to obtain and if there is relatively little capital required. Indeed, most Taiwan exports are of this type. In
other words, the high rate of export expansion means that local producers can
respond very quickly and efficiently to world market demand.

Another interesting piece of evidence about the quantity and growth of selected major export commodities in the period 1972–84 may be found in Table 9.11. For example, exports of plastic footwear were the second largest

TABLE 9.10
Growth Rate of Export of Major Commodities in Taiwan, 1972–84

Average Growth Rate* 1972–84 (%)	Number of Commodities
Negative	7
0–15	14
15–30	18
30–50	10
over 50	12
Total	61†

*Growth rate is calculated in export quantity.
†These 61 major commodities accounted for 52.5 percent of total exports in 1984.
Source:
Department of Statistics, Ministry of Finance, ROC, *Monthly Statistics of Exports
and Imports, The Republic of China*, various issues.

TABLE 9.11
Quantity and Growth of Selected Major Commodity Exports in Taiwan, 1972–84

Year	MEN'S AND BOY'S OUTER GARMENTS (NOT KNITTED OR CROCHETED) Quantity in Exports (metric tons)	Growth rate (%)	TRAVEL GOODS, HANDBAGS, AND SIMILAR ARTICLES Quantity in Exports (metric tons)	Growth rate (%)	DOLLS AND TOYS Quantity in Exports (metric tons)	Growth rate (%)	PLASTIC FOOTWEAR Quantity in Exports (1,000 pairs)	Growth rate (%)
1972	15,563	—	20,331	—	33,573	—	177,112	—
1973	10,737	−31.0	27,649	40.0	35,449	5.6	151,184	−14.6
1974	9,789	−8.8	27,801	0.5	30,514	−13.9	173,088	14.5
1975	11,306	15.5	33,822	21.7	26,114	−14.4	210,130	21.4
1976	15,460	36.7	58,153	71.9	46,244	77.1	187,553	−10.7
1977	14,594	−5.6	70,624	21.4	52,163	12.8	183,108	−2.4
1978	28,223	93.4	109,960	55.7	66,053	26.6	188,833	3.1
1979	30,983	9.8	122,836	11.7	78,382	18.7	229,658	21.6
1980	36,929	19.2	146,855	19.6	86,387	10.2	214,849	−6.4
1981	43,771	18.5	148,142	0.9	114,660	32.7	230,149	7.1
1982	52,013	18.8	150,317	1.5	122,193	6.6	258,489	12.3
1983	51,891	−0.2	166,855	11.0	148,600	21.6	340,707	31.8
1984	60,058	15.7	176,731	5.9	169,951	14.4		
Average 1972–84		15.2		22.5		16.5		7.1

	OTHER PLASTIC bACCOUNTING MACHINES ARTICLES		CALCULATING MACHINES, AND SIMILAR MACHINES*	
Year	Quantity in Exports (metric tons)	Growth rate (%)	Quantity in Exports (1,000 PCS.)	Growth rate (%)
1972	—	—	—	—
1973	—	—	—	—
1974	—	—	—	—
1975	—	—	—	—
1976	—	—	—	—
1977	—	—	—	—
1978	144,182	—	680	—
1979	176,160	22.2	923	35.7
1980	190,243	8.0	300	-67.5
1981	227,417	19.5	1,347	349.0
1982	215,857	-5.1	692	-48.6
1983	291,039	34.8	1,838	165.6
1984	365,593	25.6	5,444	196.2
Average 1972–84		17.5		105.1

*Incorporating a calculating device.

Source:
Department of Statistics, Ministry of Finance, ROC, *Monthly Statistics of Exports and Imports, The Republic of China,* various issues.

export product, amounting to $1,090 million in 1984 and accounting for 3.6 percent of the total exports. During this period, the quantity of exports fluctuated greatly. Exports of plastic footwear totalled 177 million pairs in 1973, dropped suddenly to 151 million pairs in 1974, and then increased to 173 million pairs in 1975, and further to 210 million pairs in 1976. The most interesting fact was the drop of 26 million pairs (or 14.6 percent) in 1974 as compared with the previous year and the increase of 22 million pairs (or 14.5 percent) in 1975, and 37 million pairs (or 21.4 percent) in 1976. According to the census data, there were 1,150 firms in the plastic footwear industry in 1976. We can imagine that small-scale firms dominated this industry.

Regardless of whether these firms met world market demand by increasing capacity or whether it was by the entry of new producers, we can see that factors of production such as capital, labor, entrepreneurship, and technology were mobilized from other employment or from idle usage to the production of plastic footwear for export. In particular, these mobilization efforts are managed in a very short period of time in order to respond to the order from the export market. We can also find similar evidence in the rapid increase of exports in 1983 (28 million pairs more than in 1982), and 1984 (82 million pairs more than in 1983).

Aside from the traditional labor-intensive products such as plastic footwear, electronic products also showed a similar trend. For example, calculating and accounting machines began to appear in export statistics in 1978. The quantity of exports showed a wide range of fluctuation in the first five years (1978–82). Then suddenly, these exports jumped from 0.7 million pieces in 1982 to 1,838 million pieces in 1983, and grew further to 5,444 million pieces in 1984. Clearly, such great leaps in exports required quick mobilization of the factors of production from other sectors or from new investment. Quite a number of profit-seeking entrepreneurs responded to the world market demand and were willing to take risks to invest in the production of these new products. The speed of their response has been extremely fast and the quantity of resources mobilized has been enormous. Many other examples of this phenomenon can be found in Table 9.11.

Conclusions

Economic development in Taiwan during the past three decades has been remarkable. The process of development is complicated. Many articles and books about Taiwan's development have been published. Some of the studies concentrate on the measurement of growth rates and structural changes. Others study the causes of the rapid development by concentrating on ROC's government policies. This study attempts to observe Taiwan's development through the behavior of farmers and industrial entrepreneurs.

Development in the agricultural sector is often neglected by developing countries. However, agricultural development in Taiwan is extraordinary. The contribution of two major crops—rice and sugarcane—is crucial. Because of the limited area of land cultivated per farm family, the rapid increase in the yields per hectare is undoubtedly notable. The introduction of high-yield varieties, among other factors, is a major contributor to this increase. Farmers' response to profitable new varieties, combined with the availability of an economic incentive, became the distinctive feature in agricultural development. Other factors, however, such as chemical fertilizers, irrigation facilities, improved farming techniques, credit, and training are also indispensable.

The most important factor transforming Taiwan's economy from a primarily agricultural economy to a primarily industrial economy is, of course, rapid industrial growth, which is a result of high export expansion. Exports grew very fast, and though different commodities had different growth rates (some slow or even negative, others very quick), the explanation behind this high growth rate in commodity exports is the large number of profit-seeking entrepreneurs. Taiwan's economy permits exporters to develop their strong competitiveness by organizing the factors of production to produce goods for the world market. From the high rate of exports, we know that the commodities mostly involve labor-intensive technology, the production techniques are simple, and the capital requirements are relatively small. Thus, entrepreneurs can respond to demand from the world market quickly. Of course, the conditions of a vast labor supply and high mobility are indispensable. Other relevant factors such as transportation, trading, and banking are also very important; however, the capability of entrepreneurs to employ factors of production quickly and efficiently to produce for the international market may be considered one of the distinctive features of Taiwan's development.

Notes

1. All dollar figures in this chapter are in U.S. dollars, unless otherwise indicated.
2. 14.6 percent of total exports in the period 1952–55 and 12 percent in the period 1956–60.
3. Shirley W.Y. Kuo, *The Taiwan Economy in Transition* (Boulder, CO: Westview Press, 1983).
4. S.C. Tsiang and Rong-I Wu, "Foreign Trade and Investments as Boosters for Take-Off: The Experiences of the Four Asian Newly Industrialized Countries," in Walter Galenson, ed., *Foreign Trade and Investment: Economic Growth in the Newly Industrializing Asian Countries* (Madison: University of Wisconsin Press, 1985).
5. Michael P. Todaro, *Economic Development in the Third World*, 2d ed. (White Plains, NY: Longman, Inc., 1981), p. 273.
6. Ibid.; and Theodore W. Schultz, *Transferring Traditional Agriculture* (New Haven: Yale University Press, 1964).

7. Rong-I Wu, "A Study of the Factors of Technology Diffusion in Taiwan," *Economic Study* 20, 1976, pp. 1–56 (in Chinese).
8. Z. Griliches, "Hybrid Corn and the Economics of Innovation," *Science*, July 1960, pp. 275–80; also in Nathan Rosenberg, ed., *The Economics of Technological Change* (Harmondsworth: Penguin Books, 1971), pp. 211–28.
9. Taiwan Sugar Corporation, *Taiwan Sugar Statistics*, 1975.
10. The share of the four biggest firms in total sales was only 8.74 percent; the share of the eighth largest was 14.05 percent.

10

The Distinctive Features of South Korea's Development

Kyong-Dong Kim

Recently, there seems to be a resurgence of interest in reviving the classical Weberian "Protestant Ethic" thesis, as applied to the search for explanations for the relative economic successes of select East Asian societies. As Eisenstadt[1] has pointed out earlier, Weber cannot seem to fail to come back whenever the controversy erupts, either to be supported, reexamined, or refuted. In a nutshell, this debate has to do with some connection (maybe causal in nature) between some form of religion (or pseudo-religion or ideology) and certain types of economic activities (usually of a capitalistic nature). As for the East Asian success stories, one common religious-ideological factor happens to be some form of Confucianism. And this alone seems to have sufficient drawing power to arouse the interest of social analysts to renew the controversy one way or another.[2]

My intention here is not to delve into this debate itself. Rather, a more fruitful enterprise would be to identify and lay out the more salient features of South Korea's experience of economic growth in a systematic fashion in which all the pertinent factors may be considered in perspective. Confucianism would be one of them, placed in the proper context, given no more or no less attention than it deserves. An attempt will be made to single out some "distinctive" features, often quite unique to the Korean experience. Those factors considered salient may not necessarily be distinctive to Korea, although the way they interacted to create whatever they have created in South Korea may be unique historically. This is essentially what I am attempting to unravel in this essay.

In order to carry out this task, I am going to concentrate on the human element and the principle of social organization, assuming that it is the people who achieve what is called rapid economic growth and industrialization by

197

organizing themselves and the other resources required. Broadly, this would be generally in line with the Weberian approach. But any theoretical discourse will be reserved for the final part. Up to that point, I intend to build up a rather generalized picture of what has made Korea "tick" against the backdrop of a historical overview of the major changes Korea experienced before embarking on deliberate programs of economic growth. The vantage point of my analysis, therefore, will be the early 1960s, when the Five-Year Economic Development Plan was initiated. Following a very brief descriptive reconstruction of major historical transformations before 1960, more intensive discussion of the human element and social organization will focus on motivation, quality, mobilization, and organization of human resources. It is here that the role of religious-ideological factors will be brought under consideration. Reflections on the theoretical implications will be attempted in the concluding part.

Historical Overview

Korea used to be known as a "Hermit Kingdom" in the Far East up until it was forced by the Japanese to open ports and participate in international trade in 1876. Of course, Korea had traditionally maintained a close relationship with China, mainly as a tributary state. Thus, some infiltration of modern ideas and Western culture was possible—only mediated by China—beginning in the eighteenth century. But it was in the late nineteenth century that exposure to the modern West came about, this time, primarily through Japan, with limited direct contact. Having been a kingdom ruled by the Confucian scholar-bureaucrat or gentry class for five hundred years, Korea remained a poor agrarian society when first exposed to the outside world. Torn by factional strife among the elite political groups; deprived and impoverished by corruption of the aristocrats and bureaucrats, and by the exploitation of the peasantry; stricken with peasant revolts; and with the fabric of society itself and the legitimacy of the gentry rule severely undermined and shaken, Korea was too worn out to face the challenge of the imperialistic encroachment from Japan. Some new ideas challenging the traditionalist Confucian ideology budded, off and on, from the eighteenth century on, only to be suppressed. Some rudimentary form of a capitalistic merchant class began to emerge, never to become a significant indigenous force toward the development of modern capitalism. Even some signs of reform in the agricultural sector appeared, to be wiped out eventually. Under the exploitative traditional structure, little incentives existed for any significant innovations relevant to economic development.

Before long, Japan colonized Korea (1910). The Japanese colonial authority abolished the traditional status system, replacing it with a quasi-class system of colonial capitalism. New landed, entrepreneurial, bureaucratic-professional, white-collar, commercial, service, labor, and peasant classes were formed. Nevertheless, the dominant ideology was couched in authoritarian militarism coated by the Japanese version of Confucianism. This facilitated colonial rule and economic exploitation because of the Confucian tradition of the Korean people. During the 36-year colonial occupation, Japan hardly pursued an active industrialization program in Korea, nor did Japan encourage the Korean entrepreneurs to develop industries.

When Japan left Korea after its defeat in the Second World War, Korea was almost deserted, with little industrial base, lacking well-trained managerial and engineering-technical manpower. Immediately following liberation, the nation was divided into North and South, under separate control of the United States in the South and the Soviet Union in the North. The independent republic in the South had scarcely recovered from the economic vacuum created by the desertion of the Japanese colonists and from the aftermath of political turmoil between liberation and new statehood, when the Communist regime in the North invaded in a surprise attack. All this occurred in a time span of five years: liberation in 1945, independence in 1948, and war in 1950.

Three years of war devastated the country. In the process of rehabilitation, primarily under the economic aid program of the United States, a batch of entrepreneurs emerged. They played on various political connections and special favors from the government in their growth.[3] Tainted by corruption, the abuse of power, election rigging, and other attending malaise, the regime of President Syngman Rhee crumbled in the face of nationwide student protests in 1960. The ensuing Chang Myun government did not even have enough time to settle down when General Park Chung Hee and his junta took power through a bloodless coup in May 1961.

Our benchmark for analysis is set for this period. The first Five-Year Economic Development Plan came into effect in 1962. The initial plan was drawn up by the short-lived Chang government, which did not survive to materialize the plan. Drawing upon this aborted plan, the new junta regime finalized the program and actually embarked on active economic growth policies. Typically, the growth has been attained by industrialization, and the industrial sector has been led by manufacturing, and manufacturing by exports.[4] Table 10.1 summarizes the economic changes that occurred between 1961 and 1983 in terms of some select indicators.

The above account of Korea's historical background is, no doubt, too brief and oversimplified. It is only intended to provide a time frame and a very broad picture of the changing circumstances, leading up to our benchmark of the early 1960s. This, I hope, will facilitate our understanding of the human and social forces behind South Korea's experience of growth. Since econom-

TABLE 10.1
Korean Economic Growth 1961–1983:
Major Socioeconomic Indicators

Indicator	Unit	1961 (a)	1983 (b)	Ratio b/a
GNP (market price)	billion won	297.08	58,279.7	196.18
GNP per capita (market)	US$	82	1,880	19.8
GNP Composition	%	100.0	100.0	–
Primary industry	%	40.2	13.7	–
Secondary industry	%	15.2	28.9	–
Tertiary industry	%	44.6	57.4	–
Electricity generation capacity	1,000kw	367	13,115	35.7
Coal	1,000 metric tons	5,884	19,861	3.4
Steel and iron	1,000 metric tons	86.9	591	6.8
Cement	1,000 metric tons	522.9	17,650	33.8
Unemployment	%	8.1	4.1	
Number of Schools				
Primary	–	4,700	6,500	1.4
Middle	–	1,100	2,250	2.0
High	–	600	1,500	2.5
College-University	–	58	98	1.7
Physicians	–	8,000	29,900	3.7
Culture: TV sets	1,000	31	6,960	224.5
Communication: telephone subscribers	1,000	97	4,914	50.7
Automobiles	1,000	29.2	785.3	26.9
Ratio of roads paved	%	14.9*	67.0	–
Piped water supply	%	18.5*	61.0	–

*Figure is for 1963.
Source:
Kyong-Dong Kim, *Man and Society in Korea's Economic Growth: Sociological Studies* (Seoul: Seoul National University Press, 1979); and Kyong-Dong Kim, et al., "Twelve Forces behind Social Change in Korea, 1954–1984," special issue of *Social Science and Policy Research* 6:3, 1984 (Seoul: Institute of Social Sciences, Seoul National University) (in Korean).

ics is beyond my expertise, I am going to forgo any description of the distinctive features of Korean development in its economic component. Rather, my focus will be on the human element and the principle of social organization most pertinent to the growth experience.

Traditional Elements in Korean Society

As the above summary suggests, Korea has gone through such rapid and often drastic transformations. It is therefore extremely difficult to discern the traditional features of Korean society that existed only in the premodern era and those that have lingered on to influence people's thought and behavior even today. Thus, the synopsis of traditional elements presented below necessarily mixes both elements. Also, it cannot be more than a very abstract list of human characters and organizational principles. The following are items denoting "Korean national character," typical behavioral orientations, principles of social organization, world views, and basic values of the Korean people, summarized and reorganized from works of several experts; some of these were originally drawn from observations of foreigners who either had lived or travelled in Korea during the past century or so.[5]

1. Individual personality characteristics: Extremely emotional: this may be manifested in warmth and intuitive understanding, but at the same time may cause passionate outburst, hot temper, excessive radical action, which in turn may show in daring action, or manifested in jealousy and cruelty. Lack of abstract, rational, metaphysical reasoning and value consciousness: as a corollary to the above, this tendency emphasizes the irrationality of the Korean character. Self-centered but dependent: implied here is the lack of self-reflection and of the sense of responsibility, attended by ready moral self-rationalization by individuals of any of their own behavior. Deficiencies in aesthetic sense, refinement, precision, and accuracy: well summarized in the quip, "work is done but never finished," or "creative but coarse." Suppression and concealment of emotions, desires, and impulses: discipline, asceticism, introversion, and hence lack of initiative and creativity. Strong aspirations for education (schooling).
2. Behavioral inclinations: Extravagant lifestyle, spendthrift or wasteful behavior; disguised greed and selfish desires; laziness and untidiness.
3. Interpersonal relations: Unusual hospitality, excessive, often irritating kindness even causing encroachment of privacy. Related to the above tendency is a lack of refinement in interpersonal behavior, rather crude and sometimes offensive despite good intentions. Inability to separate public and private, formal and informal, official and unofficial, due to strong emotional involvement. Weak in the spirit of obeying laws. Emphasis on saving one's own or another's face, and on moral pretext rather than the deep sense of ethical righteousness; the so-called shame-over-against-guilt culture; formalistic ritualism or ceremonialism, applying double standards depending on the other party in interaction. Sensitivity to others' judgments of and attitudes toward oneself, acting upon the assessment of "how the wind blows"; concealing one's own feelings and refraining from expressing one's own opinions or taking an unnecessary detour in

expressions, especially in front of superiors; these cause inaction and passivity, and conformity to group norms and sentiments.

4. Principles of social organization: Authoritarianism, placing strong emphasis on hierarchical relationships and order in terms of parent-child, elder-youth, male-female, superior-subordinate status positions, etc. Strong status-mobility orientation; everybody eligible wanting to become somebody by taking a position of authority, prestige in the hierarchical order. Something called "*Uri-ism*" (meaning "We-ism") or collectivism primarily couched in terms of familism; leading to a lack of strict differentiation and independence of individuality from collectivity, manifested in the inability to separate the public and private etc. "Connectionism," or the tendency to build one's social network on the basis of certain ascriptive and/or particularistic relationships. "Personalism," emphasizing close personal ties in which the element of affection looms large and parties in interaction are sensitive to each other's feelings, sharing others' feelings and emotions. Exclusivism, chauvinistic closure, and factionalism, mainly centering around immediate collectivity, primary relations, network of connections, personalized ties, such as relatives, friends from the same local origin or same school, other cohort groups, etc. Nepotism and favoritism based on the above principles. Weak sense of identity with larger organizations and the national collectivity, not in the sense of nationalism or patriotism, but in the contractual, utilitarian sense, more abstract national consciousness, related to the above listed principles.

5. World Views: Secularism, supremacy of worldly accomplishements, blessings in this world. Primacy of secular ends, with relative neglect of the just and rational means in achieving the goal. Fatalism, easy resignation. Conservatism, orientation to the past. Submissiveness to the stronger, powerful; flunkyism; inferiority.

6. General values: Value of nature; longevity; ancestors; children, especially abundance of male offspring; wealth, money; heavy eating and drinking; voracity; recognition of others; showing warm feelings toward others and sharing others' emotions, empathy and sympathy; education and learning; peace; safety and quiet.

As can be seen in the above list, there are overlaps and contradictions in the depiction of the Korean national character and organizational principles provided by both foreign and indigenous observers in the past century or so. This may be due to diversity of sources of such orientations and inclinations as well as to the enormous changes Korean society has undergone during this period. Since the nature of broad social change has already been reviewed, some consideration of the sources may be in order.

Above all, Confucianism must be mentioned as one of the most important traditional sources of Korean character and organizational principles. In Korea, the predominant ideology of the Yi Dynasty, which lasted from the late fourteenth through the beginning of the twentieth century, used to be what is known as Neo-Confucianism of Ch'eng Yi and especially Chu Hsi who were the leading figures of the so-called School of Ideas (or Platonic Ideas).[6] As adopted and practiced in Korea, it had become a very rigid ideology governing statecraft, principles of social organization and human relations, and behavioral norms, on the one hand, and a very abstract system of metaphysical ideas, on the other. However, its application was largely confined to the ruling literati class, except to exert harsh authoritarian control over the common people and menials and to justify the legitimacy of such control. As for the gentry class, Neo-Confucian ideals were summed up in the adage, "Discipline yourself, then you will be able to manage your family and kin, then you will be able to rule the state, then you will be able to subdue the entire world." In short, authoritarianism and formalistic moralism were supplemented by ceremonialism and humanitarianism of personalistic nature in the Korean version of Neo-Confucianism.[7]

If Confucianism was the predominant and almost sole ideology of the ruling class, a mixture of three sets of religious beliefs and practices governed the life of the common people and menial classes in traditional Korea. The oldest indigenous religion or folk practice was shamanism, or "worship of ten thousand gods and spirits"; the next prevalent one was Buddhism of Mahayana strain, and the third, Taoism as practiced as a folk religion not as a system of philosophy. These three played the role of subordinating the mass to the authoritarian rule or aristocratic governance, while providing an outlet for the common people to release the tensions and grievances caused by severe and rigid imposition of order and discipline, exploitation, and repression on the part of the ruling class. Buddhism was the dominant and even state religion for almost a thousand years before the Yi Dynasty, and operated as the major integrating force for the nation in the days of external invasions and calamities. Shamanism and to some extent Taoism, through their rituals, helped maintain community identity and peace of mind for the suppressed people.[8]

It is beyond the scope of this essay to detail the doctrines and practices of these religions. All I can say in summary is that whereas the authoritarian and formalistic elements presented in the above list must have their origin mostly in the Koreanized Neo-Confucianism, the nonrational, humanistic parts may have emanated from the other three religions, if we are cornered to make out some meaningful connections. One very significant element common to all four may be secularism. No religion, including Christianity, whether Catholic or Protestant, has escaped this secular tendency. And Christianity, since its introduction from the West between the eighteenth and nineteenth centuries, has had its own ups and downs vis-à-vis its confrontation with the old ways. While Protestant denominations have contributed somewhat to diminution of authoritarianism by bringing in the democratic church organization and management, Catholicism does not seem to have ameliorated the authoritarian tendency in Korean society. Neither has been successful in overcoming the very strong shamanistic beliefs and sorcerous practices prevalent in this society. Nor have Buddhism and Taoism been successful. It was only Confucianism that was able to suppress that "superstitious" element.[9]

Japanese colonialism in a way reinforced the strong authoritarian mentalities and principles through its own militaristic Confucian statism. This was done by means of education, indoctrination, and a whole variety of everyday practices. Secularism also was encouraged not only by introduction of modern culture from the West, but also by the very nature of Japanese culture itself. Even though exposure to modern science and capitalistic economic institutions through the modern educational system and economic policies of the colonial authorities may have modernized and somehow "rationalized" the thought patterns and ways of life of the Korean people, this was not sufficient to change the tenacious emotional and personalistic inclinations. Rather, under the extremely distorted circumstances of colonial rule, such tendencies may have been reinforced. To release tensions and stress, the Koreans sought comfort in more sorcerous Buddhism, Taoism, or even very fundamentalistic Christianity, let alone indigenous shamanism.[10]

It is true that liberation from Japanese colonial rule and occupation by U.S. forces brought in many cultural elements and traits that may represent the exact opposite of the traditional characteristics enumerated earlier, probably epitomized in Western democratic, rational, scientific, industrial values and modal personality stereotypes appropriate to them. Such influences from the West have continued and increased over the years, particularly during the Korean War in which a large number of international armed forces participated and during the rehabilitation efforts in its aftermath. Nevertheless, the basic traditional elements have lingered on, perhaps a bit weakened and subdued. The Korean people are still very emotional, crude, aggressive, superstitious, and untidy but may no longer be lazy. Korean society is organized basically on the principle of personalistic interpersonal relations, the intricate network of connections of a non-universalistic tint, quite individualized yet still very collectivistic in orientation and authoritarian hierarchial in organization, putting on the ritualistic facade for face-saving, and strongly status and mobility oriented and meritocratic. The major religions have had little to do with rationalization of the people and society.[11]

In spite of all this, Korea has made some outstanding progress in the economic realm, creating an interesting case of an industrial capitalist society, still compounded by all sorts of traditional traits which in general are considered inimical or at most not terribly conducive to such a development. I take it to be my task to unravel the distinctive features of South Korea's development from this twisted point of departure.

Adaptive Change Based on Nonrational Forces

In order to explain the unique performance of South Korea in the economic sphere in the past quarter century, I am going to focus once again on the human element and social organization and proceed in the following manner. I will begin by tapping the motivational forces, then looking into the quality of human resources, followed by analysis of the strategy of mobilization and organization. To state the conclusion first, in short, Korea's economic achievement is a consequence of adaptive change with various nonrational forces operating in the processes of motivating, mobilizing, and organizing the people and society.

Motivation

Acculturation. Whether you like it or not, modernization of latecomer societies should be seen as a dialectical process of international acculturation and indigenous adaptation.[12] Korea, having been a "Hermit Kingdom" for hundreds of years, came to experience modernization by these twin processes. In fact, the virtually forced opening of ports in the late nineteenth century came in the midst of adamant resistance from various sectors of the society. In this first wave of acculturation, Korea failed to make necessary adaptive changes, only to be annexed by an imperial force. Colonial rule meant distorted acculturation in whose face the native forces were again unable to make their own necessary adaptive changes, because the change agent was mainly the Japanese. After liberation, the sole change agent became the Korean people and, now, their government. Nevertheless, they still have had to meet the challenge of acculturation in a new wave. Thus far, Korea has been able to make fairly successful adaptive change in the economic sphere. But the important point here is that acculturation has provided both a stimulus or motive and the information flow needed for adaptive change. Korea has been exposed to a whole new world outside, by means of education, mass-communication media, and a variety of other channels. As the old Chinese saying goes, "seeing things arouses desires." This, of course, is the elementary stimulus offered to any latecomer society. But in the case of Korea, it has also aroused a very keen sense of shame and embarrassment. Being a nation with a long and often quite glorious history of civilization, yet downtrodden under the cruel steps of a once barbarian neighbor now equipped with modern weaponry, bureaucracy, and economic prowess, furthermore torn by a civil war, and shaken by continuing political turmoil, the Korean nation found itself still reaching to catch up with the poor nations in the global community. In this respect, the notion of world system of stratification is useful to the extent that Korea as a peripheral nation had to crawl out of that status as fast as possible. And this stimulus or impetus for adaptive change came from the process of acculturation, above all. Acculturation also furnished the basic new information required to make the necessary adaptive change to catch up with the nations of higher status (semi-core or even core nations).

Insecurity and survival. One of the distinctive features of Korean history is that it has been marred with external invasions, occupations, and incessant warfare. Also prevalent were political struggles among the contending elite groups of different backgrounds and factions. Moreover, the nation was divided into two separate states under opposing ideologies, largely as a result of the dealings among the big powers after the end of World War II. Although there are two arbitrarily divided nations in the world, Germany and Korea, the separation of the Korean nation is most unique: the two Koreas fought each other in a devastating war for three years and there has been no communication or exchange of people whatsoever, except for very limited formal government-level talks, for the past generation. On top of this, there is always the threat of another invasion from the North, whether real or concocted.

The level of insecurity has been always high in South Korea, and the value of survival as a nation-state has never been questioned. It was in the midst of a political whirlpool, in the aftermath of violent student demonstrations which toppled a regime in the early 1960s, that the military takeover was partially justified in the sense that it recovered stability. However, the legitimacy of the junta government was only consolidated when it announced and actually carried out the First Five-Year Economic Development Plan to overcome the sense of insecurity and to ensure survival as a nation in the face of constant threat from the North, unceasing political instability, and the rapidly modernizing world in which the relative position of the country was constantly slipping while a country like Japan—completely defeated in World War II—was swiftly moving ahead. The project to build the nation-state solidly on economic grounds was sufficient to hit the core of the people's motivation.[13] The idea that instigation of the people's sense of insecurity may arouse their motivation has been noted as one of the interpretations of Weberian conceptions of the psychological explanation of economic behavior.[14] The tension created by this sense of insecurity needs to be released, and the psychological force emanating from this relaxation of tension may be channeled into various spheres of social behavior. In the case of Korea, this was done in the economic realm.

The Psychology of Hahn. Perhaps the most interesting and unique factor, and one that should not be left out in explaining Korean behavior, happens to be what is called *hahn* in Korean. In fact, there is no single English word equivalent in meaning to this term. *Hahn* refers to a mixture of feelings and emotional states, including a sense of rancor, regret, grief, remorse, and revenge; and grievances or grudges. These feelings may have to do with an accumulated sense of frustration, repeated deprivation of need gratification, or constant suppression of one's own desires. Accumulated and suppressed, there may develop some hard core of grievance and rancor in the psyche of a person, and this can cause both psychosomatic and psychological malaise. Once released, however, it can become a tremendous psychic force.

Hahn has been widely mentioned as one of the very distinctive and strong psychic states of the Korean people. Depending on the class status of the person, however, the nature of social structural sources of such feelings may vary. For instance, for the nation as a whole, the state of *hahn* has been historically due to frequent invasions and occupations by foreign forces. Especially strong is the emotion of *hahn* acquired from the bitter experience of colonization by the Japanese. Also notable would be *hahn* caused by the realization through acculturation that Korea has remained too long as a poorer nation in the global society, in spite of her pride of having been a nation of high civilization for thousands of years. This kind of *hahn* must have been shared by all of the people regardless of their class position; its intensity, however, may be stronger among the general populace.

As for the mass of the population, some major structural sources of *hahn* have persisted throughout history. The *hahn* of chronic poverty is one of them. Poverty of the masses was caused not merely by low productivity of agriculture due to poor technology; it was usually a consequence of severe exploitation on the part of the traditional or colonial bureaucracy. Even after independence, the lack of resources and low productivity were compounded by excessive bureaucratic corruption. Exacerbating the situation were the destructive war, instability in its aftermath, a population explosion, urban congestion, and the like. The *hahn* of age-old poverty had never been ameliorated before deliberate economic growth plans were actually implemented.

Political oppression in the traditional setting and especially during the colonial period also helped create the state of *hahn* in the mind of the Korean people. But this was pretty much eased with independence, which has brought along with it the freedom to elect public officials, to express one's opinion, and to organize and participate in various voluntary organizations. In the political realm, the more serious issue was unrestrained abuse of power on the part of some political and bureaucratic figures. This was accompanied by the extravagant lifestyles and conspicuous consumption of the newly emerging upper class, composed of the politico-bureaucratic and the rising entrepreneurial elite. Thus, the impoverished masses began to feel excluded and alienated, accumulating the emotion of *hahn* in a new fashion.

Another important area where the feeling of *hahn* has been piling up in the psyche of the masses in Korea is that of education and status mobility. In the traditional status system, opportunity to attain status mobility and to obtain necessary education was confined to the gentry class, with very few exceptions. The channel was closed to women and sons of commoners and menials, of course. But even among the aristicrats, the offspring of concubines were prohibited from taking government examinations to become bureaucrats or military officers. Without passing this examination, status mobility was extremely limited. Education of any formal nature was limited to the gentry and to the legitimate sons of the literati. Therefore, no matter how bright an individual may have been, the door to educational and status attainment was open only to the legitimate son of an aristocrat. Restrictions were also applied to the general populace during the colonial days. This time, the privileged were the Japanese and a small minority of Koreans with vested interests in the system. The Japanese abolished the old status system and introduced the public school system, making the door to basic education, in principle, wider. But in reality, only a limited number of the Korean people enjoyed access to primary education, and the opportunity for secondary and higher education was much more restrained. Since education was almost the only channel for mobility, the chance for any Korean without proper education to move ahead on the ladder of social mobility was also extremely curtailed. Even for the better educated, the colonial system inherently imposed a certain ceiling to the probability of status achievement for Koreans.

The extraordinarily high level of aspiration for education and excessive interest in status achievement, well-noted qualities of the Korean people, happens to be an expression of *hahn* thus created and hardened in the mind of these people over the generations. Once the system of universal primary schooling was established after independence, this thirst for education began to be quenched. Nevertheless, for education to be effective as a channel for upward mobility, it had to include higher education. Competition has become extremely severe to enter colleges and universities. The long-accumulated *hahn* for education and status mobility was not to be readily relaxed. On top of this, discrimination against women has been acute in almost every conceivable aspect of social life since the early days of the Yi Dynasty. Although it has been gradually eased in selective spheres, women have been hardening the core of *hahn* for centuries. Whenever *hahn* is mentioned, one hardly fails to notice some reference to women. There is even a famous saying to the effect that the *hahn* of women can cause frost in the middle of hot summer.

Just like the sluice after a flood, an opening found may be crowded with people with long-repressed *hahn*, rushing to release it. It was in the economic arena that the Korean people finally located the outlet. Once released, *hahn* turned into an enormous force inciting and motivating the people to find ways to gratify suppressed needs. It was this deep-rooted, intense sense of *hahn* of the masses to which the junta elite was able to appeal for implementation of the economic development plan.

To complete the picture, let me comment on the nature of *hahn* most distinctive to the elite class. They too have been grinding the knife of *hahn* secretly, if they went through political struggles and purges. The history of political conflict in this country is marred with repeated give-and-take processes consisting of fatal blows and subsequent revenge, between major political opponents and their factions. Whoever is ousted from the position of power grows in their mind the seed of *hahn*, yearning and waiting for the time to strike back. Thus, in a way, the junta regime of General Park Chung Hee made the best use of the diffuse yet acute sense of *hahn* pervasive among the general populace to contain potential outburst of the *hahn* of its opponents, who they had to kick out and detain in political limbo. With the legitimacy and survival of the regime at stake, the party in power certainly could not afford to see the bomb of *hahn* concealed in the bosom of the foe blow up in their own face.

Sociological studies on Korea's economic growth and modernization have pointed out with empirical evidence that the strong achievement motive and need for status mobility played a central role in helping make the effort a success in this country.[15] Even if these conclusions are correct, they have only touched the surface without reference to the very unique psychic force called *hahn*. This must be the real force which thus far has been neglected and waits to be examined more systematically from now on.

Quality of Human Resources

Even if the motivating forces existed among the Korean people and the government of the moment was able to instigate them and channel them into realization of economic development, these forces alone are not sufficient to explain the results we have seen. In other words, the people should not only be motivated to do something, but should also be qualified to accomplish it. And it happens that Korea was fortunate to have such high-quality human resources available. This is so widely known that it is almost unnecessary to document the fact. Evidence is abundant but it may suffice to enumerate the most crucial dimensions of quality of the people relevant to our purpose.

Relative to other countries around the world in similar stages of economic growth and with a similar living standard, Korea possessed a well-educated population, to begin with.[16] As has been mentioned earlier, zeal for education has been unusually strong, and the educational system quickly expanded after independence. To show some select figures relative to education, in 1954, only one year after the truce, when GNP per capita stood at a meager $70, the illiteracy rate in South Korea was 23.2 percent. Ninety percent of primary-school age children were in school, almost 29 percent of youths were in middle schools, 17.3 percent in high schools, and 4.2 percent in colleges. Moreover, almost 100,000 young people were college students and more than 1,000 were already studying abroad, mostly in the United States and Europe. In a decade, by 1964, the illiteracy rate dropped down to 14.7 percent, the primary enrollment rate jumped to 95.7 percent, close to four out of ten youths were going to middle schools, over 25 percent were going to high schools, and 8.3 percent were in college. The number of university students increased to over 116,000, and while about half of the students returned from abroad, the number of applicants granted permission to go abroad for advanced study had risen from 48 in 1954 to 589 in 1964. The number of colleges and universities was only 44 in 1954, but had grown to 66 in ten years.[17]

Contrary to the stereotype of Koreans as lazy, as they were portrayed by most of the foreign observers travelling through Korea earlier, the Korean people in the 1960s and 1970s were found to be very industrious, aggressive, and highly committed to work and labor. Again to give an idea, I can cite a study we conducted in 1967. When asked, "If you had sufficient economic means to live on for the rest of your life, what would you do?" 97.7 percent of workers and managers responding gave positive answers, indicating they would continue to work one way or another.[18] This may be compared with the 80 percent American national sample in the 1950s who responded affirmatively to the question, "If by some chance you inherited enough money to live comfortably without working, do you think you would work anyway or not?"[19] In another study of child-rearing values conducted in the early 1970s, "achievement demand" was perceived by Korean school children to be the most important value their parents would inculcate in them.[20] Again, this may be compared with the responses of American and English children of the same age, who ranked this particular parental value sixth and eighth, respectively.[21]

Tenacity is something one could expect of a people like Koreans who have been through so much historically and yet survived as a distinct nation. Clinging to the acute sense of *hahn* cumulated by incessant external aggressions and internal conflicts, still not giving up easily, they have acquired an unusual quality of resilience. Therefore, once something valuable has been grabbed, they hang on to it to the end. This is another distinctive feature of the Korean people as manifested in the process of continued growth in the past decades.

Adaptability is another characteristic Koreans have demonstrated in their effort to modernize. If they have failed in the earlier waves of modernization, they certainly made it from the 1960s on, building something substantial almost out of scratch and weathering some of the severe storms such as oil shocks and natural disasters. As a matter of fact, the Korean people are usually very rigid in their thought patterns, behavior, and human relations; but when it comes to survival and release of *hahn*, they tend to make quick moves to adapt to the changing environment. This adaptability has been instilled through the hardships Koreans have endured throughout their turbulent history.

Discipline is also a feature which deserves mention as a quality of the Korean people. This quality of discipline, however, does not seem to have its root in some lofty ethical attitudes. Basically, Koreans have learned in the course of a stormy history the wisdom of waiting patiently, often resigned but not fatalistic—again contrary to some observations. Also, militaristic discipline has since the colonial period been inculcated from early in life starting in schools. This has continued throughout the days of war and afterwards. Ever since the truce was signed in 1953, Korea has been in a state of quasi-war without battle, at least officially. To meet the challenge of possible invasion from the North, youths have been subjected to military or quasi-military training in school, and every able young man has to serve in the military in one form or another. The reserve corps is well maintained, subject to regular roll call and drills, until the man reaches the age of 50. By law, the government conducts civil defense drills every month. All this has been maintained and reinforced by successive military or military-turned-into-civilian regimes since the 1960s. The Japanese militaristic influence still lingers on in the elite personnel in this respect.[22] It is this kind of discipline that is effective in Korea. It has a great deal to do with the attitude of obedience to authority, not exactly based on rational-legal grounds, but rather on the militaristic training and mentality inherited and buttressed over the years.

If Confucian tradition in Korea had any standing imprint on the disciplined behavior patterns of the people, my contention is that it has maintained its influence only because reinforcement came again and again from the successive militaristic cultures of Japanese colonialism, the war, and the rise of the military in the political arena. But for these latter reinforcing factors, I would argue, Confucian authoritarian discipline would have been largely attenuated in the face of acculturation from the West and the attendant rapid modernization. It should be noted that Koreans are not culturally endowed with righteous ethical orientations to enable them to discipline themselves on the moral-ethical principle. If Confucianism had anything to do with the disciplined behavior of today's Koreans, it would have been only through its strong authoritarianism combined with its face-saving ceremonialism.

Mobilization and Organization

Thus, it should now be easier to understand the strategy of mobilization and the principle of organization that Korea has employed in achieving rapid economic growth in the past quarter century or so. Considering the background forces for motivation, perhaps the most attractive carrot the newly installed military regime could offer the aspiring people was economic growth, a rather fast growth in fact. This was to help the regime retain its legitimacy as well. All it needed was a cause to mobilize the people's support and participation in the march to prosperity. Face-saving in the world community, shedding of the shameful colonial memory, and insuring security in the face of potential threat from the aggressive North were put forth as the nationalistic rationale to embark on the formidable task of economic reconstruction.

Fortunately, the people in all sectors, regions, and walks of life responded positively to the government's call for mobilization and cooperation. To organize the society for this job, the government decided to maintain a guiding hand in the affairs of the economy—in planning, implementing, and evaluating the development programs—by pronouncing the policy of "guided capitalism." This happened to be quite in line with the hitherto familiar principle of social organization in Korea. A centralized governmental system has been there for centuries, further bolstered by the Japanese colonial experience. Weathering the political turmoil and a war, the newly born republic was still able to build up a rather strong and efficient government bureaucracy and, in the process of reconstruction from the ashes of the war, entrepreneurial organizations have grown fast, mainly under the direct influence of the United States. But a great deal of the elite who manned these bureaucracies and entreprises were trained under the Japanese.[23] By 1964, when the total population in South Korea was just about 28 million, the number of public servants was 295,000, slightly over 1.5 percent. It has more than doubled in two decades, reaching 651,000 in 1983, when the total population hit the mark of 40 million, the proportion now being 1.6 percent. In 1964, there were about 9,000 enterprises employing five or more persons and the total number of workers in these organizations were 563,000, the average size of each enterprise being 42.8 employees. In 1983, the average size of enterprise had decreased to 40 employees, the number of organizations had jumped to 92,000, almost ten times that of 1964, and the total workers had grown about six times over the same period.[24]

Considering the dearth of resources and the shortage of capital required to take off, the government assumed the primary responsibility of capital formation, resource allocation, project selection, and a whole array of other activities for the sake of efficiency. The voluntary sector was not to be equal partners but targets for mobilization. In this respect, too, the Korean people happened to be used to the idea of government mobilization, such as the traditional conscription system, the Japanese programs of general mobilization, wartime emergency measures, and other programs of mobilization regularly employed by the military regime afterwards. Thus, in a way, the entire country was organized on the principle of centralized authoritarian structure.[25]

Within each unit, too, the centralized authoritarian principle of organization permeated all the bureaucracies, both in public governmental and private entrepreneurial sectors. The influence of the military should not be overlooked in this respect. The armed forces have been one of the bureaucratic organizations most extensively exposed to the modern system of management in Korea early after independence, because of the direct involvement of the United States armed forces which not only occupied the country after liberation until independence but also fought in the war. And note that the political leadership that initiated the economic development plans was of a military background.

Of course, one should also note that the traditional authoritarian, hierarchical, and collectivistic orientations had their own share in this area. Nevertheless, close analysis should reveal that the stereotypical conception of the role of the traditional element may need modification. It may be true that loyalty or commitment on the part of select managerial and supervisory personnel with distinct family or other more personalistic connections was generated by such connections. As for the majority of the members of public or private bureaucracies, however, the extent of individualization must have been much greater, requiring a different flavor of authoritarian principle. For instance, compared with the Japanese, Korean workers and managers have been found to be more individualistic in orientation,[26] and it is well noted that the turnover rate is higher among Korean workers than among Japanese. Under the circumstances, the source of commitment and loyalty must be found in immediate and concrete incentives. However, because they were short of such resources, Korean organizations had to opt for a more authoritarian principle of mobilization than either the traditional familistic one or the modern rational one. No doubt, besides the nationalistic cause, some concrete incentives were offered, chiefly in the form of status attainment, if not of plush material kind. Despite their poor salaries, civil servants were able to enjoy power and authority; despite their low wages, managers and workers could now enjoy a new status of prestige and pride. Nonetheless, the fundamental principle of organization had to be that of centralized authoritarianism.

The need for such a centralized authoritarian organizational principle may also be understood in light of the urgency of rapid growth which in turn required social and political stability more than anything else. And this sentiment is well represented in a statement of a prime minister cited in the following:

> Some argue that wealth should be evenly distributed because of extreme polarization of the poor and the rich. But our economic capacity is still in the phase of accumulation rather than distribution. If this sort of argument spreads out in an agitative manner, people will come to hate entrepreneurs and the nation will be strayed into unrest and disorder which we cannot afford.[27]

At any rate, to demonstrate what kind of organizational principle was enforced in pursuit of rapid economic growth, let me quote another statement made by a political scientist who studied labor-union leaders in Korea in the early 1970s. He said:

> It is indeed questionable whether industrial workers will continue to accept the argument that they should endure sacrifices for the supreme national interest of uninterrupted economic growth. They might even feel that successful economic progress is irrelevant to them unless its benefits are widely and fairly shared by them on the basis of social justice and political democracy.[28]

These statements only indirectly reflect the principle organization adopted by the society in general and very tangentially by management, but they are quoted here to show what kind of consequences have unfolded out of such a principle. Since our interest here is confined to the search for East Asian models of development, the discussion cannot be extended to analysis of the consequences of taking certain distinctive steps in a country at a given point in history. It seems important, however, to at least suggest what may have been the results of choosing some specific strategies over others.

Conclusions

In this essay, I have attempted to define the Korean model of development as a form of adaptive change in the encounter with the surging tide of international acculturation or modernization. From that perspective, I have shown that some very distinctive nonrational psychological forces, often uniquely experienced and defined by the Korean nation and people, have played an unusually significant part in helping the country make it economically. These forces have their roots in various experiences the nation has undergone throughout its history and in the more recent past. They have not only motivated the people but also have been conducive to their adoption of certain specific principles of organization in the course of achieving economic growth.

It has been argued that neither the rationality of Confucianism nor that of Christianity but rather, **very unusual nonrational** forces have provided the impetus for the development Korea has accomplished thus far. The kind of rationality basically needed for technological production, rational management, and all the other know-how, attitudes, and behavioral patterns have been acquired traits through acculturation processes, mainly by means of education, mass communication, and other channels of information available in the society. Despite the assumption by many Western observers that a neo-Confucian ethos must have been the common thread leading the East Asian societies on the path to rapid growth, most indigenous authors, at least in the case of

Korea, happen to have some doubt about this contention. More often than not, these scholars have stressed the negative effects of Confucian traditions on the potential propensity to modernization and development. And the sort of virtues they locate in it usually have little relevance to or affinity with the type of rational capitalist spirit Weber alluded to in his work.[29]

There seem to be two lines of reasoning prevalent in the thought of the leading observers who believe East Asian tradition must have some connection with the economic behavior of these nations in recent history. On the one hand, most Western scholars would emphasize the strong tendency of the East Asian people to strict discipline and familistic collectivism which are considered as the major source of loyalty and commitment to work. Both are the typical virtues they find in neo-Confucianism, they claim. Others add the secularism of Buddhism. This line of thinking implies a surprise at finding contrasting traditions operating to produce similar results in history. [30] On the other hand, observers of Japan, in particular, tend to interpret the role of traditional religions like Confucianism or Buddhism in the process of Japan's modernization as a special type of Weberian Protestant ethic, only made possible by ingenious modification and application on the part of the Japanese. Other East Asian countries with different historical adoption of the same traditional religions, such as China and Korea, therefore, do not fall into the same basket, according to this line of argument.[31]

Both may be on the right track. But in order to explain the experience of South Korea, and for that matter even that of North Korea, I believe, as do many of my colleagues, that the relevance of traditional religions is rather slim or at most superficial. As I have tried to show, a virtue like discipline, for example, may not necessarily mean the same thing for the good old Confucian sage and for the political or entrepreneurial leadership charged with the responsibility of organizing the people for rapid economic growth. Familistic collectivism may be fine as long as it does not create problems of favoritism, nepotism, and all sorts of corruption. Even if it does create those problems, it still may be all right as long as it is conducive to loyalty and commitment. But more often than not, familistic collectivism has been causing more problems of irrational management, a lack of identity with larger collective units, and irritating and energy-consuming factional strife in organizations and in the society at large. Authoritarianism may have deep roots in the Confucian tradition in Korea, and authoritarianism has had its positive and negative effects on the society's performance. But what is more important is that even if it had played a positive role in the incipient stage of change, that sort of authoritarianism may have emanated from something of more recent and vivid history and experience than Confucianism as such.

Overall, as far as Korea is concerned, very few Koreans genuinely believe that Confucianism has been a significant contributory factor in the effort to accomplish rapid growth, and there exists little persuasive evidence to that effect. This goes also for Buddhism and even Christianity in Korea. One could argue that Christianity, when it was first introduced around the turn of the century, must have contributed to an inculcation of democratic ideals and modern values in the minds of adherents and younger-generation intellectuals. Nevertheless, evidence is negligible that the source of entrepreneurship of the 1960s lies disproportionately in Christianity.

Professor Berger has done an admirable job in his endeavor to bring to our attention the fact that both Confucianism and Mahayana Buddism prevalent in the East Asian tradition are quite unusually this-worldly in basic characteristics.[32] Therefore, he suspects that this secular orientation of East Asian religions must have some significant bearing on the economic performance of the NICs (newly industrialized countries) in this region. It would be unjustified to flatly reject this line of assumption. What I would add, however, is that in the case of Korea, shamanism, the indigenous folk religion, which has never ceased to exert a fundamental influence on the Korean mentality and the Korean outlook on life, has as its most deep-rooted distinct feature a very strong this-worldly tendency. My argument, with other experts in Korea, is that whatever religions—Confucianism, Buddhism, Taoism, Christianity, or others—that reached Kor ea might have been Koreanized (i.e., shamanized) and become secular and this-worldly.[33]

But the distinctive nature of Korea's development is something that goes one step deeper than even this secular orientation of Eastern religions that were introduced and Koreanized. Thus, I have pursued the line of argument that it may have been a combination of the unique experiences of the Korean people throughout their history and their adaptive effort in the changing environment that has produced the recent performance in the economic sphere. As such, it is only a very preliminary and crude set of reasoning which has to be much improved. As a hypothesis, however, it deserves some attention and serious examination.

In spite of all this, a final thought is in order to do justice to the possible role of traditional religions in Korea in molding the mind of the people to acquire a propensity for economic action conducive to development. Earlier, I listed adaptability as one of the behavioral features of the Korean people. Among other things, religious syncretism, specially noted for Korean society, must have helped instill this tendency of adaptability. Syncretic orientation in adopting and indigenizing alien religions has been remarkable throughout the history of this country. It was true even during the Yi Dynasty, which of course was an extremely rigid regime in an ideological, religious respect, when persecution of other religions and ideas was often severe. This syncretism is one of the central elements of shamanistic indigenous folk religion in Korea.[34]

The basic reasoning behind this contention would be that syncretism, being an open orientation by implication, could encourage attitudes that are open-minded to adopting certain new patterns. No doubt, the this-worldiness of the Korean people and their religious inclinations also might have had their own role in enhancing their adaptability, including syncretism. In this sense, Professor Berger's hypothesis deserves due attention. Now, however, even this adaptability in itself may or may not breed the kind of "rationality" Weber noticed in the spirit of Western capitalism of modern times. Whether that particular type of rationality is a requisite for capitalist development may be debatable. But if it is so, then the future of South Korea's capitalist development will largely depend on how successfully Koreans can utilize their adaptability to acquire that rationality to the extent that is minimally required for that purpose. My emphasis here has been that the major impetus thus far has been something nonrational, rather than rational.

Finally, as for the three basic questions raised by the search for an East Asian development model, I would offer the following observations. First, to the question of whether there is an East Asian development model, my answer is both "yes" and "no." As far as economic policy orientations or principles are concerned, several different East Asian NICs may share certain common elements or traits to the extent that they may be considered as constituting "a model," in a rough sense of the term. Nonetheless, when it comes to the more complicated combination of motivational factors, human qualities, organizational principles, and the whole gamut of other noneconomic elements, each nation of the Gang of Four in East Asia should be regarded as presenting a model of its own. In this sense, there is no single model but several different models of development in East Asia.

Second, if there is a model or models, then does each model contain noneconomic elements? If so, what are those social, cultural features? A partial answer has already been given above. To elaborate a bit more, those social and cultural traits are not confined to traditional religions. Even though such traditional religions have indeed played some role, the unique historical experiences and adaptive change each society undergoes must yield a unique combination of various social and cultural factors, which includes traditional religion. It is because of this that there is no one model but several models of East Asian development.

Third, are these models transferable to other developing or less developed societies? Personally, I doubt it. Once again, some of the economic policy elements may be learned from other societies. Even in this case, extreme caution is needed. Transferability of social and cultural traits is much more difficult, especially when they affect the human element of each society. Acculturation always entails adaptive change. Creative "indigenization" must be the clue to development for any society.

Notes

1. S.N. Eisenstadt, "The Protestant Ethic Thesis in an Analytical and Comparative Framework," in S.N. Eisenstadt, ed., *The Protestant Ethic and Modernization: A Comparative View* (New York: Basic Books, 1968), pp. 3–5.
2. See Peter L. Berger, "An East Asian Development Model?" *The Economic News* (Taipei), September 17–23, 1984, pp. 1–8; Peter L. Berger, "The Asian Experience and Caribbean Development," *Worldview* 27:10, October 1984, pp. 4–7; R. McFarquar, "The Post-Confucian Challenge," *The Economist*, February 9, 1980, pp. 67–72; and Michio Morishima, *Why Has Japan Succeeded? Western Technology and the Japanese Ethos* (Cambridge: Cambridge University Press, 1982).
3. Kyong-Dong Kim, *Man and Society in Korea's Economic Growth: Sociological Studies* (Seoul: Seoul National University Press, 1979).
4. P.W. Kuznets, "Korea's Emerging Industrial Structure," ILCORK Working Paper 6 (Honolulu: Social Science Research Institute, University of Hawaii, 1971).
5. See Jae-Ho Cha, "Character and Attitudes of the Korean People," in *Studies on Continuity and Change of Culture* (Seoul: Korean Social Science Research Council, 1980) (in Korean); Jae-Ho Cha, "Measures to Revitalize National Character: A Psychological Approach," in *Ethical Conceptions of Koreans* (Seoul: The Academy of Korean Studies, 1983), pp. 319–87; Yunshik Chang, "Personalism and Social Change in Korea," in Chang Yunshik et al., eds., *Society in Transition: With Reference to Korea* (Seoul: Seoul National University Press, 1982), pp. 29–43; Jae-Sak Choi, *The Korean Social Character* (Seoul: Minjosa, 1965) (in Korean); Tae-Kil Kim, *A Study of Korean Values* (Seoul: Munumsa, 1982) (in Korean); Kyong-Dong Kim, "Characteristic Features of Korean Society: A Sociological Approach," in *Essays in Commemoration of the Seventieth Birthday of Dr. Kim Hung-Bae* (Seoul: Korea University of Foreign Studies, 1984), pp. 295–317 (in Korean); and Kyu-Tae Lee, *The Korean Psychology: Who Is Korean?* (Seoul: Munlisa, 1977) (in Korean).
6. See Yu-Lan Fung, *A Short History of Chinese Philosophy* (New York: Free Press/ Macmillan, 1966), p. 294.
7. Jae-Ho Cha, "Measures to Revitalize National Character," op. cit.; Kyong-Dong Kim, "A Study of Confucian Values: Analysis of Textbooks," in *Collected Papers in Commemoration of Prof. Sang Beck Lee on His Sixtieth Birthday* (Seoul: Ulyou Publishing Co., 1964), pp. 333–68 (in Korean); and Byong Ik Koh, *Tradition and Modernization in East Asia* (Seoul: Samjiwon, 1984) (in Korean).
8. In-Hoe Kim, "Shamanism and Imported Religions," *Ideology and Policy* 1:3, 1984, pp. 131–46 (in Korean).
9. Kyong-Dong Kim, *Man and Society in Korea's Economic Growth*, op. cit.
10. Ibid.
11. Ibid.
12. Kyong-Dong Kim, *Rethinking Development: Theories and Experiences* (Seoul: Seoul National University Press, 1985).
13. Ibid.
14. Szymon Chodak, *Societal Development* (New York: Oxford University Press, 1973).
15. Kyong-Dong Kim, *Man and Society in Korea's Economic Growth*, op. cit.; and Man-Gap Lee, *Sociology and Social Change in Korea* (Seoul: Seoul National University Press, 1982).
16. John Badgley, *Asian Development: Problems and Prognosis* (New York: Free Press, 1971).

17. Kyong-Dong Kim et al., "Twelve Forces Behind Social Change in Korea, 1954–1984," special issue of *Social Science and Policy Research* 6:3 (Seoul: Seoul National University, 1984) (in Korean).
18. Kyong-Dong Kim, *Man and Society in Korea's Economic Growth*, op. cit.
19. N.C. Morse and R.S. Weiss, "The Function and Meaning of Work and the Job," *American Sociological Review* 20, April 1955, pp. 191–98.
20. On-Jook Lee-Kim, "Parental Sex Role Patterns in the Korean Family," unpublished master's thesis, Cornell University, 1976.
21. E.D. Devereaux, Jr. et al., "Child-Rearing in England and the United States: A Cross-National Comparison," *Journal of Marriage and the Family*, 1969, pp. 257–70.
22. R.P. Dore, "South Korean Development in Wider Perspective," in Chang Yunshik, ed., *Korea: A Decade of Development* (Seoul: Seoul National University Press, 1980), pp. 289–305.
23. Kyong-Dong Kim and On-Jook Lee-Kim, "The U.S.-Educated among the Korean Politico-Bureaucratic Elite: An Aspect of American Socio-Cultural Influence," *American Studies* 6 (Seoul: American Studies Institute, Seoul National University, 1983), pp. 53–69 (in Korean).
24. Kyong-Dong Kim et al., "Twelve Forces Behind Social Change in Korea," op. cit.
25. Kyong-Dong Kim, *Man and Society in Korea's Economic Growth*, op. cit.
26. Ibid.
27. Dong-A Ilbo, article on the statement made by Prime Minister Kim Jong Pil, December 20, 1973, p. 1 (in Korean).
28. Chae-Jin Lee, "Labor Movement and Political Development in Korea," ILCORK Working Paper 2 (Honolulu: Social Science Research Institute, University of Hawaii, 1971), pp. 27–28.
29. See Chae-Sik Chung et al., "The Social Function of Religion," *Ideology and Policy* 1:3, 1984, pp. 6–25 (in Korean); Sang-Yun Hyon, *A History of Confucianism* (Seoul: Minjungsogwan, 1960) (in Korean); Kyong-Dong Kim, "A Study of Confucian Values," op. cit.; Kee-Young Lee, "An Historical Understanding and Reflection on the Status of Religions in Korea," *Ideology and Policy* 1:3, 1984, pp. 26–38 (in Korean); and Woo-Hee Park, "The Spiritual Structure of Korean Capitalism," in *Essays in Memory of Sang Chul Suh* (Seoul: Korea Economic Review, 1984), pp. 63–74 (in Korean).
30. See S.N. Eisenstadt, "The Protestant Ethic Thesis," op. cit.; Robert N. Bellah, "Reflections on the Protestant Ethic Analogy in Asia," in S.N. Eisenstadt, ed., *The Protestant Ethic and Modernization: A Comparative View*, op. cit.; R. McFarquar, "The Post-Confucian Challenge," op. cit.; Roy Hofheinz, Jr. and K.E. Calder, *The Eastasia Edge* (New York: Basic Books, 1982); Peter L. Berger, "An East Asian Development Model?" op. cit.; and Peter L. Berger, "The Asian Experience and Caribbean Development," op. cit.
31. See Robert N. Bellah, "Reflections on the Protestant Ethic Analogy in Asia," op cit.; and Michio Morishima, *Why Has Japan Succeeded?* op. cit.
32. Peter L. Berger, "An East Asian Development Model?" op. cit.; and Peter L. Berger, "The Asian Experience and Caribbean Development," op. cit.
33. In-Hoe Kim, "Shamanism and Imported Religions," op. cit.; and Chae-Sik Chung et al., "The Social Function of Religions," op. cit.
34. Kyong-Dong Kim, *Man and Society in Korea's Economic Growth*, op. cit.; and In-Hoe Kim, "Shamanism and Imported Religions," op. cit.

11

The Distinctive Features of Two City-States' Development: Hong Kong and Singapore

Pang Eng Fong

Of the four East Asian developing countries that have successfully followed the export-led path to rapid development in the past quarter century, two of them—Hong Kong and Singapore—are small, resource-poor city-economies that began as British colonies in the nineteenth century and owed their early prosperity to their role as regional entrepôts. As city-states with an economic significance much greater than their physical size, they represent a form of political organization common before the rise of the nation state some 500 years ago but rare today.[1] There is, however, a great difference in the political evolution of the two cities, a difference that accounts for their strikingly dissimilar perspectives on the role of government in the economy and society.

A colony administered by Britain since 1843, Hong Kong has been greatly influenced by developments in China. Its political machinery has remained largely unchanged since its founding: political power is concentrated in the hands of a British-appointed governor and the bureaucracy. Appointed officials form the majority of members on the Executive Council which advises the governor on policy matters, and on the Legislative Council which makes laws. Hong Kong is, therefore, not a Western-style democracy in the sense that its people have the right to elect their own representatives, but it is a free and open society. When its lease to the New Territories expires in 1997, Hong Kong will become, as a result of the Sino-British agreement reached in September 1984, a special administrative region of China, but it will retain its present economic system for 50 years after 1997 in line with China's policy experiment of one country, two systems. Unlike Hong Kong, Singapore was granted self-government in 1959, and became an independent nation with a parliamentary form of government in 1965 after its attempt at political integration with Peninsular Malaysia, its traditional hinterland, failed.

While the course of their political evolution is different, the economic features and achievements of the two city-economies are similar in many respects. They remain, as their British founders had intended them, open and outward-looking economies committed to free trade, receptive to foreign ideas and technology, and attuned to changes in regional and international economic conditions. They are among the few countries in the world whose foreign trade exceeds their GDP; Singapore's volume of imports and exports is three and a half times its GDP while that of Hong Kong is twice. Both cities diversified from entrepôt activities into the production of labor-intensive manufactures for world markets. Hong Kong did so in the early 1950s when its entrepôt trade with China was closed off by trade embargoes following China's involvement in the Korean War. Singapore's export-oriented industrialization took off only after its separation from Malaysia in 1965. In the 1970s, both city-states moved into traded services, including finance, transport and communications, and tourism. In both places, export-led growth, accompanied by slowing population growth, brought full employment and rapidly rising standards of living. Real per-capita income in both cities has risen by over five percent per year since the mid-1960s.

While impressed by the two city-states' rapid development, many analysts question the relevance of their experience to other developing countries.[2] They argue, among other things, that the two city-economies have the advantage of favorable initial conditions—a good harbor and strategic location, the absence of a large agricultural sector, a long-established free trade regime, an energetic immigrant population, and well-developed port, financial, and communications services, advantages that smoothed their industrialization path. Thus, no useful lessons for other developing countries can be extrapolated from their experience. This chapter takes the opposite view. Its central theme is that while the two city-states' development is distinctive in many respects, a few lessons can nevertheless be extrapolated from their experience. It compares first the development progress of the two cities, highlighting key similarities and differences. It then assesses the contribution of cultural, social, and economic factors to their development progress.

Development Performance

In growth terms, the experiences of the two city-states are similar.[3] Since 1960, both city-economies have expanded by an average of over eight percent per year, a performance matched only in the last quarter century by Japan and the other two newly industrializing countries—South Korea and Taiwan—with which they share a number of common characteristics, including a

Confucian-influenced majority culture and a high degree of social homogeneity. Singapore's economic performance is the steadier of the two. Its growth rate over the past quarter century has been less variable, mainly because of the government's more effective use of macroeconomic instruments to stimulate the economy when external demand weakens.[4] Reflecting its much less interventionist administration, which refrains from activist stimulatory policies, Hong Kong has an economy that is fully exposed to the vagaries of external demand. But its vulnerability also endows it with a built-in capacity to adjust more flexibly than Singapore to international economic fluctuations; declining external demand for Hong Kong's exports deflates prices and wages swiftly, making the island's products more competitive, thus stimulating exports, income, and employment.

Hong Kong, which began industrializing in the early 1950s, about a decade earlier than Singapore, outperformed its twin by an average of one percentage point per year in the 1960s and 1970s. In 1983–84 Hong Kong's growth rate faltered, mainly because of uncertainties about its political future. From 1980 to 1984 Singapore's economy benefited from continuing political stability and expansionary policies, hence its faster rate of growth compared with Hong Kong. But in 1985, it shrank by nearly two percent, partly because of weak external demand and partly because of internal problems including high operating costs, maturing key industries, an oversized public sector, and overinvestment in the early 1980s in construction. Hong Kong, too, performed badly in 1985, its economy expanding by only three percent because of a sharp decline in exports to the United States and China, its two largest markets.

The export performance of the two city-states has on the whole been impressive. Both Hong Kong and Singapore registered manufacturing export growth of fifteen percent per year in the 1960s and 1970s. Hong Kong, the largest exporter of clothing in the world, accounts for a third of the textiles and wearing apparel OECD countries import from developing countries. It is also the developing world's largest exporter of toys and watches. Singapore, whose manufacturing exports are more diversified than those of Hong Kong, is a major exporter of electronic products, including computer peripherals.

Both Hong Kong and Singapore achieved rapid growth with price stability in the 1960s. In the 1970s, their inflation rates rose because their open economies were exposed to world inflationary pressures stemming from two oil crises and international monetary instability. In the 1970s, Hong Kong's inflation rate exceeded that of Singapore, whose appreciating currency—the consequence of a consistently healthy overall balance of payments and large capital inflows—dampened imported inflationary pressures. In the first half of the 1980s, Hong Kong continued to suffer from high inflation, against a world disinflationary trend which began in 1982. In the period 1982–84, the colony's annual inflation rate averaged ten percent, twice that of Singapore. A weaker Hong Kong dollar and higher food prices charged by China, its main supplier, contributed to the island's high inflation.

High unemployment characterized both Hong Kong and Singapore when they began industrializing. By the early 1960s, Hong Kong, the earlier starter on the road to industrialization, had wiped out most of its labor surplus.[5] Singapore reached the same position in the early 1970s, thanks mainly to the large influx of labor-intensive firms from industrial countries. Since the early 1970s, both cities have enjoyed full employment, with labor demand outstripping labor supply in many sectors. Singapore has had to import large numbers of skilled and unskilled foreign workers since the early 1970s to sustain its economic expansion.[6]

Rapid growth in both city-states has apparently not worsened income disparities. The far-from-conclusive evidence for Hong Kong suggests a slight deterioration in the distribution of income in the 1960s and 1970s because of the vast expansion of job opportunities, and increased income disparities in the 1980s because of high inflation and slower growth.[7] As for Singapore, its income distribution has improved marginally since 1966 with the growth in employment opportunities and increased public spending on housing and education.[8] More impressive than the marginal improvement in income distribution is the recent absolute decline in the number of persons in low-income households: between 1977 and 1982, rapidly rising wages shrank by 36 percent the number of persons in households earning less than an inflation-adjusted monthly income of S$500 (US$230).[9]

Both city-states achieved rapid industrialization without relying on large external loans, unlike South Korea whose export-led industrial growth in the 1970s was heavily financed by foreign loans. Their open economies and stability have induced foreign capital inflows, while their efficient financial institutions, which offer real positive interest rates, have encouraged savings. In 1984 Singapore had a savings rate equal to 41 percent of its GDP, possibly the highest in the world, while Hong Kong's rate of 25 percent was twice that of most industrial countries. A rising savings rate in both cities has financed ever-increasing noninflationary domestic investment which has spurred growth and productivity. Faster growth obtained by creating and spreading wealth has in turn made greater savings possible. Thus, rising savings and fast growth have reinforced each other in a virtual circle in the two city-states.

Rapid economic growth of the two city-states is only but one facet of their extraordinary development success. Their achievements in other fields are equally remarkable. Both cities enjoy a degree of social harmony and racial tolerance uncommon among multiracial, densely-populated societies, which is a notable achievement considering their past histories and potential for social conflict. Their crime rates are low in comparison with many cities of the same size in Western industrialized countries. In both cities, educational opportunities have expanded greatly with economic growth. The quality of health care and housing has risen steadily. The Hong Kong government has built low-cost apartments for close to half of the island's population of five million. In Singapore four-fifths of the population live in public housing estates, and two in three families own the homes they live in.

Describing the development progress of the two city-states is easy, but understanding and explaining how they achieved this progress is much more difficult. Rapid economic transformation in the two city-states took place only in the last quarter century. But it would be a mistake to see it only as the consequence of successful internal responses to external conditions in the last quarter century. Past personalities, policies, traditions, and institutions all played a part in shaping the city-states' capacity to seize opportunities created by internal policies and external circumstances. The problem is to separate the effects of past conditioning factors from the effects of facilitating internal policies and external circumstances.

At one level, the rapid development of the two city-states can be "explained" in economic terms as the result of the quantitative expansion of capital and labor. But this explanation is unsatisfactory for it provides no understanding of the engine that sparked the rapid accumulation of capital and labor. At another level, the two city-states' development can be attributed to their choice of growth-inducing policies, e.g., free trade and liberal investment policies, that "get prices right" and so promote efficient resource allocation. Such an explanation identifies the various policies and programs and details the ways in which they foster efficiency and growth. While more satisfying than the simplistic, quantitative explanation of growth, this ahistorical explanation is also not complete—it does not explain how or why the right growth-inducing policies came to be chosen and effectively implemented. A full understanding of the structure and processes of decision making that led to effective growth-oriented development policies requires a historically rooted analysis of personalities, social groups, and institutions—an immense task beyond the scope of this chapter, the main focus of which is on the distinctive aspects of the two city-states' development.

Some Distinctive Features of the Two City-States

Immigrant Populations

Historically, both Hong Kong and Singapore flourished as entrepôts, the former serving China and the latter the Southeast Asian region. From the beginning, they attracted a large flow of self-selected energetic immigrants; Hong Kong drew its population mostly from China, while Singapore's immigrants came from Southern China, India, and the Malay archipelago, giving the republic a more ethnically diverse population than Hong Kong. Both societies have thus been deeply influenced by an immigrant mentality with its characteristic preoccupation with short-term goals and reliance on extensive intra-group social networks. The immigrant outlook continues to shape aspirations and behavior, more so in Hong Kong, where the population does not share a deep sense of belonging to a nation and is imbued with an abiding feeling of insecurity because of the colony's uncertain future, than in Singapore, where successful nation-building and development have instilled in Singaporeans a strong sense of nationhood and security.

Hong Kong's position as a borrowed free port living on borrowed time, administered by the British but prospering with Chinese labor and enterprise because it serves China's interests, gave people in Hong Kong little choice but to channel their abundant energies singlemindedly into wealth-creating activities. Its largely Chinese population could not aspire to high political office or top positions in the civil service, nor could they take up military careers (which do not, in any case, rank high in terms of social status in Chinese eyes). For the Hong Kong people, the private sector was, therefore, their only route to wealth, security, and social status. The island also did not have a landed gentry class which could afford to refrain from wealth-generating activities while upholding high moral, nonmaterialist values. Free of the moral strictures against an excessive concern with material wealth, its immigrant people could devote their entire energies unreservedly to the pursuit of economic gains.

Conditions in Singapore before self-government in 1959 were in many respects similar to those in Hong Kong. Reflecting its immigrant origins, Singapore's population, though taking on an increasingly settled character because of the cessation of immigration from China and India in the early 1950s, was preoccupied with economic pursuits. The people of Singapore could not aspire to political office or high posts in government. But unlike Hong Kong, there emerged in Singapore a nationalist movement that saw the island's political future as inseparable from that of the then Federation of Malaya. No one then envisioned that Singapore could survive as a separate political entity, which explains why Singapore's first elected representative government led by the People's Action Party vigorously pursued a political merger with Malaya.

Singapore's separation from Malaysia in 1965 was a traumatic event that produced in its political leaders an enduring sense of psychological insecurity and a clear-eyed awareness of Singapore's vulnerable position in Southeast Asia. On top of the daunting challenge of economic survival, Singapore's political leaders had to build a nation out of an ethnically diverse, immigrant population given to individualistic pursuits. Unlike Hong Kong, where the economic struggle consumes all energies in what was until the last few years essentially an environment of "frozen politics," Singapore's struggle for political and economic survival was one and the same thing. It led to the politics of survival, a set of policies and strategies aimed at curbing domestic dissent and promoting stability and industrial peace to attract much-needed foreign investment while instilling in the island's ethnically diverse population a sense of national identity.[10]

The Role of Government in the Economy

Reflecting their different political evolutions and the different backgrounds of their rulers, Hong Kong and Singapore have governments that differ greatly in their propensity to intervene in the economy and society. Historically, both city-states were founded as free ports to advance British commercial, not territorial, interests. In Hong Kong, the economic philosophy of laissez-faire remains essentially intact, though there has been a growing involvement of the government in the economy since the late 1960s. Taxes on both individuals and companies are low, but there are no tax concessions, as in Singapore, for desired economic activities. The government limits its economic role to the provision of basic infrastructure and to ensuring a favorable economic climate for private enterprise. It owns no industries, imposes few trade restrictions, and allows free capital flows. It also does not directly control the product or labor markets; workers are free to change jobs, trade unions which have organized only eleven percent of the workforce exert little influence on wages, and private enterprise is allowed in all sectors, including utilities.

The absence of government restrictions on capital, labor, and enterprise, however, does not make Hong Kong a classic laissez-faire economy in which the state limits itself to the administration of law and justice and to the provision of defense and public works. To begin with, the Hong Kong government is an active participant in the land market. Its land sales, which account for a significant proportion of its revenues, influence indirectly the costs of business. It has provided through its land sales low-cost housing for over half the population. The public sector accounts for a fifth of the island's GDP and employs over a sixth of its labor force. Its expenditures as a percentage of GDP amounted to a quarter of the island's GDP in recent years, a proportion comparable to that of Singapore. The Hong Kong bureaucracy, which is not small in comparison with many other developing countries, makes policies on many matters, including transportation, labor, education, and social services, that affect the business environment. For its part, the government promotes exports through such agencies as the Trade Development Council and the Hong Kong Productivity Centre. Since the late 1960s, in response to growing public pressure, it has greatly expanded social services, low-cost health facilities, and highly subsidized educational institutions, developments that belie its laissez-faire image of minimal government. In short, to Hong Kong's government, the laissez-faire philosophy is not an ironclad ideology but only a flexible guide.

The role of the government in the economy in Singapore is similar in many ways to that in Hong Kong, but it is also different in a number of significant respects. Like Hong Kong, Singapore is a free-enterprise economy with few trade restrictions. Protective tariffs on local industry are few and were not high even during the island's brief period of import-substituting industrialization in the early 1960s. Capital is allowed to flow freely, and there are few controls on private investment, which is allowed in most sectors except utilities and defense. There are no anti-monopoly laws, no approval process for foreign or local private investments (except those that seek investment incentives), no controls on technology transfer, and no domestic-content requirements. As in Hong Kong, the relative absence of official controls in the product and capital markets does not imply a hands-off government. The difference between Hong Kong and Singapore is that the Singapore government has been much more active in using the power of the state to develop the economy. If Hong Kong can be described as having a guiding philosophy of laissez-faire, where the government leans away from interventions, Singapore can be characterized as adhering to a philosophy of economic liberalism, but with selective and powerful state controls in key areas of the economy.

Beginning with self-government, Singapore's key political leaders, all of whom were influenced by Fabian ideas of social democracy, have shown a willingness to enlarge the state's involvement in the economy. When they came to power in 1959, they espoused the causes of democratic socialism. But hard realities tempered their socialist inclinations—there were few industries the government could nationalize, and Singapore's economy was too small for a policy of self-reliant development. But Singapore had few industrial entrepreneurs to realize the government's objective of diversifying the island's stagnating economy. The government, therefore, felt it had to take the initiative in setting up new development agencies and enterprises. Over the past quarter century, the government, on its own or in partnership with private interests, has become heavily involved in the production of goods and services. There are nearly 500 government-owned companies and statutory boards involved in a wide range of manufacturing and service activities, including steel mills, textiles, electronics, oil refining, hotels, shipbuilding and repairing, shipping, financial services, air transport, and property development. These government-owned enterprises range from large ones, such as Singapore Airlines and the Neptune Orient Line (the national air and shipping lines, respectively), to small ones, like Jurong Bird Park and Sentosa Development Corporation. They all operate as profit-making concerns, reflecting the government's longstanding philosophy in favor of profits and opposed to public subsidies (except for housing, health care, and education). Together they employ over a fifth of the island's labor force of 1.2 million. Their turnover in 1983 was S$8 billion, and their profits amounted to close to ten percent of turnover, which is a high rate of return compared to that of most private firms.[11]

The Singapore government's involvement in direct production is not the result of an ideological inclination but a pragmatic response to changing conditions. Unlike the Hong Kong government, the Singapore government believes that so long as its "enterprises are run on business lines, receive no special privileges and are fully competitive with the private sector, that is sufficient justification for the existence and expansion of these enterprises."[12] In the government's view, it was fruitless to argue about where the limit of government participation in the economy should lie. In the early years, the government's main reason for getting involved in direct production was to lead the way in large, high-risk projects—National Iron and Steel Mills and Jurong Shipyard are examples. The government also set up state-owned companies to take over functions from public agencies that had grown too rapidly—its motive in this case was to ensure continuing institutional efficiency and flexibility and not to create job opportunities for its political supporters as is the case in many developing countries. In keeping with its overriding philosophy of economic efficiency, the government has not been averse to abolishing state agencies that had outlived their usefulness or to withdrawing financial support from unprofitable government-owned companies.

Because of its heavy direct and indirect involvement in the economy, the government exercises considerable leverage on the domestic macroeconomy, beyond the use of conventional tax and spending policies. Over half of the domestic income passes through its hands in one way or another—through the 50 percent share of employee income that goes into the Central Provident Fund (CPF), various direct and indirect taxes, and tariffs charged by state enterprises. It influences construction activity through its public housing and property development activities and through its periodic land sales. Through the Monetary Authority of Singapore, its quasi-central bank, it regulates the financial markets and controls the domestic money supply.

Unlike the Hong Kong government, the Singapore government has been more active in employing macroeconomic policies to influence the level of aggregate economic activity and to moderate inflationary pressures. During the economic downturns that followed the world recessions in the mid-1970s and early 1980s, it greatly expanded public investments. To minimize the inflationary consequences of large net capital inflows and rapidly rising incomes, it has steadily raised CPF contribution rates, thus siphoning spending power out of the income stream while sterilizing capital inflows as foreign reserves.

While the labor market is free in Hong Kong, in Singapore it is strongly influenced by government policies on wages and foreign labor.[13] Since 1972, when it set up a tripartite wages council to recommend annual wage guidelines, the Singapore government has been able to influence the rate of money-wage increases, though in ways that reflect underlying market conditions. Until the late 1970s, it practiced a policy of wage restraint, which was reinforced by the liberal importation of unskilled foreign workers and was designed to protect the competitive edge of Singapore's labor-intensive industries. In the last few years, it has allowed wages to rise rapidly while tightening conditions on the import of unskilled labor in an effort to boost productivity and discourage the inefficient use of labor. In consequence, operating costs rose sharply, undermining its competitiveness at the same time that its key industries were maturing or facing weak external demand. While market conditions determine wages in Hong Kong, their impact on wages in Singapore is modified to some extent by government policy. The result is that wages in Hong Kong are more volatile while those in Singapore are more predictable, despite the fact that both economies face similar external economic conditions.

Unlike the government in Hong Kong, which refrains from sector-specific policies, the Singapore government offers a variety of incentives—tax holidays, research and training grants, investment credits, accelerated depreciation allowances, etc.—to induce private industry to invest in desired industries. These incentives, which have increased Singapore's attractiveness to foreign investors relative to that of many other developing countries, have helped to upgrade Singapore's industrial structure. They account in part for the wider range and different ownership pattern of manufacturing industries in Singapore as compared to Hong Kong. In Singapore, the key industries in the early 1960s were food, printing and publishing, and textiles and garments— all low value-added activities owned largely by locals and catering mainly to the domestic market. A decade later, thanks to the influx of foreign firms and government economic leadership, the dominant industries were electronics, shipbuilding and repairing, oil refining, and metal engineering—all relatively high value-added industries. A shift in ownership patterns accompanied Singapore's industrial diversification. By the late 1960s, foreign firms had become dominant in the manufacturing sector, accounting for a majority share of the sector's output, employment, and exports. Their dominance has grown over the years—in 1982 they accounted for 55 percent of the employment, 74 percent of the output, 67 percent of the value-added, and 84 percent of the exports in the manufacturing sector. Local firms, which also expanded along with the influx of large foreign firms, played a supporting role in Singapore's export-led growth.

In contrast to Singapore, Hong Kong's industrial growth has been based largely on the expansion and upgrading of textiles and garments, an industry started by refugee entrepreneurs who brought with them capital and skills from China in the early 1950s. Though Hong Kong has diversified since the late 1950s into other industries, including toys, watches, and electronics, textiles and garments remains the colony's most important industry accounting for two-fifths of its exports. Unlike in Singapore where the key industries are dominated by large firms and mostly foreign-owned, Hong Kong's major industry is characterized by a multitude of small firms owned by Shanghainese and Cantonese entrepreneurs. In Hong Kong, foreign interests are significant only in the newer industries like metal engineering, chemicals, and electronics.

Reflecting the different role of the government in the economy, the two city-states have evolved along different lines. In Singapore, with an activist government that sees its role as more than just ensuring a conducive environment for business, the development pattern could be described as the result of *managerial capitalism* because of the island's heavy dependence on domestic and foreign managers in the development process. Small entrepreneurs have played a minor supporting role. Indeed, their activities in many areas have been crowded out by the expansion of large state and foreign enterprises. Hong Kong's development pattern, which is characterized by a high dependence on small and adaptable entrepreneurs to find new business opportunities and a minimal involvement of the government in direct production, may be described as the result of *entrepreneurial capitalism.*

In recent years, both city-states have begun to realize the limits of their development models. Singapore's current perspective is that private entrepreneurship should be the engine of growth in the 1980s, and not the government as was the case in the 1960s and 1970s.[14] The Singapore government believes that government enterprises are approaching the limits of their growth and that private entrepreneurs are needed to seek out new areas of investments for Singapore's maturing economy. Accordingly, the government will divest its shares in companies in which it does not have a majority share and in which it is not essential for the government to have effective control. It will sell to the public shares in companies in which it must for national reasons maintain a controlling interest. But it will continue to invest in new priority areas, such as computers and biotechnology, where private entrepreneurs are unwilling to risk their capital. Apart from privatization, the government is also planning to reduce onerous regulations and increase assistance to local firms to stimulate entrepreneurship. The deep recession that began in 1985 has prompted it to review its basic economic policies, particularly its role in the economy.

While Singapore is encouraging the emergence of entrepreneurial capitalism, Hong Kong is increasingly aware of the problems of entrepreneurial capitalism. These problems include an excessive preoccupation of firms with short-term profit maximization, insufficient attention to product quality and technological upgrading, and inadequate public and private investments in training and capital equipment—all deficiencies that large organizations with their characteristic longer planning horizon can help to remedy, as they did in the case of Singapore. While continuing to affirm the primacy of market forces in resource allocation, the Hong Kong government has acknowledged that "there are certain services and facilities which it is either more convenient and efficient for the Government to provide or which should be provided, as a matter of policy. . . ."[15] It has thus slightly modified its resistance to enlarging the role of the government in the economy. But unlike the Singapore government, the Hong Kong government has yet to initiate new industrial policies to encourage the growth of large organizations or the merger of small manufacturing firms. Even so, the development perspective in Hong Kong appears to be slowly converging with that of Singapore: the Singapore government is actively encouraging the development of entrepreneurial capitalism while the Hong Kong government is establishing new agencies, including the recent one to promote technological innovation in industry.

The changing involvement of the government in the economy in the two city-economies has not altered the basic determinants of their economic growth. So long as both remain open economies, their future will hinge on their adaptability to new patterns of world demand. While Hong Kong's economic prospects are increasingly tied to the modernization program in China, the colony's second largest trading partner after the United States, and that of Singapore is increasingly linked to that of the Southeast Asian region, both city-states must depend on continued access to developed country markets for sustained growth.

Social interventions and political process. While the governments' perspectives of their role in the economies of the two city-states appears to be converging, their involvement in noneconomic areas remains very different. The Hong Kong government practices a policy of social noninterventionism, a policy that parallels its laissez-faire stance in the economy. Its civil bureaucracy, which is still dominated in the upper reaches by expatriates from Britain, has refrained for good reasons from trying to shape the values and norms of the Hong Kong population along British or Western lines. It understood the deeply rooted Chinese distaste for a socially interventionist government and the need not so much for political freedom as for freedom from political oppression. Also, it did not have the administrative capacity to carry out a large program of social transformation, even if it was so inclined. Instead, it has adjusted the colony's administrative apparatus to the organization of Chinese society in Hong Kong, thus minimizing conflicts with the Chinese population and ensuring a politically stable environment to give the people in Hong Kong considerable freedom to pursue their economic objectives. As a result, Hong Kong has evolved a sociopolitical system in which the polity is only weakly linked to the society at large—the British-controlled bureaucracy and the Chinese society it administers have limited contacts, despite the government's appointment of the Chinese elite to various committees (mostly wealthy businessmen whose views do not reflect that of the majority Chinese population). The weak linkages between the bureaucracy and the Chinese society do not mean that the bureaucracy is unresponsive to the aspirations and expectations of the population. On the contrary, it is fairly responsive to popular demands, though always in ways that preserve its autonomy and enhance support for its basic policies.

In contrast to Hong Kong, Singapore has developed a political system that is highly integrated with the social system. The popularly elected government has from the beginning shown a great willingness, indeed considered it vital, to intervene in the social system, both to foster new attitudes and values favorable to nation-building and to form new multiracial grassroots organizations to supplant social units organized along communal or familial lines.[17] These grassroots organizations—the community centers, the Citizens' Consultative Committees, the Residents' Committees in housing estates—serve to link the ruling political party to the people.[18] In the interests of the larger society, the government has over the years imposed various controls and regulations on many areas that affect social life in Singapore, particularly family planning, compulsory savings, public housing, education, and land transport. In consequence, the people in Singapore are subject to a much greater degree of social control and state intervention in their personal lives than people in Hong Kong. The different level of state intervention in the social realm has, however, produced the same result in both city-states, namely a long period of social and political stability which has enhanced their capacity to adjust quickly to changing external conditions.[19]

Though the political processes in the two city-states differ, the policymaking process is broadly similar. In Hong Kong, decision-making powers are concentrated in the governor and his advisers. Businessmen appointed to government advisory bodies have an indirect and sometimes strong influence on government policies, but the people's participation in decision making is small. In Singapore, decision making is also highly centralized, with a key number of political leaders, namely the prime minister and his close colleagues, making the basic policy decisions. Until last year when the ruling party lost 2 seats out of 79 in the general elections and began to be more sensitive to public feedback to its policies, the people in Singapore have not been greatly involved in the making of policies that affect their lives. In both city-states, interest and other pressure groups have not exerted a strong influence on major policies as they have in many industrial countries.

In both Hong Kong and Singapore, the style of government—impersonal in the case of Hong Kong and paternalistic in the case of Singapore—has led until the last few years to a depoliticized population. In both city-states, the government has discouraged competitive politics as disruptive and unproductive activities that undermine social harmony and economic progress. Instead, its policies have created a political process that could be called petitionary politics. In petitionary politics, the dissatisfied seek redress to problems by writing or complaining to the appropriate body. The bureaucracy responds to problems, making adjustments to policies and programs if necessary, but often acting only to diffuse or deflect the issue. This process increases the power of the bureaucracy and political leaders while enhancing their flexibility and minimizing the possibility that the problem will develop into a major political issue, which it could in a system where there are competing political parties or powerful interest groups.

Public administration in both city-states, which are largely Chinese societies increasingly subject to Western influences, is consistent with traditional Chinese ideals of good government. In the first place, both governments have been able to maintain security, order, and justice. While the Singapore government has intervened in both the economic and social realms, it has, like the Hong Kong government, given considerable freedom to its people to make individual economic decisions. Second, both governments appoint public officials on the basis of merit, not patronage, a method of selection similar to the examination system used for appointing officials in imperial China. Such a method of selection ensures that the civil bureaucracy at least has the potential to be efficient and effective. Third, the benevolent consultative paternalism that both governments practice is considered an ideal of good government in traditional Chinese thought. In this form of government, the leader—the prime minister in the case of Singapore, the governor in the case of Hong Kong—provides moral leadership and creates the conditions for material progress in return for which he receives the trust and loyalty of the people. That the characteristics of the government in the two city-states coincide with traditional Chinese ideals of good government, however, do not imply that their development progress is primarily the result of cultural factors, and therefore cannot be replicated elsewhere. As the next section suggests, external and structural factors have played a critical role in the two city-states' development success in the last quarter century.

Accounting for the City-States' Development Success

In many respects, both Hong Kong and Singapore are unique—their city-state status and entrepôt colonial origins make them atypical economies. But the immigrant character of their population and their small size are not that uncommon among developing countries. Their Confucian-influenced majority culture is shared in varying degrees by other countries, some economically successful, e.g., Japan, South Korea and Taiwan, and others less successful e.g., China, until the last few years when it began adopting more outward-looking and liberal economic policies, and North Korea. While their development progress is remarkable, so also is that of several much larger Southeast Asian states, especially Thailand, Malaysia, and Indonesia.

While the two city-states owe their early prosperity to their entrepôt role, their development success in the last quarter century is the result of export-led industrialization. Both Hong Kong and Singapore enjoyed some initial advantages when they began industrializing—good infrastructure, an effective civil service, an adaptable, outward-looking population, the absence of a large backward agriculture sector. But they also suffered from several disadvantages, including a small domestic market, the lack of resources, and a shortage of industrial skills, though the latter deficiency was more severe in Singapore than in Hong Kong.

The city-states' initial assets would have mattered little if external world conditions had not been favorable to export growth and if internal policies had not fostered the predictable, stable environment that enabled them to seize the opportunities created by favorable external circumstances. Both city-states industrialized during a period when the developed countries were enjoying fast economic growth and world trade was expanding at an unprecedented rate. Had the developed countries not expanded their demand for manufactures from developing countries, it is most unlikely that the two city-states (and also many other developing countries) would have grown as rapidly as they did. Favorable world conditions, however, are of course only part of the explanation: other countries too faced the same external environment but they did not capitalize on it. In the case of the two city-states, they were able to take advantage of favorable external conditions because of certain structural features in their societies. Both societies were able to maintain an environment conducive to the formulation of stable, predictable policies and to the pursuit of economic gains. Both believe in free trade and open competition. Neither has protected inefficient industries. Though they have intervened to different degrees in the economy, the governments of both city-states recognize the primacy of market forces in determining resource allocation. From the start, the Singapore government viewed its intervention in the economy from the objective of expanding industrial capacity and improving economic performance. It provided low-cost housing, education, and medical services, but it did not confuse the goal of economic efficiency in production with the goal of equity in distribution. The many interventions that the Singapore government made were intended therefore not to supplant market forces but to remedy clear cases of market failures.

In both city-states, had the long-established policy of economic liberalism been abandoned, the outcome would have been disastrous. In Hong Kong, the idea of discarding laissez-faire for a planned economy was never seriously debated. In Singapore, the political leadership, despite its socialist rhetoric when it came to power, did not try to alter the open nature of the Singapore economy. Instead, the government set about developing a network of efficient and flexible development organizations to realize its economic and social goals. Like the government in Hong Kong, its emphasis was on order and stability, conditions that did not obtain in Singapore in the 1950s and that the government considered crucial to the success of its industrialization program. While the Hong Kong government realized these goals by not tampering with the norms and values of the Chinese society it ruled, the Singapore government achieved them through a variety of administrative and legal measures which depoliticized the population and suppressed domestic dissent.

Some observers have suggested that the development success of Singapore and Hong Kong (and also South Korea and Taiwan) is largely due to the fact that they are Confucianist societies.[20] They argue that Confucianist values such as respect for authority, loyalty to good leaders, preference for order and harmony, and a taste for education and hard work have been crucial to their development progress. Their argument, however, is based on a selective interpretation of Confucianism. Historically, Confucianism provided a set of ideals and guides for political life. It emphasized obedience to benevolent rulers as its central value and loyalty to rulers as an extension of family loyalty. Until recently, when the economic performance of the East Asian countries began to attract world attention, many analysts (including Weber) viewed Confucianism as a conservative doctrine that stressed the maintenance of traditions, and not as a philosophy that favored economic and social progress. True, Confucianism fosters certain values that are supportive of growth— e.g., nontheistic flexibility, emphasis on self-discipline and familial group support, respect for education, and absence of ideological restraints on the pursuit of material goals, willingness to subordinate self in a hierarchy. But to highlight these positive values of Confucianism while ignoring its growth-inhibiting values is unsatisfactory for it leaves unexplained why its presumed growth-inducing values, after being dormant for centuries, should suddenly come alive in the past quarter century in four East Asian developing countries. A more satisfactory view would be to consider Confucianism as a factor that can be a positive force for development when the right set of structural conditions and economic policies are also present.

The experience of Hong Kong and Singapore, though unique in many ways and not likely to be replicated elsewhere, suggests that certain policies are helpful in creating the right environment which allows individuals and firms to take advantage of favorable external conditions. Perhaps the most important set of policies are those that favor open competition and preserve the discipline of the market. Neither Singapore nor Hong Kong, for example, introduced for reasons of economic nationalism or distributional equity, price distortions into their economies. Neither economy made extensive use of direct measures such as licenses, quotas, or price controls to influence private decision making. In consequence, both producers and consumers in the city-states had to respond to price signals from world markets. Because their governments avoided direct measures, powerful interest groups dependent on licenses and official favors did not grow and entrench themselves. In consequence, public institutions in both city-states were less constrained and could make policies that benefited the general public rather than some specific interest group. Also, public officials had less scope for arbitrary and self-seeking behavior.

Second, the experience of the two city-states suggests the critical role of efficient public agencies in economic development. Though the Hong Kong bureaucracy does not interfere directly in private economic decision making, its effectiveness ensures a healthy business climate. Reflecting its more interventionist character, Singapore has developed a wider range of public agencies to execute development policies than Hong Kong. But like Hong Kong, its public agencies have shown themselves to be flexible and efficient.

A third lesson that can be extracted from the two city-states' experience is that openness to foreign ideas and technology is vital if a country wants to develop quickly. Neither Hong Kong nor Singapore place many restrictions on the participation of foreign firms in their economies. The Singapore government does not share the view of many developing countries that its sovereignty will be kept at bay if it allows foreign interests to dominate key sectors of its economy. Its view is rather that foreign firms, far from being a threat to its sovereignty, are important to Singapore's stability and continued progress.

The experience of the two city-states underscores the importance of sound monetary and fiscal management. Throughout two decades of rapid growth, both the Singapore and Hong Kong governments practiced financial conservatism, as a result of which they have enjoyed public-sector surpluses in most years. Neither government has had to resort to deficit financing of public-sector development programs with all the inflationary consequences that such financing entails. Singapore has been able to creatively use the mechanism of the Central Provident Fund, a compulsory savings scheme for workers set up before self-government, to finance infrastructural development at low cost and to neutralize the inflationary impact of large net capital inflows.

To sum up, the cultural foundations of both Hong Kong and Singapore conceivably played a role in their rapid development in the last quarter century, but it is structural and institutional factors that have really propelled their economic engines.

Conclusions

The two city-states progressed rapidly in the 1960s and 1970s, thanks to a combination of internal growth-inducing policies and favorable external circumstances. Rapid development and rising wages have blunted their competitive edge in labor-intensive activities. Both economies are diversifying—Hong Kong's entrepreneurs are adjusting, as they have always done, to new market conditions, while the Singapore government is using incentives to push the economy into high-technology industries. Hong Kong's economy is benefiting from the modernization programs of China, but its long-term future remains clouded. In contrast, Singapore's economy slowed greatly in 1985, partly because of poor external demand but partly because of structural weaknesses including high taxes, maturing industries, and excessive regulations, weaknesses its government is trying to remedy. But it has no cloud over its long-term political future. Both city-states have so far shown a remarkable capacity to adjust their policies and institutions quickly to new challenges. There are good reasons to believe that their underlying structural features—continuity of policy, social consensus, political stability, and institutional efficiency—will enable them to overcome their present economic difficulties and help them to evolve into mature industrial economies.

Notes

1. For an analysis of Singapore as a city-state, see Pang Eng Fong and Linda Lim, "Political Economy of a City-State," *Singapore Business Yearbook 1982*, pp. 7–33.
2. See, for example, Ian M.D. Little, "An Economic Reconnaissance," in Walter Galenson, ed., *Economic Growth and Structural Change* (Ithaca: Cornell University Press, 1979), pp. 448–507; Roy Hofheinz and Kent E. Calder, *The Eastasia Edge* (New York: Basic Books, 1982); and Martin Fransman, "Explaining the Success of the Asian NICs: Incentives and Technology," *IDS Bulletin* 15:2, 1984, pp. 50–56.
3. For an analysis of Singapore's economic growth, see Lee Soo Ann, "Patterns of Economic Structure in Singapore," in You Poh Seng and Lim Chong Yah, eds., *Singapore: Twenty-five Years of Development* (Singapore: Nan Yang Xing Zhou Lianhe Zaobao), pp. 13–37; on Hong Kong's development, see A.J. Youngson, *Hong Kong: Economic Growth and Policy* (Hong Kong: Oxford University Press, 1982); and for a comparative analysis of the two city-states' development pattern, see Theodore Geiger and Frances M. Geiger, *The Development Progress of Hong Kong and Singapore* (Hong Kong: Macmillian, 1975).
4. See Pang Eng Fong and Tsao Yuan, "Macro Matters in Our Success," *Singapore Business Yearbook 1984*, pp. 24–28; and Ong Nai Pew, "Monetary and Forex Policies in an Open Economy," *Singapore Business Yearbook 1985*, pp. 24, 27–28.

5. See Laurence C. Chau, "Industrial Growth and Employment in Hong Kong," *The Philippine Economic Journal* 15:1–2, pp. 82–138; and Pang Eng Fong and Ong Nai Pew, "Labour Absorption in Hong Kong and Singapore since 1970," paper prepared for *The Philippine Economic Journal* special on Labour Absorption in East and Southeast Asia since 1970 (forthcoming).

6. See Pang Eng Fong and Linda Lim, "Foreign Labour and Economic Development in Singapore," *International Migration Review* 16:3, Fall 1982, pp. 548–76.

7. See Steven C. Chow and Gustav F. Papanek, "Laissez-faire, Growth and Equity—Hong Kong," *Economic Journal* 91, June 1981, pp. 466–85; and Tzong Biau Lin, "Growth, Equity and Income Distribution Policies in Hong Kong," mimeo, March 1985.

8. See Pang Eng Fong, "Growth, Inequality and Race in Singapore," *International Labour Review* 111:1, January 1975, pp. 15–28; Bhanoji Rao and M.K. Ramakrishnan, *Economic Growth, Structural Changes, and Income Inequality, Singapore, 1966–75*, Council for Asian Manpower Studies, Discussion Paper Series No. 77–15, December 1977.

9. *Straits Times* (Singapore), May 8, 1985; the results reported are from the 1982–1983 Household Expenditure Survey carried out by the Singapore Department of Statistics.

10. See Chan Heng Chee, *Singapore: the Politics of Survival 1965–1967* (Singapore: Oxford University Press, 1971); and Richard Clutterbuck, *Conflict & Violence in Singapore and Malaysia, 1945–83* (Singapore: Graham Brash, 1984).

11. *Straits Times* (Singapore), April 6, 1985.

12. Goh Keng Swee, "State-Owned Enterprises in Singapore," *The Mirror* 13:27, pp. 1–2, 7.

13. See Pang Eng Fong, "Labour Market Changes and Industrialisation in Singapore," ASEAN-Australian Joint Research Project (AAJRP) Economic Paper Series, June 1985.

14. *Budget Statement 1985* delivered in Parliament on March 8, 1985 by Tony Tan Keng Yam, Minister for Finance. (Singapore: Ministry of Communications and Information, 1985), p. 4.

15. A.J. Youngson, *Hong Kong: Economic Growth and Policy*, op. cit., p. 89.

16. For an analysis of mechanisms linking the bureaucracy to the Chinese society, see Lau Siu-kai, *Society and Politics in Hong Kong*, Hong Kong: Hong Kong Chinese University Press, 1984, pp. 121–55.

17. See R.K. Vasil, *Governing Singapore* (Singapore: Federal Publications, 1984).

18. See Chan Heng Chee, *The Dynamics of a One Party Dominance* (Singapore: Singapore University Press, 1976).

19. For an analysis of Hong Kong's political stability, see Lau Siu-kai, *Society and Politics in Hong Kong*, op. cit., pp. 157–82.

20. For an example of this argument but applied to Taiwan, another Confucian-influenced society, see H.J. Duller, *The Socio-cultural Context of Taiwan's Economic Development*, Academia Sinica Paper 83–5, November 1983.

INDEX

Acculturation, 205–6
African countries, 52
Agriculture, 37, 42, 43; developments in, 63
Applicability of East Asian model to other countries. *See* Lessons of East Asian experience
ASEAN countries, 106–7, 110
Asian capitalism. *See* New Asian capitalism
Ayal, E.B., 108

Baker, Hugh, 144
Bellah, Robert, 7
Benedict, Ruth, 121
Berger, Peter L., 14, 19, 216, 217
Brentano, Franz, 159
Buddhism (Mahayana), 8, 9; in Japan, 120–21, 122; in South Korea, 203–4, 215–16

Calder, Kent, 20
Capitalism, 30–31; Chinese, 9; and Christianity, 172; and Confucianism, 82, 86–87, 96; early, 147–48; European, and China, 148; modern, 172; in the West vs. the East, 131, 173. *See also* New Asian capitalism
Caribbean, 13
Charlesworth, H.K., 108
Chen, Kwan-yiu Edward, 109
China, 75, 81, 87–88; and European capitalism, 148; state-family relations in, 145; traditional, 148
Chinese: capitalism, 9; conception of state, 18; Confucianism, 93; familism, 144–46; vs. Japanese family firms, 142; family values and economic development, 134–42; impact in East Asia, 7–8, 9; vs. Japanese organizations, 106; paternalism, 137–38; religion, 9

Christianity: and capitalism, 172; in the Four Little Dragons, 130; and Japanese "inculturation," 118–30, 132n.5; and modernization, 115, 124, 132; role of, in East Asian development model, 115–32, 204; four types of, in East Asia, 116–18; in the West vs. the East, 131, 173
Collectivity, 6, 19, 87
"Comparative advantage," 11
Confucian harmony, and politics, 86–87
Confucianism, 7–8, 9, 18, 19–20, 86–87, 93, 97, 130; and capitalism, 82, 86–87, 96; and East Asian economic success, 86–87, 90, 197, 214–15, 235; and Japan, 92, 120; as a positive factor for development, 235; in South Korea, 202–4, 211, 214–16; "vulgar," 19, 20
Cultural factors in East Asian success, 19–21, 75–76
Cultural vs. economic explanation for East Asian success, 5, 11, 14, 22, 27

Deglopper, D.R., 136
Development strategies, 14, 38
Durkheim, Emile, 5–6

East Asia vs. other regions, 28–30, 31, 42, 43, 60–63, 77–79, 82, 88, 179
East Asian countries, 12–22; as anti-communist zone, 16; authoritarian systems in, 83, 88–90; common characteristics of, 28, 31–38, 43–55, 82–85; economic dynamism of, 13; economic portrait of, 28–79; role of government in, 13, 17–19, 38–40, 41, 83, 84–85; high rate of investment in, 31–37; life expectancy and, 17–18, 22; nationalism and paternalism in, 87–90; paternalism in, 88–90; novel political forms in, 82; political portrait of,

81–97; the poor in, 57–60, 63, 64; the ruling elite in, 16, 76–77, 83, 96–97; state structure of, 17–18, 22; the success story of, 12. *See also* name of individual countries

East Asian development model, 3–11, 22, 47, 52, 217; role of Christianity in, 115–32, 204; cultural features of, 19–21, 217; as a distinct model, 115–16, 217; "economic miracle" of, 11; economic success of, 10, 11, 12–13, 28–79; empirical explorations of, 12–22; the future of, 10–11; and global political-economic dynamics, 13, 14–17, 22; role of state in the, 13, 17–19. *See also* East Asian success; Modernism, New Asian capitalism; Name of individual countries

East Asian political systems, 81–97; authoritarianism and paternalism in, 83–85, 88–89, 90–94; twelve common features of; 83–85; and Confucian harmony, 86–87; and the Confucian paradox, 86–87; Hong Kong as least typical of, 83; and nationalism, 87–88; the paradox of, and capitalism, 96–97; problems of succession in, 93–94

East Asian success: comparative perspective for explaining, 75–76; cultural factors of, 19–21, 75–76; the cultural model for explaining, 100–101; economic explanation for, 28–79; economic features of, 4–5, 12, 64–65, 75; export and, 78–79; government intervention and, 78–79; industrialization and, 14–15, 43–55, 78; lessons of, 77–79; modernity and, 4, 6; and neo-Confucian ethos, 214–15; political factors for, 76–77, 100–101; political features of, 81–97; reduction of poverty by, 55–64, 78; role of culture in, 75–76, 77, 101–2; role of education in, 65–75; role of entrepreneur in, 99–110; role of technology absorption in, 72–75; sociocultural features of, 5, 14, 19–21; the structural model for explaining, 100–101; transferability of, 12–13, 64–77, 86; women's participation in labor force and, 65–75. *See also* New Asian capitalism; East Asian development model; Modernism

Economic dynamism, 12, 13, 14, 15, 19

Economic growth rate, 28–29, 33, 37, 62, 64, 74, 179; in East Asian countries, 42, 43–55, 75–76, 78, 179; and social organization, 197

Economic explanation of East Asian success, 27–79

Economic strategies, 37–43, 46, 47, 55, 63, 64, 75–76; and decline in poverty, 78; political factors and successful, 76–77; successful, 77–78

Economic success, 77. *See also* East Asian success; Economic strategies; Education's role in; Government intervention and; names of individual countries

Economic timing, 15–17, 21

Economists, 11

Education's role in economic success, 65–75

Eisenstadt, S.N., 197

Endland, Joe and Rear, John, 137

Entrepreneurship: and familism outside China, 146–48; and family values in Hong Kong, 142–46; functions of, 103–4, 108–110; nature of, 102–4; and new Asian capitalism, 99–110; patterns of, in East Asia, 104–8

Family values, 87

Family values and economic development: Asian, 134–48; Chinese, 134–42; of Chinese in Hong Kong, 135–39, 142–46; in developing countries, 147; Japanese, 170; outside China, 146–48; Overseas Chinese, 146–47

Folk culture, 131, 133n.19; and modernism, 131

Four Little Dragons (Hong Kong, Korea, Singapore, Taiwan), 4, 15, 52, 82, 130, 179, 217

Four "Little Tigers." *See* Four Little Dragons

Freedman, Maurice, 145

Gang of Four. *See* Four Little Dragons

Gold, Thomas, 16

Government intervention: and economic success, 31, 38–39, 40–41, 64–65, 77, 78; and national development, 83, 88–90, 97; problems of, 91–97; and social services, 91

Hamilton, Gary, 138
Hofheinz, Roy, 20
Hong Kong: Chinese family firms in, 135–42; Chinese family values and economic development in, 135–39, 142–46; development success of, 233–36; economic features of, 4, 12, 13, 15, 27, 30, 31, 33, 36, 38, 40, 46, 55, 56, 65; "entrepreneurial familism" in, 138–39; government role in the economy of, 226–33; immigrant population in, 224–26; nepotism in, 138–39; political features of, 81, 82, 83, 220–21, 231–33; as purest private-enterprise economy, 31; role of state in, 145; sex differences in education in, 142–43; common features of Singapore and, 220–36. See also East Asian countries; Two city-states
Hsu, Francis, 145

Illiteracy, 67, 73
Imai, Kenichi, 105
Income distribution, 55–64
India, 31, 52, 67, 74
Individualism, 5, 87, 130, 131; and modernization, 6, 131–32; and social organization, 197–98, 205–215; and Western development, 131
Indonesia, 52
Industrialization, 12, 14–15, 18, 22, 38; and East Asian success, 43–55, 78; and labor, 37; transition to, 147
Inoue Kowashi, 163, 166
Investment rate, 31–37, 76, 78
Itō Hirobumi, 163, 164, 166
Itō Miyoji, 163
Iwakura Tomini, 163

Japan: Buddhism in, 120–21, 122; bun (compartment) in, 121–25, 128, 129; and Confucianism, 92, 120; Christianity in, 118–30, 132n.5; cultural features of, 119, 125, 129; as a development model for East Asia, 118–30; economic development of, since 1945, 168–72; economic features of, 4, 7, 12, 15, 27, 29, 31, 33, 36, 41, 43, 46, 52, 55, 56, 60, 63, 65, 169; effect of U.S. occupation on 89, 94; encounter with the West, 125; entrepreneurship in, 105, 106, 109; musubi-faith (fertility) in, 126–29, 133n.15; the new communities

of, 125–30; political features of, 81, 82–83, 87–88, 92, 93, 94, 96; Postdam Declaration of, 168–169; pragmatic religion in, 118–19, 121–22; results of rapid industrialization of, 176; Shinto in, 121, 122, 128; transition toward state-run welfare, 91; wa (harmony) in, 119, 121, 123, 125, 128, 129. See also East Asian countries; Japanese; Japanese modernization, Meiji
"Japan Inc.," 31, 39
Japanese: cultural disintegration, 176; family patterns, 170; ideological transferability, 175; industrialized enterprises, 170–72, 174, 177nn.20,21; model of "inculturation," 118–30, 132n.5; value transferability, 170–71, 174. See also Japanese modernization
Japanese modernization, 124, 130; absolutist ideology and, 165–68; basic cultural patterns of, 155–57, 162, 172–73; distinctive features of, 155–76, economic development and, 168–72; governmental reform since 1945 and, 168–72; history of, 161–72, 174–75; Kokutai ideology and, 164–65, 177n.15; and the Meiji Constitution, 164–65; and the Meiji government, 160; political and economic features of, since the Meiji era, 161–72; sociocultural perspectives of, 172–76; symbolic immanentism in, 157–58, 159, 168, 169, 172–74, 175 176n.2; Tokugawa feudal system and, 160–61; transition from Tokugawa feudalism to the Meiji government and, 161–63, 175; transferability of endogeneous cultural values and, 159–61, 169
Johnson, Chalmers, 101–2, 105, 109; MITI and the Japanese Miracle, 101
Jones, L.P. and Sakong, I.L., 103, 104, 108

Kahn, H., 101
Kerr, Clark, 134
"Korea Inc.," 39
Korean model, the, 27, 29
Kuomintang, the, 89, 94–96

Labor, 37–38, 39, 52, 65, 73, 77; vs. government, 90; -intensive, 13, 37, 43–55, 63, 64, 65, 78–79, 237; women's participation in, 65–75

Lasserre, P., 108
Latin America, 9, 13, 15, 16, 31, 52, 73, 83
Lessons of East Asian experience, 77–79, 146–48, 221, 235–36
Levy, Marion J., 45–46, 135, 148
Liang Shu-ming, 137
Little, I.M.D., 13, 109
Low-income countries, 28–30, 31, 52, 57, 60, 63

Meiji: absolutist ideology of, and an authoritarian state, 165–68; Constitution, 163–65, 166–67, 169, 175, 177n.15; emperor, 160, 162, 166; government, 87, 88, 160, 165, 166–67, 175; ideological anguish of leaders, 175; restoration, 160, 162, 168
Middle-income countries, 52, 57, 179
Modern technology: and culture, 87–88; and traditional social institutions, 147
Modernity. See Modernization
Modernization: Asian spiritual aspects of, 8; Christianity and, 115, 124, 132; collective features and, 6, 87; as a dialectic process, 205; distinctive features of Japanese, 155–76; divergent patterns of, 148; and East Asian industrial capitalism, 4, 130; and East Asian political authority, 85; and folk culture, 131; and individualism, 6, 131–32; in Japan, 124, 130; and nationalism, 87–88; and paternalistic authority, 91; as a Western phenomenon, 3–4, 5–6, 124. See also East Asia development model
Morishima, Michio, 20
Myrdal, Gunnar, 13

Nationalism: and Confucian tradition, 90; and modernization, 87–88; and paternalism, 89–90
Neo-Confucian ethos, See Confucianism
Nepotism, 138–39
New Asian capitalism: and Confucianism, 86–87, 90, 97; economic portrait of, 28–79; effective management key in, 37–43; equitable income distribution and, 55–64, 78; indices of success of, 28–30; high rate of investment and, 30–37; mercantilism becomes corporatism in, 90–91; paternalistic authority and, 83–85, 88–89, 90–94; political portrait of, 81–97;

political systems of, 96–97; and private enterprise, 78; rapid industrialization and, 43–55; resources and, 30–31; role of entrepreneur in, 99–110; transition to, 87–91. See also Capitalism; East Asian development model; East Asian success
New classes in East Asia, 18, 21
NICs (newly industrialized countries). See East Asian countries

Ōkuma Shigenobu, 163
"Outer limit" and East Asian countries, 15–16, 17
Overseas Chinese, 105–6; family values and economic development of, 146–47; entrepreneurship of, 106, 109; vs. Japanese organizations, 106

Pakistan, 52, 67, 76
Parsons, Talcott and Smelser, Neil, 147–48
Paternalistic authority, 88–94; and Confucian tradition, 97; and new Asian capitalism, 83–85, 88–89, 90–94; problems of, 91–97
Preindustrial European societies, 147
Private-enterprise economy, 37, 38–40, 41, 78, 88

Redding, S.G. and Hicks, G.L., 106
Roesler, Hermann, 163, 177n.14
Ryan, E.J. 108

Salaff, Janet, 142–43
Schumpeter, J.A., 102, 108
Singapore: development success of, 233–36; economic features of, 4, 10, 12, 13, 15, 27, 30, 31, 33, 42, 46, 47, 52, 56, 65, 75; features of economic development common to Hong Kong and, 220–36; government role in the economy of, 226–33; immigrant population in, 224–26; political features of, 81, 82, 93–94, 220, 231–33. See also East Asian countries; Two city-states
Smith, Tony, 17
Social scientists, 3–4, 11, 12, 21, 75
"Soft" states, 13, 83
South Asia, 29, 52, 60–63, 67, 73; the poor in, 60–63
Southeast Asia, 52, 60, 63, 65, 73, 82, 234
South Korea: Christianity in, 116, 203; Confucianism in, 202–4, 211, 214–16;

development model of, 214; economic
features of, 4, 12, 13, 15, 18, 27, 29, 31,
33, 36, 39, 42, 43, 46, 47, 52, 55, 56,
63, 65; economic reform in, 75, 77, 204;
effect of war on, 89; entrepreneurship in,
104–5, 109; Five-Year Economic
Development Plan, 198, 199, 206;
government intervention in the economy,
90–91, 92; a "Hermit Kingdom," 198,
205; historical overview of, 198–99, 206;
industrialization and social organization in,
197–98, 202, 205–215; national and
organizational characteristics, 201–4,
206–9, 210–14; political features of,
81–82, 87–88, 89, 91–92, 93–94, 95–97;
religion in, 202–4; religious syncretism in,
216–17; secularism in, 203–4; traditional
social elements in, 201–4. *See also* East
Asian countries; "Korea Inc.,"; Korean
model, the; South Korea modernization
South Korean modernization: achievement,
status mobility needs and, 208–9;
adaptability as a model for, 204–214,
216–17; authoritarian principle and,
212–14, 215; distinctive features of,
205–214; education and, 208–210;
economic growth and, 204, 211–14;
human resources quality and, 209–211;
Korean War and, 204; mobilization,
organization and, 211–14; motivation and,
205–9; neo-Confucianism and, 214–16;
political changes and, 198–99; psychology
of *hahn* and, 206–9, 210; traditional
religions and, 214–15; Western influences
and, 198–200, 204
Syncretism, 216–17

Taiwan: agricultural features in, 186–88,
195; dependency on foreign trade in,
183–86; distinctive features of the
development in, 186–94; economic
development of, 179, 180–86, 194;
economic features of, 3, 4, 9, 12, 13, 15,
18, 27, 31, 33, 36, 43, 46, 47, 52, 55,
56, 63, 65, 75; effect of Kuomintang's
defeat on, 89; government intervention in
the economy of, 90–91, 92; high growth

rate in, 180; the Nationalists in, 89;
political features of, 81, 82, 88–89,
91–92, 93, 94–95, 96; rapid industrial
growth in, 190–94, 195; structural change
in, 180–83. *See also* East Asian countries;
Kuomintang, the
Technology. *See* Modern technology
Toennies, Ferdinand, 5
Tokugawa keiki, 161–62, 166
Two city-states (Hong Kong and Singapore),
30, 41; development performance of,
221–24; development success of the, 223,
233–36; distinctive features of
development of the, 224–37; differences
in political evolution of the, 220;
economic growth and social achievements
in, 223–24; enterpreneurial capitalism in,
230–31; financial conservatism and
economic growth in, 236–37; government
role in the economy of the, 226–33;
immigrant population in the, 224–26;
industrial growth in, 229–30; political
policies of, 231–33; political systems in,
231–32; transferability of experience of,
221. *See also* Hong Kong; Singapore

Underdevelopment, causes of, 37
United States, 30, 33, 21–22; as capitalist
world center, 15–16; Cold War ideology,
15; and East Asian countries, 15–16, 17,
22, 77, 82; market for East Asian goods,
15; support for East Asian countries, 18

Wages, 55–56, 57, 60–63, 73; government's
control of, 90; rising, 237
Weber, Max, 6–7, 130, 134–35, 145, 172,
197
Women's participation in the economy,
65–75
West, the, 3, 4, 6, 88, 115, 130;
Christianity in, 131; vs. the East, 131,
138, 147–48, 223–24; and Japan, 125
Western feudalism, 147–48; and traditional
China, 148

Yang, C.K., 135
Yew, Lee Kuan, 10

For Product Safety Concerns and Information please contact our EU
representative GPSR@taylorandfrancis.com Taylor & Francis Verlag GmbH,
Kaufingerstraße 24, 80331 München, Germany

Batch number: 08153766

Printed by Printforce, the Netherlands